Happy Father's Day to a
very special father —
June 17, 1984
Terry, BettyLynn
Rick, Jeanie, Cassi
Karen, Ken
Diane

A Book of MORMONS

A Book of MORMONS

Richard S. Van Wagoner and Steven C. Walker

© Copyright 1982 by Signature Books
Salt Lake City, Utah
All Rights Reserved
ISBN 0-941214-06-0
Printed in the United States of America

*Dedicated to the men and women
who made Mormon history*

Contents

Introduction	ix	Orson Hyde	125
Elijah Abel	1	Anthony W. Ivins	130
Almon W. Babbitt	5	Heber C. Kimball	135
John C. Bennett	10	J. Golden Kimball	141
John M. Bernhisel	15	Jesse Knight	145
Sam Brannan	19	Harold B. Lee	150
George H. Brimhall	24	John D. Lee	155
Fawn M. Brodie	29	Amasa Lyman	162
Hugh B. Brown	34	Amy Brown Lyman	167
Abraham H. Cannon	40	Francis M. Lyman	172
Frank J. Cannon	44	Karl G. Maeser	177
George Q. Cannon	49	Thomas B. Marsh	182
Martha Hughes Cannon	57	David O. McKay	187
Butch Cassidy	61	Edward Partridge	192
J. Reuben Clark	67	David W. Patten	196
Oliver Cowdery	72	Romania Pratt Penrose	200
Matthew Cowley	78	W. W. Phelps	204
Richard L. Evans	82	Orson Pratt	210
Green Flake	86	Parley P. Pratt	217
Susa Young Gates	89	Alice Louise Reynolds	224
William S. Godbe	93	Willard Richards	228
Heber J. Grant	98	Sidney Rigdon	232
Jedediah M. Grant	104	B. H. Roberts	239
Jacob Hamblin	108	Porter Rockwell	249
Martin Harris	113	Aurelia Rogers	254
Bill Hickman	118	Ellis Shipp	257

Emma Smith	262	John Taylor	353
George A. Smith	269	John W. Taylor	361
George Albert Smith	276	Moses Thatcher	366
Hyrum Smith	282	Chief Walker	371
Joseph Smith	288	Daniel H. Wells	376
Joseph F. Smith	295	Emmeline B. Wells	382
Joseph Fielding	303	David Whitmer	386
Lucy Mack Smith	309	John A. Widtsoe	392
Reed Smoot	314	Wilford Woodruff	395
Eliza R. Snow	320	Brigham Young	402
Erastus Snow	326	Brigham Young, Jr.	411
Lorenzo Snow	332	Zina D. H. Young	415
Fanny Stenhouse	339	Bibliography	419
James E. Talmage	343	Photographic Sources	441
Annie Clark Tanner	348	Index	443

Introduction

"The past," wrote William Faulkner, "is not dead; it is not even past." But much of it is buried. Five years of digging into archives has convinced us that details in the lives of many men and women who made Mormon history—people whose tastes conceived our architecture and set the shape of our cities, whose voices echo in our speech patterns, whose passion for improvement invites us into their footsteps whether we walk in Salt Lake City or Tokyo or Sao Paulo—are difficult to find. Orson Pratt, well-known figure though he was, accurately prophesied: "Should my history ever be written, it will be the result of a laborious task."

Apostle Pratt was the least of our problems. Our search for the other seventy-seven pivotal personalities in *A Book of Mormons*—prophets, pioneers, politicians, physicians, professors, apostles, authors, outlaws, even an Indian chief—led us through thousands of letters, hundreds of books and periodicals, dozens of personal interviews, through documents and rumors and legend and surmise.

We found in that labyrinth of 150 years of Mormon history vivid moments: Stroke-stricken Thomas B. Marsh, once president of the Quorum of the Twelve, limping his way back into the Church in 1856; "Prophetess, Presidentess, Priestess" Eliza R. Snow healing the sick by the laying on of hands; black Elijah Abel, ordained elder and seventy as early as 1836; Parley P. Pratt bleeding to death in Arkansas dust from knife and bullet wounds at the hand of a jealous husband; aging Hugh B. Brown lamenting, "My bifocals are wonderful,/ My hearing aid's a find,/ My dentures come in handy,/ But how I miss my mind!"

A Book of Mormons attempts to make accessible those elusive moments, those highlights of the lives of the people we met most and liked best in Mormon history. Having come to those essential facts at such cost, we were determined to put them at the fingertips of the readers of this volume. Alphabetical arrangement, marginal dates, and frequent subtitles are designed to make information easy to locate. Brevity—we cut the text to half its original length—further focuses salient fact; our "highlights of life" format is intended to allow concentration through illustrative fact rather than interpretive summary. Over a hundred photographs inform immediately.

—And, we think, accurately. Our other major passion in writing the book has been historical reliability. Seeing so much of folklore in what passes for Mormon history, and so much more of unabashed slanting, we have been anxious to stick steadfastly to primary documents and original witnesses. We allow historical figures to speak for themselves whenever possible; we quote our Mormons frequently, preserving even original spelling. Where there is controversy or conflicting fact, we've included spokespersons from both sides—when Brigham Young and Emma Smith quarreled, for example, we thought it fair (and far more interesting) to hear from both the Lion of the Lord and the Elect Lady.

But concern for objectivity is not the only reason we've invited our Mormons to speak for themselves. We like the way they talk. Listen, for instance, to Orson Hyde and Parley P. Pratt: "When dancing was first introduced in Nauvoo among the Saints, I observed Brother Parley standing in the figure and he was making no motion particularly, only up and down. Says I, 'Brother Parley, why don't you move forward?' Says he, 'When I think which way I am going, I forget the step and when I think of the step I forget which way to go.'"

We've left the warts on our portraits, presenting these individuals as the historical documents made them appear to us, without minimizing or ignoring incidents in their lives which some may consider embarrassing or controversial. We have written *A Book of Mormons* out of our conviction that people are best loved, and best learned from, when they are most truly known.

We are grateful not only to the authors we've cited in notes, but to many who have shared with us unpublished expertise or inside information about historical figures, notably Maureen Gates on Bill Hickman, Hampton Godbe on William S. Godbe, Steven K. Madsen on Green Flake, Linda King Newell on Emma Smith, Barbara McKay Smith on Fawn Brodie, and Scott Kenney on Joseph F. Smith. We are deeply appreciative of the patience of Mary Van Wagoner and Ardith Walker.

Richard S. Van Wagoner
Steven C. Walker

Elijah Abel

(1810-1884)

First Black Elder
Personal Friend of Joseph Smith
Builder on Kirtland, Nauvoo, and Salt Lake Temples

Family Background:

1810   July 25: Born in Washington County, Maryland. Married Mary Ann Adams; they had eight children.

First Black Elder:

1836   March 3: Ordained an elder—the first black to hold priesthood office in the Church. At the time of his ordination, he was given a patriarchal blessing by Church Patriarch Joseph Smith, Sr.: "Thou has been ordained an Elder. . . . Thou shalt be made equal to thy brethren, and thy soul shall be white in eternity and thy robes glittering: thou shalt receive these blessings because of the covenants of thy fathers."

First Black Seventy:

1836   December 20: Ordained a member of the Third Quorum of Seventy in Kirtland, Ohio. His ordination was certified in Nauvoo. In 1902 President Joseph F. Smith recalled a seventies meeting held in Utah on March 4, 1879: "Bro Elijah Able [sic] gave an outline of his history and experiences during a period of forty years. Of his being in Kirtland. Of his appointment an[d] ordination as a Seventy, and a member of the 3rd Quorum. He related some of the saying[s] of the prophet Joseph who told him that those who were called to the Melchisadec [sic] Priesthood and had magnified that calling would be sealed up unto eternal life."

First Black Missionary:

1838   Listed as a "minister of the gospel" in an 1837 *Messenger and Advocate,* Abel served missions to Canada and New York in 1838, and another mission to Ohio shortly before his death.
       His Canadian mission provoked concerns at a seventies conference in Quincy, Illinois, where Jedediah M. Grant "communicated to the council a short history of the

conduct of Elder Elijah Abel, and some of his teachings etc. such as . . . that in addition to threatening to knock down Elder Christopher Merkley on their passage up Lake Ontario, he publicly declared that the Elders in Kirtland made nothing of knocking down one another."

Friend of Joseph Smith:

While living in Joseph Smith's Nauvoo home, he was given "the calling of an undertaker" by the Prophet.

When Joseph Smith was illegally detained by Missouri and Illinois lawmen near Quincy, Illinois, Abel and six others attempted unsuccessfully to rescue him.

Temple Builder:

1841   A skilled carpenter, Abel and others formed a partnership called "The House Carpenters of the Town of Nauvoo." He worked on the Kirtland, Nauvoo, and Salt Lake temples.

Missionary to Blacks:

1843   Abel's desire to engage in missionary work in Cincinnati, Ohio, presented special difficulties for a traveling high council comprised of Apostles John E. Page, Orson Pratt, Heber C. Kimball, and Lorenzo Snow. Despite their respect for "a coloured Bro.," the brethren felt "wisdom forbids that we should introduce [him] before the public . . . [but] Bro Abels [sic] was advised to visit the coloured population."

Hotel Manager and Minstrel:

After arriving in Salt Lake Valley with his family in 1853, Abel worked at many trades, including managing the Salt Lake Farnham Hotel. He also performed minstrel shows with his family while living in Ogden.

Denied Sealing Privileges:

1870s Abel had received washings and anointings in the Kirtland Temple in 1836, before the complete endowment ceremonies had been established. Though he acted as proxy in baptisms for the dead in Nauvoo and Salt Lake City, Brigham Young denied his request to be sealed to his wife and family: that was a "privilege" he "could not grant," a decision later reaffirmed by President John Taylor.

Death:

1884 Died Christmas Day at the age of seventy-four, only two weeks after his return from a proselyting mission in Ohio, where he had become ill through exposure. He is buried in Salt Lake City Cemetery.

Almon W. Babbitt

(1813-1856)

Church Legal Defender

Family Background:

1813   October 1: Born Almon Whiting Babbitt in Berkshire County, Massachusetts. Married Julia Ann Hills Johnson in 1833. They were parents of four children.

Missionary:

1831   Immediately after his baptism at age eighteen, Babbitt was called to serve a mission to New York. He later served another mission to New York, as well as missions to Canada and to Indiana-Pennsylvania.

In and Out of the Church:

Although Babbitt's Church commitment was evidenced by his service in Zion's Camp (1834), the First Quorum of the Seventy (1835), and as Kirtland's stake president (1841), he frequently clashed with other Church leaders.

When brought before the Kirtland High Council in 1835 for failing to keep the Word of Wisdom, Babbitt claimed that he "had taken the liberty to break the word of wisdom, from the example of President Joseph Smith, Jr., and others," whereupon the Prophet charged him with "traducing my character." Babbitt was disfellowshipped and later received back into fellowship after "confessing his error."

1839   Apparently pleased with his work on a committee to "gather up and obtain all the libelous reports and publications which have been circulated against the church," Joseph Smith appointed him Kirtland Stake president, with instructions to "do what you can in righteousness to build up Kirtland, but do not suffer yourselves to harbor the idea that Kirtland will rise on the ruins of Nauvoo."

1840   In Nauvoo, Joseph Smith charged that Babbitt had claimed members of the First Presidency were financially extravagant. These charges were eventually dropped, but in 1841 he was disfellowshipped for teaching new members of the Church to locate in Kirtland rather than Nauvoo—a "doctrine contrary to the revelation of God, and detrimental to the interests of the Church."

Two years later he was restored to fellowship and appointed presiding elder in Ramus, Illinois.

1849   Disfellowshipped in Kanesville (Council Bluffs, Iowa) for opposing Orson Hyde's use of the *Frontier Guardian* to support the Iowa Whig Party, he was received back into fellowship six months later.

In 1851 he was again disfellowshipped for "profanity and intemperance in the streets of Kanesville; for corrupting the morals of the people ... by giving them liquor to beguile them from the path of duty and honor."

Finally excommunicated in May, 1854.

Church Legal Defender:

1844   During the troubled days prior to Joseph Smith's death, Babbitt served as legal counsel to the Prophet, recommending the actions which resulted in the destruction of the anti-Mormon *Nauvoo Expositor*.

After the Prophet's death, Babbitt served on a committee with Brigham Young, Willard Richards, Orson Pratt, W.W. Phelps, and John M. Bernhisel that unsuccessfully petitioned President James K. Polk to "convene a special session of Congress and furnish us an asylum where we can enjoy our rights of conscience and religion unmolested."

When the main body of Saints left Nauvoo, he remained behind to serve with Joseph Heywood and John S. Fullmer as trustee-in-trust for Church property.

Politician:

1844   A member of the Council of Fifty, Babbitt was elected to the Illinois Legislature, where he argued gallantly but unsuccessfully against repeal of the Nauvoo Charter in 1845.

1849   Elected by the "General Assembly of the State of Deseret" to petition Congress for statehood. Brigham Young wrote Orson Hyde in Council Bluffs, informing him of Babbitt's selection and alluding to their differences over the *Frontier Guardian*: "Babbitt . . . is somewhat acquainted with the rules of legislation and has formed a considerable acquaintance with many of the members of Congress, especially on the other side of politics. . . . Brother Babbitt came here rather soured in his feelings in relation to certain differences of opinion and policy in your region. . . . Let the past be buried."

Hyde responded, "Brother Babbitt, I believe, is a good hand to manage a dirty law suit; but I think, for a representative, you can send a man to Washington who will do you and himself more honor than Mr. Babbitt."

Congress refused to seat Babbitt, and created the Territory of Utah instead of the State of Deseret. Thomas L. Kane advised "against returning Mr. Babbitt as your delegate." And John M. Bernhisel, Babbitt's colleague, observed, "The Senators in Congress could not comprehend how we could select such an immoral man as Babbitt for our delegate."

Babbitt took such criticism philosophically: "When I came here I was chosen their humble servant to go back, and ask for admission into the Union. I went, and did so. I laboured faithfully. I went back with all the prejudices of this people against me. I stood between the wind and the water and combatted the opposition."

1852   Established the *Western Bugle* at Council Bluffs. Orson Hyde editorialized in the *Frontier Guardian*: "We welcome Friend Babbitt to the editorial corps, and wish him every success in every undertaking except his political exertion."

In 1853 President Franklin Pierce appointed Babbitt Secretary of Utah Territory.

Ambushed by Indians:

1856   Murdered by Cheyenne Indians on the Wyoming plains in late August at the age of forty-four. He had sent a government supply train from Florence, Nebraska, to Utah, but an Indian attack near Fort Kearney left only one survivor. Babbitt regrouped the train, against the advice of

Porter Rockwell: "Porter, perhaps the next thing you will hear of me will be in my grave, but I must go."

The statement proved prophetic. Ambushed again, apparently by the same band of Cheyenne, Colonel Babbitt and his entire train were wiped out. It was later reported that "after the colonel had fired his double-barrelled gun and his two revolvers, one of the Indians crept behind the wagon and tomahawked the colonel.... Babbitt fought like a grizzly bear." Nothing was found of his remains "but a few bones."

"Mormon Marauders" Accused of His Death:

1856   In his resignation letter as Associate Justice of Utah Territory, William W. Drummond claimed that Babbitt had been killed by a band of "Mormon marauders sent from Salt Lake City for that purpose ... under direct order of the presidency of the Church of the Latter-day Saints."

Babbitt's widow, Julia Ann, wrote in the *New York Herald*, August 1, 1857: "I have not a shadow of suspicion that white men were any way concerned in his death—the newspaper story that he was killed by the 'Mormons' to the contrary notwithstanding."

Nevertheless, Babbitt's estrangement from Brigham Young had become so severe that President Young told a combined meeting of the Quorum of the Twelve and Salt Lake High Council on October 4, 1856: "Speaking of Babbit's [sic] death—thank God for that I will acknowledge the hand of the Lord in *that* at all events."

John C. Bennett

(1804-1867)

Soldier of Fortune
Physician
Member of the First Presidency
Author of An Expose' of Joe Smith

Family Background:

1804   August 3: Born John Cook Bennett in Fairhaven, Massachusetts. He married Mary A. Barker, who bore him four children. He divorced her in 1842 on grounds of desertion, and five years later married Sarah Rider.

Appearance:

5'5" tall, 142 pounds, dark complexion, dark eyes, with a Roman nose. By the age of thirty-eight he had lost his upper front teeth.

Physician:

1825   Bennett studied medicine with his uncle, the president of the Ohio Medical Convention, and was licensed to practice medicine by the Ohio Twelfth District Medical Society. He served as president of a medical college at Willoughby, Ohio, and was instrumental in founding the Illinois State Medical Society. He also taught at Cincinnati's University of the Literary and Botanico-Medical College, as "Professor of Mid-wifery, and the Diseases Peculiar to Women and Children."

In Nauvoo he became interested in the medicinal effects of the tomato, proposing that "much of the bilious affections to which our citizens are subjected during the hot season, can be prevented by the free use of the Tomato." He also helped initiate the drainage of nearby swamps—a major health hazard to Nauvoo.

Preacher:

1826   After serving as a Methodist preacher for three years, he became a follower of Alexander Campbell. Like Sidney Rigdon, Bennett gained prominence as a Campbellite preacher.

Educator:

Though his attempt to found Methodist University in Ohio was unsuccessful, he secured a charter for Wheeling (Ohio) University in 1829. Later he helped found Indiana University at New Albany, and was its first president. In 1841 he was appointed chancellor of the University of Nauvoo. Classes in the sciences, literature, philosophy, history, music, foreign languages, and religion were taught in private homes, the Masonic Hall, and the uncompleted temple.

Church leader:

He first met Joseph Smith and Sidney Rigdon when he was living at Willoughby, Ohio. When he heard of Church difficulties in Missouri, he wrote encouraging letters to Joseph Smith and was later baptized by him in Nauvoo.

On April 8, 1841, John C. Bennett replaced the ailing Sidney Rigdon as "Assistant President" of the Church. For a time he was the Prophet's constant companion, confidant, and advisor, and was praised in Doctrine and Covenants 124: "I have seen the work which he hath done, which I accept if he continues, and will crown him with blessings and great glory."

Military Leader:

1839   Known in military circles as "42-pounder" for his aggressive tactics, Bennett was appointed brigadier general in the Invincible Light Dragoons of Illinois. In addition to serving as quartermaster general of Illinois, he was commissioned major general in the Nauvoo Legion by Illinois Secretary of State Stephen A. Douglas. During the Civil War he organized the Tenth Iowa Infantry and later served as field and staff surgeon of the Third U.S. Infantry.

Nauvoo Civic Leader:

1841   Unanimously elected the first mayor of Nauvoo, he also served as secretary of the Nauvoo Masonic Lodge. He engineered the Illinois Legislature's approval of the Nauvoo Charter, Nauvoo Legion, and the University of Nauvoo.

Apostate:

1842   After eighteen months of membership in the Church, he was accused of teaching an adulterous system of "spiritual wifery" and was asked to "withdraw his name from the Church record." At the time of his excommunication he was expelled from the Masonic Lodge, cashiered from the Nauvoo Legion, and forced to resign as mayor of Nauvoo—although the city council approved a vote of thanks "for his great zeal in having good and wholesome laws adopted for the government of this city; and for the faithful discharge of his duty while Mayor."

Author of *An Expose' of Joe Smith*:

1842   Declaring that he had only become a Mormon in order to "get behind the curtain, and behold, at my leisure, the secret wires of the fabric and likewise those who moved them," he wrote *The History of the Saints: Or An Expose' of Joe Smith and the Mormons*. "I felt myself an humble instrument in the hands of God to expose the Imposter and his myrmidons, and to open the eyes of my countrymen to his dark and damnable designs. I have done my duty."

Supporter of Mormon Splinter Groups:

1844   After Joseph Smith's death, he returned to Nauvoo with a letter purportedly given to him by the Prophet which stated that Sidney Rigdon was to be president of the Church in the event of Joseph Smith's death. In 1844-1845 he joined the disciples of William Law and Sidney Rigdon. Baptized into James Strang's Mormon group in 1846, he was excommunicated a year later for sexual licentiousness and disagreements over management of the sect's affairs. Despite his excommunication, however, Bennett continued to advise Strang, particularly on matters of pomp and ceremony, such as Strang's public coronation in 1850.

Wished to Command the Utah Expeditionary Forces:

1858   Aware of President Buchanan's plans to send an army to Utah, Bennett sent a letter to his friend Stephen A. Douglas volunteering his service: "That the conflict with Utah will be most sanguinary, there is little doubt. I desire to be in the most bloody and terrible battle. You know my military capacity well. When I commanded the Legion it was the best disciplined body of troops in the Union, so admitted on all hands. I can now select and take against them as formidable a Regiment as America can produce, if President Buchanan will only give me the *authority* to do so."

Chicken Expert:

1866   Bennett was well known in the Polk City, Iowa, area as a poultry expert. He wrote *A Treatise On Breeding & General Management Of Domestic Fowls*, and is credited with having created the Plymouth Rock strain of chicken.

Death:

1867   Died August 5, at the age of sixty-three. He was buried with Masonic honors in Polk City Cemetery.

John M. Bernhisel

(1799-1881)

Copyist of Joseph Smith's Bible Revision
Pioneer Physician
Mormon Congressman

Family Background:

1799   June 23: Born John Martin Bernheisel in Tyrone, Pennsylvania, he later changed his name to John Milton Bernhisel.

Much-Married Monogamist:

When he was forty-four, Bernhisel was sealed to ten deceased female friends and relatives by Joseph Smith, but he did not enter into a temporal marriage until 1845, when he married Julia Ann Haight Van Orden, a forty-year-old widow with six children.

The following year he married plural wives Dolly Ranson, Catherine Paine, Fanny Spafford, Melissa Lott Smith, and Catherine Burgess Barker and her sixteen-year-old daughter, Elizabeth. Bernhisel apparently considered the first three plural wives as a "spiritual charge," for he never lived with any of them. His marriage to Melissa Lott Smith was for "time only"; she had been sealed to Joseph Smith in 1843. Melissa left Bernhisel, though apparently never divorcing, and married Ira Willes in 1849. Bernhisel's marriages to Julia Van Orden and Catherine Burgess Baker were dissolved by mutual agreement in the Salt Lake Valley. Thus by 1851 he had reverted to monogamy with his youngest wife, Elizabeth, who bore him eight children.

In addition to the sealings performed by Joseph Smith, and the seven wives married in Nauvoo, Bernhisel was sealed to eighty-three deceased women in the Salt Lake Endowment House in 1868, plus an additional twenty-three wives one year later.

Physician:

1827   Graduated from the medical department of the University of Pennsylvania, specializing in apoplexy (strokes). He set up a private practice in Philadelphia, and later in New York. In Nauvoo he discontinued the practice of medicine until after retirement from public office in 1863, when he resumed private practice.

Patients remembered him as an "urbane, cultured, and refined physician, making his professional visits in a long frock coat and a high silk hat—a rather formidable antiquarian." At the conclusion of his examination of female patients, he would often advise: "Cultivate, my dear Madam, as far as possible, a cheerful, happy and contented disposition, and all will be well."

Friend of Joseph Smith:

1843   Though he was baptized in 1837 and ordained a bishop in New York City in 1841, it was not until 1843 that the Prophet could convince him to migrate to Nauvoo. On his arrival, Joseph Smith insisted that he board in the Smith home. He became a respected friend and adviser to the family, serving as Joseph's personal emissary to Governor Ford in 1844 and attending to Emma Smith after the birth of her son, David Hyrum, five months after the Prophet's death.

1845   Emma Smith offered to let Bernhisel read the manuscript of the Bible revision Joseph Smith and Sidney Rigdon had prepared in 1830-1833. He borrowed the manuscript for three months, copying the manuscript markings into his own Bible, which he later presented to Brigham Young.

Council of Fifty Member:

A charter member of the Council of Fifty, Bernhisel helped Joseph Smith prepare his 1844 political treatise, "Views on Government." Later he was selected by the Council to help dispose of property in Nauvoo after the main body of Saints had left. In 1848 the Council appointed him to "treaty with Congress on behalf of Deseret."

He became vice-president of ZCMI, which was established in 1868 by the Council of Fifty to combat the anticipated economic threats of the transcontinental railroad and William Godbe's "New Movement."

Five-term Congressman:

1849 Selected by the Council of Fifty to pursue territorial status for Deseret, Bernhisel left for Washington on May 3, 1849. But by July Brigham Young and his advisers decided to petition for statehood instead. As Colonel Thomas L. Kane put it, the Saints would be "better off without any government from the hands of Congress than with a territorial government." Almon Babbitt was dispatched with the statehood petition.

Bernhisel believed that Congress was unlikely to grant statehood "on account of the sparcity of population," and he proved correct: statehood was denied; Utah was given territorial status.

Shortly before his departure for Washington as Utah Territory's first Congressional delegate, Bernhisel decided to revert to monogamy. Though he accepted plural marriage in principle, he opposed its open promulgation and practice. He realized that his political colleagues viewed polygamy as repugnant to the laws and mores of the country. In 1852 he admonished Brigham Young, "Not one in a thousand will be convinced that the 'Doctrine' is at all consistent with chastity, or even morality, much less that it is a pure and righteous one."

Death:

1881 September 28: Died of "intermittent fever" in Salt Lake City at the age of eighty-two; buried in Salt Lake City Cemetery.

Sam Brannan

(1819-1889)

Early Church Newspaperman
Leader of California Mormons
California's First Millionaire

Family Background:

1819   Born Samuel Brannan in Saco, Maine. He married Ann Eliza Corwin and they had five children. After his wife divorced him in 1870, he married Carmelita de Llaguno.

Early Mormon Convert:

1833   He first heard of Mormonism from Apostles Heber C. Kimball and Orson Hyde. Settling near Kirtland, Ohio, he was baptized and apprenticed as a printer. The collapse of the Kirtland Safety Society and surrounding banks ruined him financially, and he was forced to travel the country seeking newspaper work, finally finding employment in Painsville, Ohio.

Church Newspaperman:

1844   Though he had been ordained an elder in 1838 and served a mission to Ohio, his chief contributions to the Church were as a newspaperman.

    He was called to help found the *Prophet* in New York City with Joseph Smith's brother William. Following Joseph's death, Brannan, William Smith, and George J. Adams were charged with using the *Prophet* for personal gain. According to Wilford Woodruff, "Their whole influence has gone throughout the eastern Churches to gratify their own propensities, rob the Churches for themselves, set up as great men, to gain influence unto themselves."

    They were also accused of teaching "a principle that they call the spiritual wife doctrine. . . . If any one says anything against practising or preaching it, they think he is an old granny and weak in the faith." Brannan was disfellowshipped for marrying a plural wife in Massachusetts, but the woman died shortly thereafter. When he asked for forgiveness from the Council of the Twelve, he was quickly reinstated and sent back to New York City to assist New England Mission President Parley P. Pratt in publishing a new Church periodical, the *Messenger*.

California Pioneer:

1846   February 4: Encouraged by Brigham Young, Brannan loaded 238 Saints, mostly farmers and mechanics, and the *Messenger* press on board the *Brooklyn*. Sailing from New York around Cape Horn, the *Brooklyn* weathered two severe storms. Ten passengers died but two babies were born—one named "Atlantic," the other "Pacific."

          Arriving in Yerba Buena (San Francisco) on July 29, the Saints established a settlement called New Hope. Unaware of the decision of Brigham Young and the Twelve to settle in the Great Basin, the California settlers anticipated the arrival of the pioneer company in their new community.

          Brannan published the first newspaper, preached the first English sermon, performed the first white marriage, and was defendant in one of the first jury trials of northern California, having been accused of misappropriating funds from the *Brooklyn* Saints' "common stock."

1847   June 6: Received his first communication from Brigham Young since the *Brooklyn* Saints left New York: "The camp will not go to the west coast or to your place at present; we have not the means.... Any among you who may choose to come over into the Great Basin or meet the camp, are at liberty to do so; and if they are doing well where they are, and choose to stay, it is quite right."

          Brannan traveled to meet Brigham Young on the Green River and argued unsuccessfully for settlement in California rather than the Great Salt Lake Valley.

          Returning to California, he met the mustered-out Mormon Battalion, and advised, "The Saints could not possibly subsist in the Great Salt Lake Valley, as according to the testimony of mountaineers, it froze there every month in the year, and the ground was too dry to sprout seeds without irrigation, and if irrigated with the cold mountain streams, the seeds would be chilled and prevented from growing, or, if they did grow, they would be sickly and fail to mature."

California's First Millionaire:

1849   His published cries of "Gold! Gold! Gold from the American

River!" started the California gold rush. Though not directly involved in "golddigging," he became California's first millionaire in merchandising, hotels, real estate, lumber, and shipping.

Mindful of Brannan's financial success, President Brigham Young advised him, "If you want to continue to prosper, do not forget the Lord's treasury, lest he forget you; for with the liberal, the Lord is liberal. And when you have settled with the treasury, I want you to remember that Brother Brigham has long been destitute of a home, and suffered heavy losses and incurred great expenses in searching out a location and planting the church in this place. He wants you to send him a present of twenty thousand dollars in gold dust, to help him in his labors. This is but a trifle when gold is so plentiful, but it will do me much good at this time."

When Apostles Amasa M. Lyman and Charles C. Rich visited the California Saints, they asked for the tithes. Brannan, who had invested the money in personal and "common stock" ventures, replied: "I'll give up the Lord's money when he [Brigham Young] sends me a receipt signed by the Lord, and no sooner."

Prominent San Francisco Citizen:

1851   Organized "Committee of Vigilance" to combat incendiarism and lawlessness in San Francisco. Presiding over the committee's first lynching, rope in hand, he encouraged, "Every lover of liberty and good order, lay hold." He was the leading spirit in the Odd Fellows, the Society of California Pioneers, the Marion Rifle Corps, the Eureka Light Brigade, and the E. Clampus Vitus—"for the benefit of widows and orphans but primarily of widows."

Excommunication:

1851   September 1: Newly arrived Pacific Mission President Parley P. Pratt excommunicated Brannan for "a general course of unchristianlike conduct, neglect of duty, and for combining with lawless assemblies to commit murder and other crimes"—the "Committee of Vigilance" lynching.

Founder of Calistoga:

1859   Purchased 2000 acres of prime Napa Valley lands on which he built a huge resort, Calistoga, where Merino sheep and blooded Spanish horses grazed, and a distillery turned out an annual 90,000 gallons of brandy made from the grapes of 100,000 vines. "Calistoga" was coined when Brannan, in an inebriated state had declared he would make the resort the "Calistoga of Sarafornia."

Pauper:

1868   Severely wounded during a violent property dispute at Calistoga, he suffered permanent partial paralysis of his left side. Two years later, Brannan's enchantment with dancer Lola Montez, Lillie Hitchcock Coit, and others resulted in divorce, which forced Brannan to liquidate his holdings. Increased drinking eventually precipitated total collapse of his financial empire.

        He traded his last $1.5 million in Mexican war bonds for 1,687,585 acres in Sonora, but was unable to colonize the arid, Indian-infested region and returned to San Diego—deserted by his Mexican wife, penniless, and wracked with arthritic pain.

Death:

1889   May 6: Died at the age of seventy of inflammation of the bowels. His remains were interred in a pauper's holding vault for sixteen months prior to his family's securing final burial in San Diego's Mount Hope Cemetery.

George H. Brimhall

(1852-1932)

*Brigham Young University President
Middleman in BYU "Modernist Controversy"*

Family Background:

1852   December 9: Born George Henry Brimhall in Salt Lake City. In 1874 he married Alsina Elizabeth Wilkins; they had six children. After her death in 1884 he married Flora Robertson; they became the parents of nine children.

Education:

1870   Every Sunday night or Monday morning, Brimhall walked twelves miles from his home in Spanish Fork to attend "Timpanogos University," a Provo high school. He worked for Principal Warren Dusenberry for board and did janitorial work for tuition. At the end of the year he gave the valedictory address "with considerable vehemence, I presume, as for the first time I *was applauded* although my pants were patched."

1877   Received a "normal diploma" (teaching certificate) from Brigham Young Academy in Provo, where he studied under Karl G. Maeser. "Judge Dusenberry showed me the road to higher education," Brimhall recalled, "but Karl G. Maeser showed me the way to a higher life."

Principal:

1890   After serving as principal of Spanish Fork schools, district superintendent of Utah County schools, and superintendent of Provo community schools, Brimhall became head of the intermediate department and preparatory school at Brigham Young Academy for twenty dollars a month. He later became principal of the normal department and completed a bachelor's degree in pedagogy, graduating in Brigham Young Academy's first college commencement in 1893. Later that year he was awarded the bachelor of didactics by the Church Board of Education.

BYU President:

1900   Having served as a member of the Church Board of

Education since 1898, Brimhall was designated acting president of Brigham Young Academy in the spring of 1900 when President Benjamin Cluff left on an expedition to South America. Brimhall planned to "improve . . . but not . . . radically revolutionize the school," for he believed the academy "depends not on man, or any set of men. God planted it and we are but gardeners to take care of it."

Brimhall purchased seventy-four acres of "Temple Hill," where the upper BYU campus was built. The academy became Brigham Young University in 1903, and Brimhall was appointed permanent president in 1904. He introduced B.S. degrees in 1904, B.A. degrees in 1907, and the M.A. in 1919.

During his presidency, five buildings were constructed on campus—the Training School (1902), Art Building (1904), Maeser Memorial (1911), Mechanic Arts Building (1919), and Women's Gymnasium (1913)—one of few buildings in the United States devoted exclusively to physical education for women.

"Modernist Controversy":

1909   Critics charged that BYU was "lacking in genuine scholarship" and that most of its teachers were a "bunch of farmers who gave their leisure time only to teaching."

To upgrade the level of scholarship, Brimhall hired four Mormon professors trained at Harvard, Chicago, Cornell, and the University of California. The popular, articulate professors quickly won the minds and hearts of many students with their lectures in eugenics, communism, socialism, Darwinism, and "higher criticism" of the Bible.

1910   "Many stake presidents, some of our leading principals and teachers, and leading men who are friends of our schools . . . expressed deep anxiety" to Church Commissioner of Education Horace Hall Cummings. Brimhall, though an initial supporter of the professors, changed his view when some BYU students "told him they had quit praying because they learned in school there was no real God to hear them." A dream about the issue charged Brimhall with "enthusiastic support thereafter in setting things right." Both he and Cummings advised the four professors "not to press their views with such vigor," and Cummings took a report to the university trustees which ultimately led to the dismissal or resignation of the four.

BYU students petitioned in behalf of the professors. Caught in the crossfire, Brimhall feared loss of funding for the university and declared, "The school follows the Church."

Ecologist:

Brimhall was responsible for developing a bird sanctuary in Provo Canyon and was a strong advocate of placing elk, caribou, and mountain sheep in the Wasatch and Uinta mountains.

Honors:

An active supporter of the Utah National Parks Council of the Boy Scouts of America, he received the first Silver Beaver awarded by the council.

In addition to receiving honorary doctorates from the Church Board of Education and Brigham Young University, he was president of Utah Educational Association (1897-1898), National Educational Association life member, and American Red Cross director. A BYU building was named in his honor in 1935.

Author:

Brimhall wrote numerous articles for Church magazines and composed several songs, including "Old Glory" and "I Love Thee, Utah Valley." He also published a collection of sayings and speeches entitled *Long and Short Arrows*.

Retirement and Death:

1921 After twenty-one years as President of Brigham Young University, Brimhall retired in 1921.

1932   July 29: After several months of ill health, Brimhall became depressed. "His restless spirit chafed under the long seige which had sapped his strength." While his wife was out of the house on a short shopping trip, Brimhall killed himself with a hunting rifle. Apostles George Albert Smith, Richard R. Lyman, and Melvin J. Ballard participated at his funeral program. He was buried in Provo Cemetery.

Fawn M. Brodie

(1915-1981)

Author of **No Man Knows My History**
Psychohistorical Biographer

Family Background:

1915   September 15: Born Fawn McKay in Ogden, Utah, she was the niece of Church President David O. McKay and the granddaughter of BYU President George H. Brimhall. Married Bernard Brodie; they had three children.

Education:

1934   Graduated from the University of Utah with a B.A. in English at the age of eighteen. "I was devout until I went to the University of Utah. . . . Being exposed to the great literature of the past . . . was a very quiet kind of liberation. . . . There was no active trauma. It was a quiet kind of moving out into . . . the larger society and learning that the center of the universe was not Salt Lake City as I had been taught as a child.

"It was not really until I went away to graduate school at the University of Chicago that I understood how much of a liberation the university experience in Salt Lake City had been, because then the confining aspects of the Mormon religion dropped off within a few weeks. As I've said before, 'it was like taking off a hot coat in the summertime.'"

1936   Received an M.A. in English literature from the University of Chicago the same day she and Bernard Brodie were married. He was to become a noted international political strategist and professor of political science at UCLA.

They had met in the student cafeteria: "Because I was tall and could easily be seen, and because I needed work to help pay school expenses, I was given a special job at the University of Chicago cafeteria. I carried a big coffee pot and poured second cups of coffee. When I poured an extra cup for Bernie, he gave me two red carnations. He brought me flowers every day for the next six weeks, when we were married."

No Man Knows My History:

1936   While employed at the University of Chicago library, she began research on the life of Joseph Smith. She submitted the first five chapters to Alfred Knopf Publishing Company and in 1943 was awarded a $2500 Fellowship in Biography.

1945   *No Man Knows My History: The Life of Joseph Smith the Mormon Prophet* was published. She tried to prepare her parents by writing: "It is only fair to you both that I tell you quite frankly and honestly in advance that the book is likely to get a good bit of hostile criticism from the authorities of the Church. Certain things which I feel should be included to tell the whole story of the man, you will feel should better have been left buried. You will probably be criticized for having raised a wayward daughter."

The best-known criticism was Hugh Nibley's *No Ma'am, That's Not History*, which argued that another biographer could use the same facts to support a different set of conclusions. To her parents, Brodie wrote in 1946: "Thank you for sending the Hugh Nibley pamphlet. I had expected better things in this 'scholarly reply to Mrs. Brodie.' It is a flippant and shallow piece. He really did me a service by demonstrating the difference between his scholarship and mine. If that is the best a young Mormon historian can offer, then I am all the more certain that the death of B.H. Roberts meant the end of all that was truly scholarly and honest in orthodox Mormon historiography."

Heretic:

1946   "I was excommunicated for heresy—and I was a heretic—and specifically for writing the book. My husband was teaching at Yale at the time and we were living in New Haven. Two Mormon missionaries came to the door and presented me with a letter asking me to appear before the bishop's court in Cambridge, Massachusetts, to defend myself against heresy. I simply told them, or wrote a letter telling them, that I would not go because, after all, I was a heretic."

The letter announcing the bishop's court charged "apostasy, in this among other matters: That in a book recently published by you, you assert matters as truths which deny the divine origin of the Book of Mormon, the restoration of the priesthood and of Christ's Church through the instrumentality of the Prophet Joseph Smith, contrary to the beliefs, doctrines and teachings of the Church."

Psychohistorical Biographer:

1951   The Brodies moved to California, where Fawn actively pursued her literary career. During the next thirty years she wrote *Thaddeus Stevens, Scourge of the South* (1959)—the life of a radical Republican leader of Civil War Reconstruction; *From Crossbow to H-Bomb* (co-authored with her husband, 1962); *The Devil Drives: A Life of Sir Richard Burton* (1967)—Nile explorer, translator of the *Arabian Nights*, soldier, and poet; second edition of *No Man Knows My History* (1969); and *Thomas Jefferson: An Intimate History* (1974). She also edited *The City of the Saints* (1963)—an account of Sir Richard Burton's 1860 trip to Utah, and *Route from Liverpool to Great Salt Lake* (1963)—Frederick Piercy's 1853 narrative of a visit to Utah, as well as publishing more than forty book reviews and articles.

Her publications, particularly the Joseph Smith and Thomas Jefferson books, generated both acclaim and criticism. Criticisms centered on the use of psycho-biographical techniques to ascertain a historical figure's experiences and motivations through psychological interpretation. Mindful of the pitfalls of her profession, Brodie commented, "Even the most dispassionate historian, trying to select fairly with intelligence and discretion, manipulates in spite of himself, by nuances, by repudiation, by omission, by unconscious affection or hostility."

Social Critic:

"She attacked civic problems, she attacked political problems, she was a wonderful letter writer to the *Times*," a neighbor eulogized. "We always felt joy when we felt a letter coming on, seeing it snap in her dark eyes before she would attack the typewriter. . . . You'd see Fawn stalking the moors like Boadicea out on a Roman charge. She was really a warrior lady about our hill; she was a fierce defender of it. And when she saw something evil creeping up on us, in the way of either civic injustice or some pollution that was in the offing, she fought. She was a wonderful fighter."

Honors:

She was awarded several prestigious awards during her lifetime, including the Commonwealth Club of California Literature Award in 1959, the Utah Historical Society 1967 Fellow of the Year, the 1974 Alumni Emeritus Award at the University of Utah, and the 1975 *Los Angeles Times* "Woman of the Year." She was appointed senior lecturer in the UCLA history department, though her academic credentials were in English literature.

Retirement and Death:

1977 Retired from UCLA to write *Richard Nixon: The Shaping of His Character.* One year later, her husband died of cancer.

1981 January 10: Died of cancer at the age of sixty-five in Santa Monica, California, having refused pain medication to finish the final draft of her Nixon biography. She was cremated, her ashes scattered over the Pacific Palisades area she loved and protected.

Hugh B. Brown

(1883-1975)

Member of the First Presidency
Utah State Democratic Party Chairman

Family Background:

1883   October 24: Born in Granger, Utah, the fifth of fourteen children. He married Zina Young Card, a granddaughter of Brigham Young, in 1908. They were the parents of eight children, including a son, Hugh Card Brown, RAF pilot lost over the North Sea during World War II.

Nicknamed "Dutch":

As a young boy he acquired the nickname "Dutch" because of a speech impediment. He later became one of Mormonism's most respected orators.

Transplanted Canadian:

1899   The family moved to Alberta, Canada, where, except for studies at the Brigham Young College in Logan, Utah, and a mission to Great Britain, he lived for twenty-eight years.

Military Career:

1915   Served for three years as a Canadian Army major in World War I, with overseas duty in France.
        At the outbreak of World War II he became an army coordinator for the Church, visiting military installations and conferring with Latter-day Saint leaders and servicemen. The LDS Servicemen's Committee was organized on his advice in 1943.

Lawyer:

1920   Served as a barrister and solicitor in Lethbridge, Alberta. In 1927 he joined the Salt Lake City law firm which included J. Reuben Clark, Preston Richards, and Albert E. Bowen.

Stake President:

1921   The first president of the Lethbridge Stake at the age of thirty-eight, Brown was at that time the youngest stake president in the Church. Two years after arriving in Salt Lake City, he was called to preside over Granite Stake.

Democrat:

1927   When Brown moved to Utah, President Heber J. Grant, Anthony W. Ivins, and B.H. Roberts "told me at different times and separately that if I wanted to belong to a party that represented the common people, I would be a Democrat, but if I wanted to be popular and be in touch with the wealth of the nation, I would be a Republican."

1934   Left the Clark-Richards-Bowen firm because of political differences. Though he considered J. Reuben Clark his mentor in law and religion, Brown knew they were poles apart in politics.

        Elected state chairman of the Democratic Party, Brown decided to run for the U.S. Senate. He placed third, behind incumbent Senator William H. King and Herbert Maw: "I entered, in fact, against the advice of my wife, which I have regretted ever since."

        As a general authority, Hugh B. Brown advised Church members to "develop a maturity of mind and emotion and a depth of spirit which enables you to differ with others on matters of politics without calling into question the integrity of those with whom you differ. Allow within the bounds of your definition of religious orthodoxy variations of political beliefs. Do not have the temerity to dogmatize in issues where the Lord has seen fit to be silent."

State Liquor Chairman:

1935   Appointed chairman of Utah's first liquor commission: "We must find a condition that will not be ideal for the bootleggers. . . . I had a lot of experience with this in Alberta . . . and with that background and experience and observation, I am unalterably opposed to the licensing system and in favor of state control."

Mission President:

1937   Called to preside over the British Mission. At the outbreak of World War II, Brown was appointed coordinator of LDS servicemen in the U.S. and Great Britain. When the war ended, he was again appointed president of the British Mission.

Educator:

1946   Though he did not complete his college education, he taught political science and religion for a short time at Brigham Young University.

1962   Awarded an honorary doctor of humanities degree from BYU, he advised students: "Be dauntless in your pursuit of truth and resist all demands for unthinking conformity. ... Tolerance and truth demand that all be heard and that competing ideas be tested against each other."

He stressed the study of literature: "While making a lifetime study of the standard works of the Church, one should also become familiar with the classics, with Shakespeare, Milton, Tennyson, and Wordsworth.... One should know something of the writings of Plato, Aristotle, Socrates, and the later philosophers, who while they err in many respects, will start a man thinking independently and courageously on the meaning of life and its purpose."

During a 1969 BYU commencement address he said, "You young people live in an age when freedom of the mind is suppressed over much of the world. We must preserve it in our Church and in America and resist all efforts of earnest men to suppress it.... Preserve, then, the freedom of your mind in education and in religion and be unafraid to express your thoughts, and insist upon your right to examine every proposition. We are not so much concerned whether your thoughts be orthodox or heterodox as we are that you shall *have* thoughts."

Author of many books, including *Eternal Quest, You*

and Your Marriage, Abundant Life, Continuing the Quest, Vision and Valor.

General Authority:

1953   Called to be an assistant to the Twelve. Five years later he was called to the Quorum of the Twelve by President David O. McKay, and in 1961 he was called to be counselor to the First Presidency due to the ill health of J. Reuben Clark. Following President Clark's death in October, he became second counselor. Two years later he was named first counselor to President McKay.

As a member of the First Presidency, he often voiced sentiments on controversial matters, as in his 1963 conference address on civil rights: "We believe that all men are the children of the same God, and that it is a moral evil for any person or group of persons to deny any human being the right to gainful employment, to full educational opportunity, and to every privilege of citizenship, just as it is a moral evil to deny him the right to worship according to the dictates of his own conscience."

Businessman:

Brown served as president of the Richland Oil Development Company in Edmonton, Alberta, in the early 1950s. His skills proved useful in his Church assignments, which included service on the boards of directors of Beehive State Bank and Deseret Federal Savings and Loan Association, plus vice-presidencies of Beneficial Life Insurance Company, Hotel Utah Corporation, ZCMI, Utah-Idaho Sugar Company, and KSL Radio.

Endurance:

Though suffering from trigeminal neuralgia, which caused extreme facial pain for nearly fifty years, President Brown never lost his sense of humor:

My bi-focals are wonderful,
My hearing aid's a find,
My dentures come in handy,
But how I miss my mind!

"There are, of course, physical limitations imposed by increasing years," he said, "but we should not yield or surrender to them, or give up in despair with the first twinge of stiffening joints in mind or body. Life will continue to have an alluring and increasing wealth of interest all the way down its western slopes for him who keeps a cutting edge on his awareness."

Death:

1975   December 2: Died at the age of ninety-two in Salt Lake City of causes incident to age. Epitaph in Salt Lake City Cemetery: "From Man to God."

Abraham H. Cannon

(1859-1896)

Publisher
Apostle
Post-Manifesto Polygamist

Family Background:

1859   March 12: Born Abraham Hoagland Cannon in Salt Lake City to George Q. Cannon and Elizabeth Hoagland. He worked as an errand boy for the *Deseret News*, apprenticed as a carpenter and architect on the Salt Lake Temple, and graduated from the University of Deseret.

Having married Sarah A. Jenkins in 1878, Abraham married his first cousin Wilhelmina M. Cannon in 1879, and his step-sister Mary E. Croxall in 1887. Although both plural wives expressed dissatisfaction with polygamy, "Mina" threatening divorce repeatedly, Abraham remained committed to "the principle."

General Authority:

1882   Returning from a three-year mission to Europe, he was ordained and set apart to the First Council of Seventy: "In the Council of the Twelve . . . the remark had been made that we did not fully tend to our duties. The proposition was also made to pay us a salary . . . so that we might devote less time to business and more to our ministry. I told Father I would prefer to receive no salary, and as for neglect of duty I had tried to do my best. It would, however, please me very much if I could be honorably released."

Called to the Quorum of the Twelve in 1889, at age thirty.

Publisher:

1882   After his European mission, Cannon became the business manager of the *Juvenile Instructor* and developed a small printing office into a major publishing house, Cannon & Sons. In 1892 he became editor and publisher of the *Contributor*, the same year he and his brother John assumed control of the *Deseret News*.

He was the author of many books, including *A Handbook of Reference to the History, Chronology, Religion and Country of the Latter-day Saints, Including Revelation on Celestial Marriage, for the Use of Saints and Strangers*;

and *Questions and Answers on the Book of Mormon, Designed and Prepared Especially for the Use of the Sunday Schools in Zion.*

Businessman:

In addition to promoting the Salt Lake-Pacific and the Utah-California Railways, he was a director of Bullion-Beck Mining Company, State Bank of Utah, Utah Loan and Trust Company, and Co-op Furniture Company. He was also vice-president of George Q. Cannon & Sons Company and the Salt Lake City Chamber of Commerce, and owned a large book and stationery store in Ogden.

Prisoner for Conscience Sake:

1886   When asked if Sarah and Wilhelmina were his wives, he replied, "They are, thank God," and he was immediately convicted of "unlawful cohabitation."

Fined $300 and sentenced to six months in prison, Cannon served his time in the Utah "Pen" at Sugarhouse. "For some few days the men have been complaining about the poor coffee sent in to them," he wrote, "and on it being mentioned to the Warden, he said that a bottle of carbolic acid had accidentally been dropped into the coffee, and the kettle in which the drink was made had not been cleaned out for some time. But this had now been remedied. The bread for two days has been so sour that we could scarcely eat it. Radishes that were sent in last night were so tough that they could scarcely be eaten, and lettuce sent in the night previously was nearly covered with worms. It is something new for us to receive anything green to eat from the Penitentiary ranch, but it would be better to have it in an eatable condition."

Post-Manifesto Polygamist:

1896   Despite the Wilford Woodruff Manifesto (1890), Cannon married Lillian Hamblin: "Father [President George Q. Cannon] also spoke to me about taking some good girl and raising up seed by her for my brother David. . . . He told me to think the matter over, and speak to him later about it. Such a ceremony as this could be performed in Mexico, so Pres. Woodruff has said."

With the assistance of Joseph F. Smith, Abraham married Lillian off the coast of California, and sired one child on behalf of his deceased brother. The child, named "Marba" ("Abram" spelled backwards), was born in 1897, eight months after Cannon's death.

Death:

1896 July 19: Died of meningitis at the age of thirty-seven after contracting a post-surgical inflammation subsequent to a chronic mastoid infection. He was buried in Salt Lake City Cemetery.

At his funeral Church authorities discouraged the custom of viewing the body: "It is needless to say to intelligent Latter-day Saints that all this is repugnant to that spirit and decorum which ought to characterize the laying away of the earthly tabernacles of those whom we have loved or respected; and the general authorities of the Church have felt called upon to exert an influence to check this evil, and have advised the Saints not to expose their dead to public view."

Frank J. Cannon

(1859-1933)

Publisher
Utah's First United States Senator
"Furious Judas"

Family Background:

1859   January 25: Born Franklin Jenne Cannon in Salt Lake City to George Q. Cannon and Jane Jenne. He married Martha Brown in 1878; they had four children. After Martha's death in 1908, Frank married her sister May.

A Wayward Cannon:

1882   Spared excommunication for fathering an illegitimate child only through a reluctant public confession. For years afterward, Cannon continued his drunken sprees at Kate Flint's brothel in Salt Lake City.

1886   In an attempt to obtain evidence against George Q. Cannon, District Attorney Dickson ruthlessly grilled plural wife Martha Telle Cannon. Frank J., his brother Hugh, and cousin Angus M. assaulted the prosecutor as he was leaving the Continental Hotel in downtown Salt Lake. Frank served a brief prison sentence before his brother Abraham arranged bond.

Author:

1886   A gifted writer, Cannon apparently wrote most of the *Life of Joseph Smith the Prophet* shortly after his release from prison. Because of his unsavory reputation, the biography was published under his father's name.

Church Lobbyist:

1890   Sent to Washington by his father, Cannon worked to prevent passage of the Cullom-Strubble Bill, which would have disfranchised all Mormons. He argued, "It is a poor reward that this bill proposes to bestow—to inflict the same political deprivations on the men who are obeying the law as have been imposed upon offenders."

    Cannon later claimed that assurances given to national leaders by him and his father regarding the abandonment of plural marriage were decisive in Wilford Woodruff's decision to issue the Manifesto.

Utah's First United States Senator:

1891   Cannon was prominent in the organization of the Republican Party in Utah. He was a delegate to the national convention in 1892 and 1896, and served as Utah's territorial delegate to Congress from 1895 to 1896.

As Utah neared statehood, Cannon hoped to become Utah's first senator. On January 4, 1896, President Grover Cleveland proclaimed Utah a state, ending Cannon's service as a territorial delegate. That evening he received a coded telegram from President Woodruff which translated: "It is the will of the Lord that your father shall be elected Senator from Utah. We want you to tell us how to bring it about."

"President Woodruff," Cannon replied, "you have received the revelation on the wrong point. You do not need a voice from heaven to convince anyone that my father is worthy to go to the Senate, but you will need a revelation to tell how he is to get there."

President Woodruff pointed out, "The legislators are pledged to you. Will you not release them from their promises and tell them to vote for your father?" "No," Cannon responded. "And my father would not permit me to do it, even if I could. He knows that I gave my word of honor to my supporters to stand as a candidate, no matter who might enter against me. He knows that he and I have given our pledges at Washington that political dictation in Utah by the heads of the Mormon Church shall cease." George Q. Cannon, with President Woodruff's approval, withdrew from the race. Frank J. Cannon was elected Utah's first United States Senator.

"Silver Republican":

1896   During his three years in the Senate, Cannon denounced Spanish rule in Cuba. He was one of the Senate leaders of the first ill-fated movement against the control of the Republican Party by financial interests he viewed as "piratical."

Cannon was a militant advocate of the remonetization of silver, an issue which gained national attention during the presidential campaign of 1896. Cannon delivered a strong speech at the Republican National Convention which nominated William McKinley, but unable to have their way, Cannon and the other "Silver Republicans" left the floor and threw their support behind Democrat William Jennings Bryan.

1898   Cannon's platform contained fourteen "Reasons for Voting for Cannon"—seven of which pertained to silver. But silver was not the issue in Utah; sugar was. The Church had extensive sugar interests. Cannon's 1897 vote against the Dingley Tariff was, in the words of his father, "a great mistake . . . alienating the friends who have done so much for us. . . . When a man's head is high, it is easily hit."

Cannon was the sole Republican voting nay. His vote cost him Church support and the election of 1898. In 1900 he joined the Democratic Party, serving as the Utah State Democratic Chairman in 1902.

The last decade of Cannon's life was devoted almost exclusively to bimetallism. He served as chairman of the International Silver Commission, and as president of the Bimetallical Association in Denver, Colorado.

"Furious Judas":

1903   As editor of the Democrat *Utah State Journal*, Cannon tried to gain "restoration of political freedom in Utah and to remonstrate against the new polygamy." When the *Journal* failed, Cannon became editor of the *Salt Lake Tribune*. Believing that the Reed Smoot confirmation hearings provided ample evidence that "the tyranny of the Prophet's absolutism had been re-established with a fierceness I had never even seen in the days of Brigham Young," Cannon began a relentless editorial attack on Church leaders—especially Joseph F. Smith.

Requested by friends Ben Rich and J. Golden Kimball to formally withdraw from the Church, Cannon refused. His February, 1905, editorial charged that President Smith "violated the laws [revelations] of his predecessors," took "the bodies of the daughters of his subjects and bestowed them upon his favorites," and "impoverished his subjects by a system of elaborate exactions [tithes] in order to enrich 'the crown.'"

1905 President Smith, privately referring to his nemesis as "Furious Judas," proceeded against him in the Church tribunals. Cannon refused to attend a meeting of his stake's high council convened to hear his case. He was excommunicated on March 14 for "unchristianlike conduct and apostasy." He responded in a *Tribune* editorial: "To be disfellowshipped by littleness is to be parted from dragging things. To be excommunicated by bigotry is to be set free to dwell in grandeur."

1911 Cannon published *Under the Prophet in Utah*, a vituperative attack on President Joseph F. Smith: "I undertake, in fact, in this narrative, to expose and to demonstrate what I do believe to be one of the most direful conspiracies of treachery in the history of the United States." In 1913 he wrote *Brigham Young and His Mormon Empire*.

Death:

1933 July 25: Cannon developed a serious infection following a minor surgical procedure and died in Denver. He was buried in the Ogden, Utah, Cemetery.

George Q. Cannon

(1827-1901)

Counselor to Four Prophets
Church Publisher

Family Background:

1827　January 11: Born George Quayle Cannon in Liverpool, England. In 1854 he married Elizabeth Hoagland, and later married plural wives Jane Jenne, Eliza Lamercia Tenny, Martha Telle, and Caroline Young Croxall, daughter of Brigham Young.

His thirty-five children included John Q., counselor to the Presiding Bishop; Abraham H., member of the Quorum of the Twelve; and Frank J., Utah's first U.S. Senator.

On one occasion he stopped in a cutlery shop in London and ordered three of their finest Sheffield razors for three sons who were turning twenty-one that month. "Triplets?" asked the clerk. "Why no, indeed," replied Cannon, "they were born several days apart throughout the month."

Orphan:

1842　George's family was converted to the Church by his uncle John Taylor. His mother died on the ocean voyage from Liverpool and his father died in Nauvoo. George was taken into the Taylor home and worked for his uncle on the *Times and Seasons*. He was adopted to John Taylor in the Nauvoo Temple in 1846.

Missionary:

1849　Two years after arriving in the Salt Lake Valley, Cannon was called on a gold-mining mission to California. "There was no place I would not rather have gone to at that time than California. I heartily despised the work of digging gold."

1850　Cannon and nine others were called to open missionary work in the Sandwich Islands (Hawaii). Discouraged when white settlers would not listen, five elders returned to Utah.

"I felt resolved to stay there, master the language and warn the people of those islands, if I had to do it alone." Through the efforts of the remaining missionaries, four thousand native Hawaiians joined the Church in four years.

Printer, Editor, and Publisher:

He began translating the Book of Mormon into Hawaiian after hearing the language for only one month. "In the beginning my method was to translate a few pages ... and explain to Brother Napela [a Hawaiian judge] the ideas. I would then read the translation to him ... and learn from him the impression the language conveyed to his mind. In this way I was able to correct any obscure expression which might be used, and secure the Hawaiian idiom."

After a brief trip to Salt Lake City to be married, he returned to San Francisco, where he and Parley P. Pratt published the Hawaiian Book of Mormon. He also published and edited the Church's *Western Standard* in San Francisco.

1858   With the approach of the Utah Expeditionary Force, the *Deseret News* press was moved to Fillmore and Cannon was appointed editor. Later in his life he edited and published in the *Millennial Star* and *Juvenile Instructor*, and with his sons established the George Q. Cannon & Sons Publishing Company.

General Authority:

1858   On one day's notice Cannon was sent to preside over the Eastern States Mission, with the special charge to influence Eastern editors against the rising "anti-Mormon feeling." At the time, Cannon's "family had no place to live in ... I had not time to do anything in relation to a house and they were left to shift for themselves."

1860   Returning from the East in August, Cannon was ordained an apostle by Brigham Young. He later testified, "I know that God lives. I know that Jesus lives, for I have seen him."

Six weeks after his return from the East, Cannon started for England with Charles C. Rich and Amasa M. Lyman to preside over the European Mission.

1862   Called home to serve as a "senator" to petition for statehood, Cannon had no legal standing with Congress, but represented the "state of Deseret" with W.H. Hooper. When the petition was denied and the first federal anti-polygamy legislation was enacted, Cannon returned to England.

By 1871 a tradeoff was being considered in which Utah would become a state in exchange for Church abandonment of plural marriage. Brigham Young sent Cannon east again to convince editors and Congressmen that the Church would not compromise "the principle."

Served as a member of the general superintendency of the Deseret Sunday School Union from 1867 to his death in 1901.

Beginning with a call as special counselor in the First Presidency, he served as counselor to Presidents Brigham Young (1873-77), John Taylor (1880-87), Wilford Woodruff (1889-98), and Lorenzo Snow (1898-1901).

Brigham Young Estate Executor:

1864   As Brigham Young's personal secretary, Cannon was appointed chief executor of the will.

Settlement of the estate was complicated by a suit filed by several Young heirs, resulting in three weeks imprisonment for Cannon and his co-executors Brigham Young, Jr., and Albert Carrington. In prison Cannon entertained many visitors and frequently granted inmate requests to "preach to the spirits in prison."

Council of Fifty Member:

1885   February 4: At an informal Council of Fifty meeting attended by seven apostles and two secretaries, George Q. Cannon anointed John Taylor "King, Priest, and Ruler over Israel on Earth." The ordination was in response to a revelation President Taylor had received and written, but never published.

A member of the council since 1867, Cannon served as recorder and for many years had the only key to the safe which contained council minutes since 1844.

Congressional Delegate:

1872   Elected Utah's territorial delegate with "voice but no vote." In Congress he came forward with the rest of the delegates to be sworn in, when, according to an Ohio Representative, "a fool from the other side jumped up and objected, and afterward offered a resolution. Mr. Cannon walked out cooly to one side and stood there, and I was struck with admiration at the manner in which he went through the scene; he showed such pluck and betrayed so little agitation. He looked as though he didn't care a damn whether they swore him in or not."

After nine years in the House of Representatives, Cannon was expelled as a polygamist in violation of the 1882 Edmunds Act.

Church Benefactor:

1878   "I have been desirous to . . . restore to the Church all I had ever drawn from it for services, so my labors might be gratuitous. I have paid tolerably heavy tithing and I felt if I could square up these credits I should be grateful," Cannon said. For twenty years of Church service and the funds he had drawn to build his "Big House," Cannon's "debt" totaled $39,914. He offered the $75,000 house to cancel the amount, but his fellow apostles declined the offer. Finally he deeded the house to the Church, his account was cancelled, and he received a credit of $20,000.

On the Underground:

1886   Due to his commanding presence, President Taylor's advanced age, and Joseph F. Smith's "exile" in Hawaii, George Q. Cannon was considered "the power behind the throne." Non-Mormons referred to him as "the Mormon Richelieu," and a bounty was offered for information leading to his arrest on "unlawful cohabitation" charges.

At one point Cannon proposed to President Taylor

that every man living in plural marriage should surrender himself to the court, pleading: "I entered into this covenant of celestial marriage with a personal conviction that it was an order revealed by our Father in Heaven for the salvation of mankind. I have kept my covenant in purity. I believed that no constitutional law of the country could forbid this practice of a religious faith. As the laws of Congress conflict with my sense of submission to the will of the Lord, I now offer myself, here, for whatever judgment the courts of my country may impose."

President Taylor, concerned for his counselor's safety, sent him to Mexico to negotiate a land contract. En route, he was apprehended by federal marshals near Humbolt Wells, Nevada. The returning party occupied a stateroom in the rear of one of the railroad cars. During a night-time bathroom trip, Cannon stepped outside the rear of the car to assess the possibilities of escape. The train lurched; he was thrown from the car and later recaptured in a dazed condition, bleeding profusely from a badly broken nose.

Boasts were made that Cannon would be imprisoned for life and that he would be sent to a distant prison where his condition would be "unbearable." On the advice of President Taylor and with the approval of his bondsmen, Cannon returned to the underground and forfeited a $45,000 bond.

1888 Frank J. Cannon persuaded President Grover Cleveland to replace punitive federal judges in Utah with more lenient judges. As part of the agreement, George Q. Cannon voluntarily appeared before Judge Elliott Sandford, pleaded guilty to two charges of "unlawful co-habitation," and was fined $450 and sentenced to 175 days in the Utah Territorial Prison.

In his own words, entering prison proved that "the leading men are willing to suffer but not to concede." His presence among other Mormon prisoners created a feeling that the Church was making no concessions on plural marriage. While imprisoned, he wasted no time. He collaborated on a biography of Joseph Smith with his sons, wrote magazine articles, organized a Sunday School and taught a Bible class, acquired an organ for the prison, and entertained hundreds of visitors.

George Q. Cannon (center, front row) at territorial penitentiary.

Businessman:

Director of the Bullion-Beck and Champion Mining Company (from which most of his wealth was derived), Union Pacific Railroad, Co-op Wagon and Machine Company, and Grant Central Mining Company; vice-president of ZCMI and Zion's Savings Bank and Trust Company; and president of George Q. Cannon Publishing Company, Utah Sugar Company, Brigham Young Trust Company, and Utah Light and Power Company.

Author:

Cannon's writings include *My First Mission, The Life of Nephi, The Latter-day Prophet: Young People's History of Joseph Smith,* and *Life of Joseph Smith the Prophet* (written primarily by his son Frank J.), three hundred discourses, and thousands of editorials.

Death:

1901   April 12: Died of "la grippe" (influenza) in Monterey, California, at the age of seventy-four. Buried in the Salt Lake City Cemetery.

A family publication honored him as a "Dedicated Apostle—Grimy Gold-Miner! Distinguished Statesman—Energetic Emigration Agent! Spell-Binding Missionary—Intransigent Federal Prisoner! Brilliant Writer and Orator—Thirteen-year-old 'school dropout.'" They remembered him, too, as a faddish dieter and health food enthusiast, a lover of ice baths, a man prone to seasickness and abnormally afraid of mice.

Martha Hughes Cannon

(1857-1932)

Physician
Plural Wife
First Female State Senator in the United States

Family Background:

1857   July 1: Born Martha Hughes. Her family joined the Church in Wales and emigrated to America a few months after her birth. Her father's ill health prevented their continuing to Utah until 1860. He died just two days after their arrival in Salt Lake City.

Physician:

As a child, Martha dreamed of being a doctor. When she was fifteen, Church leaders called her to set type for the *Deseret News* and the *Woman's Exponent*. She attended the University of Deseret and saved her typesetting wages to go to medical school.

1878   Set apart for medical training by President John Taylor, she entered the University of Michigan Medical School, where she received an M.D. on her birthday in 1880. Two years later she graduated from the University of Pennsylvania and the National School of Elocution and Oratory with bachelor of science degrees. She was the only woman in her graduating class.

1882   Dr. Cannon opened a private medical practice in Salt Lake City, but was soon called to serve as a resident physician at Deseret Hospital. Attempts to continue her medical practice were interrupted throughout her life by the birth of her three children, exile in the face of polygamy persecution, and political activities.

Plural Wife:

1884   Secretly married Salt Lake Stake President Angus Cannon in the Endowment House. He was twenty-three years her senior; she was his third plural wife. Each time she became pregnant, she was forced to leave the city to prevent her husband's arrest; she visited Europe to avoid detection in 1886-87.

Cannon described her marriage as "a few stolen interviews thoroughly tinctured with the *dread of discovery.* . . . Oh for a home! A husband of my own because he is my own. A father for my children whom they know by association. And all the little auxiliaries that make life worth living. Will they ever be enjoyed by this storm-tossed exile. Or must life thus drift on and one more victim swell the ranks of the great unsatisfied!"

If she had not believed that plural marriage, rightly lived, would enable her to associate with the elect in eternity, she said, she would "undoubtedly have given plural marriage a wide berth except perhaps as first wife."

But she also noted the advantage of a plural wife: "If her husband has four wives, she has three weeks of freedom every month."

Women's Rights Advocate:

1893 As a suffragette, Cannon addressed the Columbia Exposition and, in 1898, lobbied in Washington, D.C., for women's right to vote.

"You give me a woman who thinks about something besides cook stoves and wash tubs and baby flannels," she declared, "and I'll show you, in nine times out of ten, a successful mother."

First Female State Senator:

1896 Running against her Republican husband, Democrat Martha Hughes Cannon won one of five Utah State Senate seats, becoming the first woman in the United States to be elected a state senator.

1896 As a member of Utah's first senate, Cannon championed public health, sponsoring "An Act to Protect the Health of Women and Girl Employees," "An Act Providing for the Compulsory Education of Deaf, Dumb, and Blind Children," and "An Act Creating a State Board of Health and Defining its Duties."

In 1897 Dr. Cannon ignored her husband's political views and supported Moses Thatcher for the U.S. Senate. Thatcher had been dropped from the Quorum of the Twelve for refusing to sign a "political manifesto."

According to the *Salt Lake Tribune*, Cannon's endorsement speech was so eloquent that "despite parliamentary decorum and the rigid rules against demonstrations she was cheered and cheered again at its conclusion."

She refused to support her husband's nephew Frank J. Cannon for the Senate in 1899 because, she said, she had been elected a Democrat and intended to support the Democratic candidate, Joseph L. Rawlins.

Death:

1932   July 10: Died at the age of seventy-five following surgery in Los Angeles. She had lived during the last years of her life near her children in California, where she worked in the orthopedic department of General Hospital and at the Graves Clinic. She was buried in the Salt Lake City Cemetery.

Butch Cassidy

(1866-1937)

"*King of the Wild Bunch*"

Mormon Background:

1866   April 13: Born Robert LeRoy Parker in Beaver, Utah, the eldest of thirteen children. He was baptized at the age of eight. Temple work was performed in his behalf by his brother-in-law in 1945.

Horse Thief:

1884   When the family moved to Circleville, Utah, near Bryce Canyon, young Parker was influenced by a local outlaw, Mike Cassidy. After his initial horse-stealing venture, Parker escaped to Telluride, Colorado.

Jack-of-All-Trades:

When he was not robbing banks or trains, Parker worked as an ore packer in the Telluride mines, as a ranch hand, cowboy, and even as a butcher in Otto Schnauber's Meat Market in Rock Springs, Wyoming. This latter job, coupled with his outlaw mentor Mike Cassidy's last name, is apparently the source of his best-known alias—"Butch Cassidy."

An excellent handler of horses, he won many horse-races in Telluride and later in Brown's Park on the Utah-Colorado border.

As a ranch hand with the Eugene Amaretti outfit in Wind River, Wyoming, he was described as a "crack shot, and the best there was with a rope. . . . He could ride around a tree full speed and empty a six-gun into the tree, putting every shot within a three-inch circle."

Caught:

1892   July 15: Arrested with Al Hainer on a horse-theft complaint. The arresting officer, Bob Calverly, reported: "I told him I had a warrant for him and he said: 'Well get to shooting,' and with that we pulled our guns. I put the barrel of my revolver almost to his stomach, but it missed three times, but owing to the fact that there was another man between us, he failed to hit me. The fourth time I snapped the gun it went off and the bullet hit him in the upper part of the forehead and felled him. I then had him and he made no further resistance." Cassidy was acquitted.

1893   While still in custody, Cassidy was tried and convicted on a second charge of horse-stealing and on July 15, 1894, was sentenced to two years of hard larbor in the Wyoming penitentiary—the only jail sentence he ever served.

Prison description: "Height, 5'9"; Complexion, Light; Hair, Dark Flaxen; Eyes, Blue; Wife, No; Parents, Not Known; Children, No; Religion, None; Habits of Life, Intemperate; Education, Com. School; Relations Address, Not Known; Weight 165#; Marks, Scars; Features regular, small deep set eyes, 2 cut scars on back of head, small red scar under left eye, red mark on left side of back, small mole on calf of left leg, good build."

Pardon:

1896   Wyoming Governor W.A. Richards pardoned Cassidy on the promise that he would stop robbing Wyoming banks and rustling Wyoming cattle. As a "gentleman outlaw," Cassidy was a man of his word. He turned to robbing Wyoming trains and non-Wyoming banks.

"King of the Wild Bunch":

In the five years after his pardon, Cassidy masterminded bank and train robberies in Montpelier, Idaho; Castle Gate, Utah; Folsom, New Mexico; Winnemucca, Nevada; and Wagner, Montana—robberies that netted over $270,000. His "Wild Bunch," perhaps the largest group of outlaws in the West, operated out of the Brown's Hole and Robbers Roost areas of Colorado and Utah.

After the Winnemucca job, members of the gang escaped to Fort Worth, Texas, where they posed for a formal photograph which they sent to the Winnemucca Bank, "thanking them for their contribution."

Butch told his family, "There were a lot of good friends, but Elzy Lay was the best, always dependable and level-headed. Sundance and I got along fine, but he liked his liquor too much and was too quick on the trigger."

When his father asked if he had ever killed a man, Butch claimed, "No, thank God. But some of my boys had itchy trigger fingers. I tried to control 'em. I feel real bad about some posse men who got shot."

Wild Bunch at Ft. Worth, Texas. Standing, L-R: Bill Carver, Harvey Logan. Sitting, L-R: Harry Longabough, Ben Kilpatrick, Butch Cassidy.

South American Rancher-Robber:

1902   After a five-year crime spree, Cassidy, Harry Longbaugh (the Sundance Kid), and the Kid's girlfriend, Etta Place (described in Pinkerton Detective files as "a refined type"), embarked for Argentina. They bought "four square leagues" of land in Cholilo, Chubert Province, and established a large ranch with thirteen hundred head of sheep, five hundred head of cattle, and thirty-five horses.

1905   The three robbed the Bank of Loudres and Tarapaco at Rio Gallegos, Argentina, of 20,000 pesos and an undetermined amount of gold. They also successfully robbed the bank of Via Mercedes in San Luis in 1906.

Report of His Death Greatly Exaggerated:

1909   Mistakenly reported killed in a gun battle with Bolivian police and soldiers in San Vicente. The false reports were based on Arthur Chapman's poem, "Out Where the West Begins," which colorfully recounts that Cassidy and Sundance had robbed the payroll of the Aramayo Mines near Quechisla, Bolivia.

         Surrounded by police and Bolivian cavalry, Chapman claimed, the two decided to shoot their way out rather than be captured. Sundance was seriously wounded. After dragging him to cover, the "King of the Wild Bunch" fired a bullet into the Kid's head and a second into his own. According to this account, the outlaws killed twenty Bolivians and wounded forty more.

"William Phillips":

1908   After a year of working in the Concordia Tin Mines near Tres Cruces, Bolivia, Cassidy returned to the U.S. and settled in Michigan. As "William Thadeus Phillips," he married Gertrude Livesay in Morenci, Michigan. In 1919 they adopted a son, William Richard Phillips.

1912   Cassidy unsuccessfully hunted for gold in Alaska and eventually established the Phillips Manufacturing Company in Spokane, Washington. He developed an adding machine and invented parts for farm equipment, an automatic garage-door opener, and an automobile gas-mileage indicator.

Hard Times:

1930   He lost his business in the Depression and tried in vain to locate buried caches of money hidden during his outlaw days.

         According to his younger sister, Lula Betenson, Cassidy visited his father in Circleville, Utah, in 1925 and told him that he had tried to leave his life of crime on several early occasions, but "when a man gets down, they won't let him up. He never quits paying his price."

1934 Butch wrote *The Bandit Invincible, the Story of Butch Cassidy,* but failed to find a publisher for his life's story. This unpublished manuscript, along with an inscribed ring, Cassidy's marked guns, and other compelling evidence, welds the link between Butch Cassidy and William Phillips in Larry Pointer's book *In Search of Butch Cassidy.*

Death:

1937 July 20: Died of rectal cancer in Spokane at the age of seventy-one. He was cremated and his ashes scattered over the Little Spokane River.

J. Reuben Clark

(1871-1961)

Ambassador to Mexico
Member of the First Presidency
Statesman

Family Background:

1871   September 1: Born Joshua Reuben Clark, Jr., the eldest of ten children, in Grantsville, Utah. In 1898 he married Luacine Annette Savage, daughter of prominent photographer C.R. Savage; they had four children.

Intense Student:

His father, a school teacher, remarked that Reuben "would rather miss his meals than miss a day from school." After completing the eighth grade, the extent of educational opportunity in Grantsville, he returned to repeat the grade twice more: "I was not quite that dull, but there was nothing to do, so I went to school in the winter time and went over the same ground."

1890   Enrolled in the Latter-day Saint College in Salt Lake City. Principal James E. Talmage, recognizing Reuben's potential, as well as his poverty, offered him a job at the new Deseret Museum. When Talmage became president of the University of Utah in 1894, he named Clark as his assistant.

1898   In addition to working for Talmage, Clark edited the *University Chronicle*, served as student body president, and completed six years of study in four, graduating first in his class. His valedictory address was filled with enthusiasm for the Spanish-American War.

Teacher:

1898   Served as principal of the Heber, Utah, school system for one year. In 1899 he taught at the Salt Lake City Business College for a year, and then served as principal of the University of Utah's Southern Normal School in Cedar City. Differences of opinion with the board of trustees over granting four-year recognition for the school led to his replacement and return to Salt Lake City.

Law Student:

1902   Clark's dream of going to law school was fulfilled when his Salt Lake Business School mentor Joseph Nelson picked up the tab as a "loan...without interest, terms, or penalties." When Clark left for Columbia University, Talmage remarked, "He possesses the brightest mind ever to leave Utah."

1906   Received his L.L.B. from Columbia University, where he was editor of the law review.

State Department Solicitor:

1906   Shortly after graduation, Clark was appointed assistant solicitor with the State Department under Secretary of State Elihu Root. Dominating the State Department legal bureau, he was appointed solicitor in 1910 and was responsible for settling the legal difficulties encountered during the Mexican Revolution.

Lawyer:

1913   When Democrat Woodrow Wilson swept into power, Clark left the State Department for private law practice, but his international clientele and service on the American-British Pecuniary Claims Commission kept him abreast of American foreign policy.

1917   At the outbreak of World War I, he joined both the office of the United States attorney general and the headquarters of the army provost marshal. For his military service he was awarded three silver chevrons and the Distinguished Service medal.

1921   With Staynor Richards and Albert Bowen, he established a prestigious law firm in Salt Lake City.

Ambassador to Mexico:

1927   Having served on the United States-Mexico Mixed Claims Commission, Clark was appointed legal counsel to the ambassador to Mexico by Herbert Hoover. After a temporary assignment as undersecretary of state, he was named ambasador to Mexico in 1930.

"I am an American because this nation has no scheme or plan of conquest," he said, "because it has a respect for the rights of other peoples and of other nations, because it promotes justice and honor in the relationships of nations, because it loves the ways of peace as against war."

During his government career, he at one time or another opposed virtually every major political figure he worked with, including Theodore Roosevelt, Elihu Root, William H. Taft, Henry Cabot Lodge, Woodrow Wilson, Herbert Hoover, Franklin D. Roosevelt, and Reed Smoot. He described himself as "anti-internationalist, anti-interventionist, anti-meddlesome busybodiness, in our international affairs. In the domestic field, I am anti-socialist, anti-communist, anti-Welfare State."

Of his fierce opposition to the League of Nations, he declared: "I am a confirmed isolationist, a political isolationist, first I am sure, by political instinct, next from experience, observation, and patriotism, and lastly, because while isolated, we built the most powerful nation in the world, a nation that provided most of prosperity to all its citizens, with the full measure of resulting comfort, most of popular education, most of freedom, most of peace, most of blessing by example to other nations."

General Authority:

1923 Concerned with her husband's passivity toward the Church, Luacine Clark commented, "I don't see why you can't do a little church work. . . . Everyone loves to hear you talk, you would be such a big help if you would take hold. You have been nearly twenty years out of it. . . . I have hired you, I remember, more than once to go to church with me, but now you are of age."

1925 Appointed to the general board of the YMMIA. The following year he became a member of the advisory editorial committee of the *Improvement Era*.

1931 At the funeral of Second Counselor Charles W. Nibley,

President Grant whispered to First Counselor Anthony W. Ivins that he knew who could fill the vacancy in the Presidency: "This man Clark, the ambassador to Mexico." "You can't get him, Heber," Ivins advised, "he is a $100,000-a-year man." Replied the President, "We can ask him."

1933   Called as Second Counselor to President Grant. Ordained an apostle and called as first counselor on the death of President Anthony W. Ivins in 1934. He also served in the First Presidency during the administrations of Presidents George Albert Smith and David O. McKay—a total of twenty-eight years.

Conservative Philosopher:

"We are of the view that the so-called inefficiency of democracies . . . is evidence of their highest virtue, which is a regulation of the civic, social, and economic life of the nation by the experience of all the people, crystallized into their mass wisdom. We know that this must mean a slow development, but we know also that it means a sure one."

"On more than one occasion our Church members have gone to other places for special training in particular lines; they have had the training which was supposedly the last word, the most modern view. . . . Before trying on the newest fangled ideas in any line of thought, education, activity, or what not, experts should just stop and consider that however backward we may actually be in some things, in other things we are far out in the lead, and therefore these new methods may be old, if not worn out, with us."

Death:

1961   October 6: Died at the age of ninety in Salt Lake City; buried in Salt Lake City Cemetery.

Oliver Cowdery

(1806-1850)

Joseph Smith's Scribe
Book of Mormon Witness
Associate President of the Church

Family Background:

1806   October 3: Born in Wells, Vermont. In 1832 he married Elizabeth Ann Whitmer, daughter of Peter Whitmer, Sr. Only one of their six children lived to adulthood. Cowdery was brother-in-law to Brigham Young's brother Phineas and to Book of Mormon Witnesses David Whitmer, Jacob Whitmer, and Peter Whitmer, Jr. He was a third cousin to the Prophet Joseph Smith.

Book of Mormon Scribe:

1829   A rural school teacher, he became aware of the gold plates while boarding in the home of Joseph Smith, Sr. As the Prophet's scribe, "I wrote with my own pen, the entire Book of Mormon (save a few pages), as it fell from the lips of the Prophet Joseph Smith, as he translated it by the gift and power of God."

Book of Mormon Witness:

1829   As one of the Three Witnesses, Cowdery testified, "We, through the grace of God the Father, and our Lord Jesus Christ, have seen the plates which contain this record.... And we also testify that we have seen the engravings which are upon the plates; and they have been shown unto us by the power of God, and not of man. And we declare with words of soberness, that an angel of God came down from heaven, and he brought and laid them before our eyes, that we beheld and saw the plates."

Early Church Leader:

Cowdery is mentioned in twenty-seven sections of the Doctrine and Covenants, which include references to his ordination by John the Baptist (section 13), his gift of faith and power equalling that of the Prophet (section 17), and his appointment as "first preacher to the Church" (section 21).

Cowdery was one of the six original members of the

Church, the first person baptized, and the first ordained to the priesthood in this dispensation.

1830 According to Joseph Smith's 1838 journal history, as they neared completion of the Book of Mormon, they became concerned about the restoration of priesthood authority. "We had not long been engaged in solemn and fervent prayer, when the word of the Lord came unto us in the chamber, commanding us; that I should ordain Oliver Cowdery to be an Elder in the Church of Jesus Christ; and that he also should ordain me to the same office, and then to ordain others as it should be made known unto us, from time to time: we were however commanded to defer this our ordination untill, such times, as it should be practicable to have our brethren, who had been and who should be baptized, assembled together, when we must have their sanction to our thus proceeding to ordain each other, and have them decide by vote whether they were willing to accept us as spiritual teachers or not."

April 6: Designated "second elder" at the organization of the Church, Cowdery was called on a mission six months later with Parley P. Pratt, Peter Whitmer, Jr., and Ziba Peterson "into the wilderness among the Lamanites" (D&C 32).

1834 December 5: Ordained "to assist in presiding over the whole church, and, to officiate in the absence of the President," a position that gave him authority over Joseph Smith's counselors. Church historian Joseph Fielding Smith coined the term "associate president" to describe Cowdery's office.

1835 With Martin Harris and David Whitmer, Cowdery selected twelve elders to constitute the first Quorum of the Twelve.

1836 In the Kirtland Temple Cowdery administered endowments and, on April 3, shared with Joseph Smith a vision of Christ, Moses, Elias, and Elijah.

Editor:

Editor of the *Messenger and Advocate* and of the edited

republication of the *Evening and Morning Star* in Kirtland, Ohio.

Alleged Polygamist:

1832   According to Brigham Young, "While Joseph And Oliver were translating the Book of Mormon they had a revelation that the order of Patriarchal Marriag and the Sealing was right. Oliver Said unto Joseph, 'Br Joseph why dont we go into the Order of Polygamy, and practice it as the ancients did? We know it is true, then why delay?' Joseph's reply was 'I know that we know it is true, and from God, but the time has not yet come.' This did not seem to suit Oliver, who expressed a determination to go into the order of Plural Marriage anyhow, although he was ignorant of the order and pattern and the results. Joseph said, 'Oliver if you go into this thing it is not with my faith or consent.' Disregarding the counsel of Joseph, Oliver Cowdery took to wife Miss Annie Lyman cousin to George A. Smith. From that time he went into darkness and lost the spirit. Annie Lyman is still alive, a witness to these things."

This statement by President Young seems to have been either to discredit Oliver Cowdery or to enhance polygamy. No charges of sexual misconduct were made against Cowdery during his 1838 excommunication trial. However, one of the charges brought against him, was seeking to destroy the prophet's character by "insinuating that he was guilty of adultery." Cowdery had openly condemned the Prophet for that "dirty, nasty, filthy affair of his and Fanny Alger's."

Excommunication:

1838   Excommunicated in Far West, Missouri, for (1) persecuting the brethren by urging on vexatious lawsuits against them; (2) accusing Joseph Smith of adultery; (3) not attending meetings; (4) not being governed by ecclesiastical authority in temporal matters (charge withdrawn); (5) selling land in Jackson County against the wishes of Joseph Smith (charge withdrawn); (6) sending an insulting letter to Thomas B. Marsh (charge withdrawn); (7) leaving his calling to practice law; (8) being in the "bogus business"; (9) dishonestly keeping notes that had been paid.

Left Missouri after he, David Whitmer, John Whitmer, W.W. Phelps, and Lyman E. Johnson received a letter signed by eighty-four Church members ordering the dissenters to leave the country or "face a more fatal calamity." For Cowdery, there was a special irony in his fleeing Missouri under Church duress. In November, 1836, he had joined with sixty-nine other Church leaders who signed a petition warning a hostile justice of the peace to leave Kirtland.

Lawyer:

1840s Practiced law for several years in Ohio and Wisconsin. He described his 1842 practice as "steadily increasing—nothing operates against me, except the fact that I have been formerly connected with, what is now an important church."

A contemporary described him as "an able lawyer and great advocate. His manners were easy and gentlemanly; he was polite, dignified, yet courteous. He had an open countenance, high forehead, dark brown eyes, Roman nose, clenched lips and prominent lower jaw. He shaved smooth and was neat and clean in his appearance. He was of light stature about five feet, five inches high and had a loose easy walk. With all his kind and friendly disposition there was a certain degree of sadness that seemed to pervade his whole being."

Return to the Church:

1848 Though he joined the Methodist church in Tiffin, Ohio, he kept in constant communication with his brother-in-law, Phineas Young, who encouraged him to travel to Council Bluffs, Iowa. He was permitted to address the Saints when he arrived, and the next day he was rebaptized by Orson Hyde.

Brigham Young wrote him in 1849, "congratulating him on his return to the Church, admonishing him to righteousness and informing him of their [The First Presidency's] desire that he should accompany Mr. Babbitt [Almon] to Washington and endeavor 'to obtain the admission of the state of Deseret' into the union."

Death:

1850   Wishing to visit his in-laws, the Whitmers, Cowdery left Council Bluffs for Richmond, Missouri. He wrote Phineas Young, "I am poor, very poor, and I did hope to have health and means sufficient last spring to go West and get some gold, that I might so situate my family, that I could be engaged in the cause of God; but I did not succeed."

Neither Cowdery's financial status nor his health improved. Suffering from consumption (tuberculosis), he complained, "My lungs are very bad, with considerable cough. I have been careful to take exercise in the open air and flatter myself that my cough is less severe and that I raise less also. I have spit no blood during this attack as last winter."

Died March 3 at the age of forty-three. David Whitmer, who was present, said he died "the happiest man I ever saw." Buried in the "old" Richmond, Missouri, Cemetery.

Matthew Cowley

(1897-1953)

Child of Promise
"Apostle to the South Pacific"

Child of Promise:

1895   July 28: Moses Thatcher dedicated the Cowley home in Preston, "That herein might be born prophets, seers, and revelators to honor God."

Family Background:

1897   August 2: Born in Preston, Idaho, to future Apostle Matthias F. Cowley and Abbie Hyde. In 1922 he married Elva Eleanor Taylor; they had one child and adopted a Maori son.

Missionary:

1914   At the age of seventeen he began a five-year mission to New Zealand, where he learned Maori in three months by studying eleven hours a day.

       Soon after his arrival, Cowley was summoned to the bedside of a Maori man suffering from typhoid fever. "All I could do was pray, and I knelt down beside that suffering native, and I prayed to God, and opened up my heart to him; and I believe the channel was open; and then I placed my hands upon that good brother; and with the authority of the priesthood which I as a young boy held, I blessed him to be restored to health."

       Shortly after his mission, he was called by President George Albert Smith to translate the Doctrine and Covenants and Pearl of Great Price into Maori, and to revise the Maori translation of the Book of Mormon.

Lawyer:

1925   Graduated from George Washington Law School. As a student he had worked for Senator Reed Smoot on the U.S. Senate Finance Committee.

       Following graduation, Cowley began practicing law in Salt Lake City. Five years later he became Salt Lake County Attorney.

       "Law is a wonderful profession. I never made much

money at it.... When you are an honest lawyer and you represent criminals, it isn't long until you have lost all your clients. They are in jail.... They never did pay me. Many of them offered to pay me at times, but with stolen property."

"Apostle to the South Pacific":

1939   Began a six-year term as mission president in New Zealand. Maoris called him "Tumnaki," or "great leader."

On one occasion Cowley was asked to name a fourteen-month-old child and give it a blessing. Matter-of-factly the father added, "'While you are giving it its name, give it its sight.' The child was born blind...

"Well, I was scared. I never had that faith. The thing came to me suddenly like lightning out of the blue. But I went on and blessed the baby with a name. It was the longest blessing I think I have ever given. I was using all the words I could think of and had ever thought of. I was trying to get enough inspiration—enough nerve, if you want to call it that, to bless that child with its vision. I finally did.

"Eight months later I saw the child, and the child saw me.... Never let this simple faith get away from your life, never let it get away from you. It is the most precious thing you have in your life."

Of healing by the power of the priesthood, Cowley said, "Miracles are evidence of the efficacy of the priesthood of God, to bring his power and blessing to the children of men. Everywhere you go among the people you see the blessing of the sick, making the blind to see, and the deaf to hear. Let us appreciate the priesthood we hold and magnify it so that God will magnify us. He wants us to do his work for him."

1945   October 5: Called to the Quorum of the Twelve by President George Albert Smith.

1946   Called to preside over the Pacific Islands Mission, consisting of Hawaii, Tonga, Tahiti, New Zealand, and Australia.

1947   Reopened the Japanese Mission.

1949   Introduced missionaries into Hong Kong.

Humorist:

> To a friend running for political office: "I would rather see you running for the position of janitor of the St. John's post office on the Republican ticket than for the position of Chief Justice of the Supreme Court of Arizona on the Democratic ticket. Repent, brother, repent, before it is too late, and it becomes too well-known that you have temporarily descended to the lowly ranks of the Democratic Party."
>
> To his parents-in-law, shortly after his marriage: "I had long flattered myself on being one of the few remaining he-men of the present generation, until Christmas morning, when I received among other things, from you know where, a beautiful rubber gown to be worn by men in the very holy of holies of the woman—the kitchen. . . . Woe is me, the mantle of femininity has fallen on these masculine shoulders!"

Counselor to Alcoholics:

> Spent much of his life serving in alcoholic rehabilitation programs, counseling alcoholics and their families, and speaking to Alcoholics Anonymous groups.

Death:

1953   December 13: While attending the dedication of the Los Angeles Temple, he suffered a massive heart attack and died at the age of fifty-six. Buried in Salt Lake City Cemetery.

Richard L. Evans

(1906-1971)

"Voice of the Mormon Tabernacle Choir"
Apostle

Family Background:

1906   March 23: Born Richard Louis Evans in Salt Lake City. His father died from injuries received in a streetcar accident when Richard was only ten weeks old. When he was thirteen, his left eye was destroyed by a pellet from a playmate's BB gun.
In 1933 he married Alice Ruth Thornley; they had four sons.

Editor and Author:

Evans edited his high school yearbook, and as a nineteen-year-old missionary to Great Britain, served as assistant editor of the *Millennial Star* under mission presidents James E. Talmage and John A. Widtsoe. In Evans's copy of *Evidences and Reconciliations* Widtsoe wrote, "To me this volume is another evidence of your goodness to me. No son could do more than you have done for me in our association together."

He began fourteen years as managing editor of the *Improvement Era* in 1937 followed by twenty-one years as senior editor. He was instrumental in the creation of the *Ensign, New Era*, and *Friend* magazines.

Evans wrote seventeen books in addition to fourteen volumes of his "Spoken Word" sermons. He also wrote a weekly editorial for William Randolph Hearst's national King Features for five years.

KSL Director:

1928   Shortly after graduating from the University of Utah, Evans began working as an announcer on KSL radio. He soon became publicity director, production manager, and eventually station director.
"I spend a full seventy hours a week working here," he said. "I never have a day off, not excepting Sundays or holidays. At one time I went two years without a vacation or a single day off, except one day spent in bed under doctor's orders."

"Voice of the Mormon Tabernacle Choir":

1929 "Once more we welcome you within these walls, with music and the spoken word, from the Crossroads of the West," was the sign-on heard by millions of Americans every Sunday as they tuned in Richard L. Evans and the Mormon Tabernacle Choir.

To his vast audience, Evans was "a personal friend who dropped in Sunday mornings to introduce the selections to be performed by the Mormon Tabernacle Choir and organ and to share his short, inspirational messages. Many people throughout the world have claimed membership in Richard L. Evans's church. . . . Their only 'religion,' an enjoyable half-hour weekly with 'Music and the Spoken Word.'"

Evans delivered more than two thousand sermons during the forty-one years he produced and announced the program. *The Spoken Word* messages were short, to the point, and filled with suggestions for improving one's life: "There are some fine distinctions to be found in the now immortal phrase, 'life, liberty, and the *pursuit* of happiness.' Life is an eternal fact; liberty, an inalienable right. But with happiness—we are offered only the right to *pursue* it! We can give man his liberty. He may not use it well or keep it long, but we can give it to him. But not so his happiness. We can help, but ultimately he has to help himself to happiness."

General Authority:

1938 October 7: At thirty-two, Evans became the youngest general authority in over thirty years when he was called as a president of the First Council of the Seventy.

1947 Appointed director of Temple Square.

1953 October 8: Called to the Quorum of the Twelve by President David O. McKay. His committee responsibilities included Church magazines, Temple Square activities, world fair exhibits and other Church information centers, the Tabernacle Choir and the Choir broadcast, general conference broadcasts, the Hill Cumorah pageant, Church historical sites, management of Church communications, public relations, publications, translation and distribution, and temple ceremonies.

Rotary President:

Elected president of the Salt Lake Rotary Club in 1949. A year later he was elected president of the University of Utah Alumni Association. Three years later he was elected president of the Salt Lake Bonneville Knife and Fork Club. After his calling as an apostle, he was elected International Rotary president.

Death:

1971   November 1: Died of a viral infection of the central nervous system at the age of sixty-five; buried in the Salt Lake City Cemetery.

Green Flake

(1828-1903)

Black Pioneer
"Human Tithing"

Family Background:

1828 January 6: Born into slavery on the Jordan Flake plantation in Madsburr, Anson County, North Carolina. Married Martha Crosby (later known as Louise, "Liz," Hazel), daughter of Vilate Litchfield. They had two children, Abraham Green Flake and Lucinda Vilate Flake Stephens. The Flakes also raised Lewis Flake, a white foster son.

Mormon Convert:

1844 James M. Flake, Green's owner, was baptized in Mississippi during the winter of 1843-44. After visiting Illinois in the spring of 1844, the family decided to move to Nauvoo. John Brown recorded in his pioneer journal that he "baptized two black men, Allen and Green, belonging to Brother Flake," in April, 1844.

Black Pioneer:

1847 "When Brigham Young commenced fitting out a train to take the first of the Pioneers across the Great Plains, he needed the very best teams and outfits to be had. James M. Flake, who had put his all upon the altar, sent his slave, Green, with the mules and mountain carriage, to help the company to their destination. He told Green to send the outfit back by some of the brethren, who would be returning, and for him to stay and build them a house. Like the old slaves he faithfully carried out his instructions."

One of three black servants in the pioneer company, Green drove James Flake's white-topped carriage used by Brigham Young during the trek and entrance into the Salt Lake Valley. By Green's own account, he was "in the first wagon through Emigration Canyon."

Human Tithing:

1850 When Green's owner was killed in an accident in California, Mrs. Flake moved to San Bernardino with

Charles C. Rich and Amasa M. Lyman. Before leaving Salt Lake, she gave her "Negro slave Green Flake to the Church as tithing. He then worked two years for President Young and Heber C. Kimball, and then got his liberty."

Settler:

1851   A free man, Green moved his family to the Union area of Salt Lake County, where he farmed and mined ore from the Cottonwood Canyons. He was an active member of the Union Ward. Friends and neighbors remembered his neighborly deeds, his fine singing voice, and his participation in dances at the old Union Co-op Hall.

1885   Upon the death of his wife, he moved to Gray's Lake, Idaho, to be near his son Abraham's family. He returned to Salt Lake in 1897 to attend the Utah Pioneer Jubilee on July 24, where he received a certificate honoring him as a surviving member of the Brigham Young pioneer company.

Death:

1903   October 20: Died in Idaho Falls, Idaho, at the age of seventy-five. Buried in the Union, Utah, Pioneer Cemetery.

Susa Young Gates

(1856-1933)

*Women's Rights Advocate
"The Thirteenth Apostle"*

Family Background:

1856   March 18: Born in the Lion House in Salt Lake City, Susa Amelia Young was Brigham Young's forty-first child. When told she was a girl, Susa's mother, Lucy Bigelow, exclaimed: "Shucks." "No!" cried midwife Zina D. H. Young, "It isn't all shucks, it's wheat, and full weight too!"

Student:

1869   At thirteen, she entered the University of Deseret, but her father soon banished her to Saint George for helping her sister Dora elope.

A few months later she recorded this self-portrait: "5'3". 115 lbs. Dark blue or grey eyes, light 'rather curly' brown hair. I must confess my teeth are the only redeeming feature of my face."

In 1877 Susa became the first person to be baptized for the dead in the newly completed Saint George Temple.

Returning to Salt Lake City, she mastered courses in telegraphy and shorthand. As Church recorder David W. Evans's "star pupil," Susa attained such proficiency that she occasionally served as her father's clerk at conferences.

Troubled Marriage:

1872   Married Saint George dentist Alma Dunford. Sixteen years old at the time, she was psychologically unprepared for the intimacies of married life. Her husband's drinking problem complicated their relationship. In 1877, while Dunford was serving a mission intended to rehabilitate him from alcoholism, Susa filed for divorce. He returned and raised their two children. Even on her deathbed more than fifty years later, she worried, "I hope I have not wronged Dr. Dunford."

1880   Married Jacob Gates; they had eleven children, seven of whom died in childhood accidents or illnesses: Simpson Mark and Heber died shortly after birth, Joseph Sterling at the age of five. Jacob Young and Karl Naham died in Hawaii, where Elder Gates had been called on a mission, of "diptheriatric croup." Sarah Beulah was shot to death in childhood play. Three-year old Brigham died of dye poisoning from a candy wrapper. Baily Dunford, her eldest son was blown up in adulthood in a powder factory explosion in Butte, Montana.

Susa and Jacob Gates with descendents.

"The Thirteenth Apostle":

1899 Though she "admitted to not having a spiritual conviction of the Gospel until her fortieth year," Gates was called to the general board of the Young Ladies Mutual Improvement Association, and twenty years later to the general board of the Relief Society.

The only woman given an office in the Church Office Building at 47 East South Temple, she was jokingly referred to as "the thirteenth apostle." She advised, "Provoke the brethren to good works, but don't provoke the brethren while doing so."

Women's Rights Advocate:

1901 Delegate to the International Council of Women in Copenhagen and London. In England she presented a paper, "Scientific Treatment of Domestic Science," and was invited to tea with Queen Victoria.

"In times past," she wrote to her colleagues, "women have . . . done many improper things; and one of them is they often preferred men's opinions to their own and even yielded points of conscience for the sake of pleasing them, until, very naturally, they are looked upon by men as shallow, weak, and contemptible. . . . A course of self-reliance and self-assertion will restore our credit."

She organized the music department at Brigham Young Academy when she was twenty-two, and nineteen years later established the domestic science department. She served on the boards of directors of both the Brigham Young Academy and the Utah Agricultural College.

1904 As president of the Daughters of the Utah Pioneers, Gates established the Hall of Relics. Acclaimed "founder of modern Mormon genealogical research," in 1923 she became head of the Genealogical Society of Utah's Library and Research Department.

Author and Editor:

She founded the *Young Woman's Journal* (1889), edited the *Relief Society Magazine*, and, under the pen name of "Homespun," wrote many articles for the *Deseret News*, *Juvenile Instructor*, *Woman's Exponent*, and *Young Woman's Journal.*

She also wrote several books, including *Lydia Knight's History*, *John Steven's Courtship*, *History of the Young Ladies Mutual Improvement Association*, *The Prince of Ur*, *Surname Book and Racial History*, and, with her daughter Leah Dunford Widtsoe, *The Life Story of Brigham Young*.

Death:

1933 May 27: Died of cancer at the age of seventy-seven in Salt Lake City. Buried in the Provo, Utah, Cemetery.

William S. Godbe

(1833-1902)

Mormon Businessman
Dissident
Founder of the Church of Zion

Family Background:

1833 June 26: Born William Samuel Godbe in Middlesex, England. In 1855 he married Annie Thompson; he later married plural wives Mary Hampton, Rosina Colborn, and Charlotte Ives Cobb. The last marriage, through which Godbe became a son-in-law to Brigham Young (Charlotte's mother was a plural wife to Young), ended in divorce. In 1873, by mutual agreement with his wives, he returned to monogamy with Annie Thompson, providing financially for his other wives and his twenty children.

Conversion:

1849 Godbe was converted to Mormonism as an apprentice sailor in England. Before emigrating to America, he traveled in Egypt, Greece, Turkey, Russia, Germany, Africa, Brazil, France, and Denmark.

Arriving in America, he worked his way across the Great Lakes from Buffalo to Chicago, then walked to Council Bluffs, Iowa, where he joined Thomas Williams's wagon train to Salt Lake City.

Salt Lake Merchant:

1851 He began as a store clerk for Thomas Williams, eventually established his own "states goods" importing company, and became one of the wealthiest men in Utah Territory. As a Latter-day Saint, he donated over $50,000 to the Church.

Dissident:

1868 Godbe served as a counselor to Bishop Edwin D. Woolley in the Salt Lake Thirteenth Ward, and was a member of the Salt Lake School of the Prophets. But, concerned about the economic and political control Brigham Young exercised over Utah Territory, he established the *Utah Magazine* with E.L.T. Harrison. Later he founded the *Mormon Tribune*, forerunner of the *Salt Lake Tribune*.

The first issue of *Utah Magazine* declared, "For some years we have felt that a great encroachment of power was being made by the ruling Priesthood of our Church, beyond that allowed by the spirit and genius of the Gospel. We have also perceived that a steady and constant decline was taking place in the manifestation of the spiritual gifts, as well as in the spirituality of our system as a whole, and that as a Church we were fast running into a state of most complete materialism."

Excommunication:

1869   October 16: Disfellowshipped for "irregular attendance" at the School of the Prophets. Godbe and Harrison continued to argue for "the right of, respectfully but freely, discussing all measures upon which we are called to act. And, if we are cut off from this Church for asserting this right, while our standing is dear to us, we will suffer it to be taken from us sooner than resign the liberties of thought and speech to which the gospel entitles us." They were excommunicated within the week for "apostasy."

President George Q. Cannon editorialized in the *Deseret News*, "We could conceive of a man honestly differing in opinion from the authorities of the church and yet not be apostate; but we could not conceive of a man publishing those differences of opinion, and seeking by arguments, sophistry and special pleading to enforce them upon the people to produce division and strife, and to place the acts and counsels of the church, if possible, in a wrong light, and not be apostate; for such conduct was apostasy as we understood the term."

Spiritualist:

1870   While on a business trip to New York, Godbe and Harrison claimed to have received divine instruction regarding the "future of Mormonism": "At last the light came, and by the voice of angelic beings. . . we were each of us given personally to know that, notwithstanding some misconceptions and extremes wisely permitted to accommodate it to the weaknesses of mankind, 'Mormonism' was inaugurated by the Heavens for a great and divine purpose; its main objective being the gathering of an inspirational people, believing in continuous revelations, who with such channels opened up, could at any period be moulded to any purpose the Heavens might desire."

Godbe and others founded the Church of Zion, the religious element of the "New Movement," or "Godbeitism," which disavowed religious authoritarianism. The movement soon disintegrated.

Mormon Advocate:

1870 As a self-appointed emissary, Godbe traveled to Washington, D.C., to lobby against the anti-Mormon Cullom Bill. In interviews with Vice-President Colfax and President Ulysses S. Grant, he "pleaded for kindly treatment of the Mormon people by the general government."

According to Mormon historian Orson F. Whitney, "the result of all these movements was that the Cullom Bill, after its passage by the House of Representatives, died, like its predecessor, the Cragin Bill, in the Senate."

Bankruptcy and Recovery:

1871 The School of the Prophets voted "that those who dealt with outsiders should be cut off from the church," and a few days later the boycott was approved at general conference. The School of the Prophets established Zion's Cooperative Mercantile Institution, and within two years Godbe "saw his 15 years of work evaporate and he was over $100,000 in debt."

Determined to overcome all obstacles, Godbe vowed, "Though I well know that he [Brigham Young] can break me up for a time, I will show him that even in Utah, which he has so long carried in his pocket, I can leap out and walk without his let or hindrance."

Brigham Young regretted his estrangement from Godbe, often commenting, "I loved William Godbe."

1873   With English financial backers, Godbe organized the Chicago Silver Mining Company, the beginning of mining ventures in Utah, Wyoming, and Nevada which reestablished much of his lost fortune.

Poet:

As a patron of literature, he donated over $200,000 to support the arts during his lifetime. His own poetic works often had a spiritualistic theme:

> Charms of the sensuous alluring and fair,
> Fade from our sight as the clouds of the air,
> Whilst spiritual beauty, like truth's holy ray,
> Shall shine forth in splendor forever and aye.

Death:

1902   August 1: Died of "cardiac exhaustion" at the age of sixty-nine, while vacationing in his cabin at Brighton, Utah. Buried in the Mt. Olivet Cemetery in Salt Lake City.

Heber J. Grant

(1856-1945)

Financier
Seventh President of the Church

Family Background:

1856   March 22: Born Heber Jeddy Grant to Apostle Jedediah M. Grant and Rachael Ridgeway Ivins in Salt Lake City. He was first cousin to Apostle Anthony W. Ivins, son-in-law of Brigham Young's Counselor Daniel H. Wells, and brother-in-law to Apostles Orson F. Whitney, Joseph Fielding Smith, and Reed Smoot.

Persistence:

Eight days after Heber's birth, his father died of pneumonia. As a student in Brigham Young's family school, his severe astigmatism and resulting headaches interfered with his early education. He overcame childhood taunts of "sissy" with determined efforts to play baseball: "I spent hours and hours throwing the ball at Bishop Edwin D. Woolley's barn, which caused him to refer to me as the laziest boy in the Thirteenth Ward. Often my arm would ache so that I could scarcely go to sleep at night. But I kept on practicing ... and eventually played in the nine that won the championship of the territory."

Businessman:

1871   Grant began his business career as an office boy and policy clerk for H.R. Mann Company, selling insurance in his spare time.

1880   Formed a syndicate to purchase $350,000 worth of ZCMI stock. Later he served as assistant cashier at Zion's Savings Bank and Trust Company; vice-president of the Salt Lake Herald Company; director of Provo Woolen Mills, Deseret National Bank, Oregon Lumber Company, and ZCMI; and president of the State Bank of Utah, Home Fire Insurance Company, Salt Lake Theatre Company, Co-op Wagon and Machine Company, and the Heber J. Grant Insurance Company.

Polygamist:

1877   Married Lucy Stringham. In 1884 he married Hulda Augusta Winters and Emily J. Harris Wells. Lucy died in 1893, Emily in 1908, and Hulda in 1951. He was the father of twelve children.

After the Wilford Woodruff Manifesto of 1890, Elder Grant sought permission from President Joseph F. Smith to marry Fanny Woolley, but his request was denied.

Stake President:

1880   Called to be president of the Tooele, Utah, Stake at the age of twenty-four, Grant delivered a short speech because, "I ran out of ideas."

Joseph F. Smith commented, "Heber, you said you believe the gospel with all your heart, and propose to live it, but you did not bear your testimony that you know it is true. Don't you know absolutely that this gospel is true?"

"I do not."

"What, you! a president of a stake?"

"That is what I said."

"President Taylor," said Smith, "I am in favor of undoing this afternoon what we did this morning. I do not think any man should preside over a stake who has not a perfect and abiding knowledge of the divinity of this work."

To this Grant replied, "I am not going to complain." "President Taylor," Grant recalled, "had a habit, when something pleased him excessively, of shaking his body and laughing," and he said to President Smith, "Joseph, Joseph, Joseph, he knows it just as well as you do. The only thing that he does not know is that he does know it. It will be but a short time until he does know it. He leans over backwards. You do not need to worry."

Apostle:

1882   October 10: Called to the Quorum of the Twelve by President John Taylor after Orson Pratt's death. He was only twenty-five, and the first native Utahn to serve in the Quorum.

When Heber was fifteen, Eliza R. Snow prophesied in tongues and Zina D. H. Young interpreted: eventually Heber would be one of the leading men in the Church. On October 6, 1881, photographer Charles R. Savage told Grant "that within one year [he] would be a member of the Twelve Apostles"; one year and seven days later President John Taylor announced a revelation calling Heber J. Grant to the apostleship. During an 1883-1884 mission to the Moquis Indians in Arizona, Grant reported a vision in which he learned he had been called to be an apostle because his natural father J. M. Grant, and the Prophet Joseph [Heber's father by sealing], had requested it.

Youngest and Last Member of the Council of Fifty:

1882   October 10: Accepted as member of the Council of Fifty—its youngest member—just days before the revelation naming him as one of the new members of the Quorum of the Twelve.

         So far as is known, the Council of Fifty never convened after its October, 1844, meeting. Grant was the last surviving member of that body.

Civic Career:

Served in the Tooele City Council (1881-84), Salt Lake City Council, and the Utah Legislature (1884-85).

1896   His boyhood dream to become the first governor of the State of Utah seemed fulfilled when he received a telegram from the state Democratic convention: "Sixty percent of the convention in Ogden has agreed to vote for you on the first ballot, you are sure to be nominated. We believe it will be unanimous before we get through voting."

         He took the telegram to President Wilford Woodruff and asked him how he should respond. President Woodruff replied: "Haven't you, an apostle of the Lord Jesus Christ, sufficient wisdom to answer a telegram without bothering me?"

         Grant responded, "Thank you, Brother Woodruff; thank you. Had you thought that I could do any good for the people, you would have said, Heber, the Lord bless you. I hope you will be elected. I shall send a telegram that it will be a personal favor to me if my name never comes before the convention."

Missionary to Japan:

1901　The moment he heard President George Q. Cannon announce in general conference the decision to open a mission to Japan, Grant felt he would be called to preside. But when the call actually came in a meeting of the First Presidency and Quorum of the Twelve, he was gloomy. "I was owing a little over one hundred thousand dollars. I had two wives, neither one having a home; my mother's home was mortgaged at that time for three thousand dollars."

After the meeting, John W. Taylor prophesied privately to Heber, "You shall be blessed of the Lord and make enough money to go to Japan a free man financially." Through deft financial maneuvers, he "went to Japan a free man, financially."

As mission president (1901-1903) Grant was unable to learn Japanese and saw only two persons baptized, both of whom soon left the Church. His sense of personal failure was assuaged only by the fact that a generation of missionaries had little more success in Japan.

In 1924 Church President Heber J. Grant closed the mission to Japan.

Seventh President of the Church:

1918　From 1903 to 1906 he had served as president of the British and European Missions. In 1916 he became President of the Quorum of the Twelve, and on the death of Joseph F. Smith became seventh president of the Church. His term of almost twenty-seven years is second only to the tenure of Brigham Young.

President Grant ushered the Church into an era of prosperity and popularity. Missionary work increased dramatically and Church membership grew from under 500,000 to more than 950,000. In 1922 he became the first

Church president to deliver a gospel message by radio. He dedicated the Hawaiian Temple (1919), the Alberta Temple (1923), and the Arizona Temple (1927).

He regretted his inability to sing on key: "I have, all the days of my life, enjoyed singing very much. When I was a little boy ten years of age I joined a singing class, and the professor told me that I could never learn to sing. Some years ago I had my character read by a phrenologist and he told me that I could sing, but said he would like to be forty miles away while I was doing it. I was practicing singing a few weeks ago in the Templeton building, and the room where I was doing so was next to that of a dentist. The people in the hall decided that someone was having his teeth extracted."

During the Depression, President Grant inaugurated the Church Welfare Program: "Work is what keeps people young.... We should have an ambition, we should have a desire to work to the full extent of our ability. Working eight or nine hours a day has never injured me, and I do not believe it will injure anyone else. Work is pleasing to the Lord."

Bedridden President:

1940   Due to a stroke, President Grant was a semi-invalid the last five years of his life. Despite a brief and dramatic recuperation, he was increasingly unable to attend public meetings. For several years he did not attend regular meetings of the First Presidency or the weekly temple meetings of the Quorum of the Twelve. Although John Taylor had been bedridden during the last months of his life, Grant was the first Church president to be physically incapacitated for years. He was informed of administrative developments at his home by Counselor J. Reuben Clark.

Death:

1945   Died of cardiac failure in Salt Lake City at the age of eighty-eight. Buried in Salt Lake City Cemetery.

Jedediah M. Grant

(1816-1856)

First Mayor of Salt Lake City
Apostle of the "Mormon Reformation"
Member of the First Presidency

Family Background:

1816   February 21: Born Jedediah Morgan Grant in Windsor, New York. "Frontier schooling gave him only a shaky command of commas, periods, and the perplexing science of orthography; yet as a teenager he ambitiously read from such religious and philosophical thinkers as Wesley, Locke, Rousseau, Watts, Abercrombie, and Mather."

Convert:

1833   Baptized by John F. Boynton in water so cold his clothing immediately froze to his body when he left the water.

1834   Shortly after his eighteenth birthday, Grant joined Zion's Camp. He later served missions in New York, North Carolina, Illinois, Virginia-North Carolina, and Pennsylvania.

1835   Ordained a seventy by Joseph Smith.

1845   Called to the First Council of Seventy by Brigham Young.

Polygamist:

1844   Married Caroline Van Dyke, who died crossing the plains in 1847. Grant brought her body to the Salt Lake Valley, where she was the first white woman to be buried.
       Between 1849 and his death, Grant married six plural wives. He was the father of nine children, including Heber J. Grant, born just eight days before Jedediah's death.

First Mayor of Salt Lake City:

1851   Respected as brigadier general of the Nauvoo Legion (Deseret territorial militia), he was elected as the first mayor of Salt Lake City. Until his death, he served as both mayor and a member of the Utah Legislature.

Apostle of the "Mormon Reformation":

> "I am not one of that class which believes in shrinking; if there is a fight on hand, give me a share in it. I am naturally good natured, but when the indignation of the Almighty is in me I say to all hell, stand aside and let the Lord Jesus Christ come in here."

1854   Ordained an apostle by Brigham Young, but never a member of the Quorum of the Twelve, Grant served as President Young's second counselor, succeeding Willard Richards.

As the instigator of the "Mormon Reformation," Grant, with other Church leaders, stressed cleanliness of property and person, confession and repentance, and home industry. The keystone to the reformation movement was renewed commitment to the Church.

"The Church needs trimming up," Grant charged, "and if you will search, you will find your wards contain branches which had better be cut off. The kingdom would progress much faster, and so will you individually, than it will with those branches on. . . . I would like to see the works of reformation commence, and continue until every man had to walk to the line."

Death:

1856   December 1: After baptizing hundreds in the cold waters of City Creek, fifty-year-old Jedediah M. Grant collapsed of exhaustion and exposure. He died a few days later of pneumonia.

At his funeral Brigham Young mused, "I was reflecting upon how many bands attended Jesus to the tomb; upon how many there were to lament when he went out of the world. . . . Suppose Brother Grant could speak to us this day. He would deprecate to the lowest degree the fuss and parade we are making. He would say: 'Away with you! Stop your blowing of horns, beating of drums, and hoisting of colors.'"

Buried in the Salt Lake City Cemetery. Hosea Stout eulogized in his journal,

As a Major General he was buried in the honors of war
As a Master Mason he was buried as such
And above all as a Saint he lived, died and was
   buried as such.

Jacob Hamblin

(1819-1886)

Pathfinder and Peacemaker
"Apostle to the Lamanites"

Family Background:

1819   April 2: Born Jacob Vernon Hamblin in Salem, Ohio, his family later homesteaded a large tract of land in Wisconsin. When he was nineteen, Hamblin worked in a lead mine but quit when the mine caved in, killing a co-worker.

         He married Lucinda Taylor in 1839 and later, Rachel Judd Henderson (1849), Priscilla Leavitt (1857), and Louisa Bonelli (1865). He was the father of twenty-four children.

1842   Hamblin was converted by the preaching of Elder Lyman Stoddard. When he told Lucinda that he intended to be baptized, she threatened to leave him.

1844   After two years in Nauvoo and a short mission in behalf of Joseph Smith's presidential candidacy, Hamblin moved his family west to Pottawattamie County, Iowa. Two years later, Hamblin and his three older children returned from a short trip to Council Bluffs to be met by Lucinda, who shoved thirteen-month-old Lyman under the fence to Jacob and screamed, "Take your little Mormon brats." "The family saw her for only one brief visit after this."

Polygamist:

1849   Hamblin married widow Rachel Judd Henderson of Council Bluffs eight months later. Having dreamed that he would marry her, he knocked on her door and announced, "My name is Jacob Hamblin, I was impressed to come to your home and ask you to be my wife." She replied, "I am Rachel Judd, and am willing to marry you, but it will be impossible for us to have children." Hamblin responded, "My name is Jacob, yours is Rachel, we will have two sons and shall name them Joseph and Benjamin." They also had three daughters.

Peacemaker:

1850   Sent to colonize Tooele the day of his arrival in Salt Lake. Though Indian depredations were common, Hamblin had a strong aversion to killing Indians. Assigned to bring in some Indian prisoners, he promised them safe conduct. Local authorities wanted to execute them on the spot, but Jacob stood between the Indians and the settlers, warning that it would be necessary to kill him first.

1853   Called to the Southern Indian Mission in Washington County, Utah. Four years later he established a Paiute mission in Santa Clara. He failed to convert many but suppressed the desire to give up and instead "gave vent to the mission impulse by making peace and by engaging in pathfinding and other services short of the redemptive effort."

He became the "Mormon Leatherstocking" to Paiute, Piede, Moquis, Navajo, and Hopi Indians.

"Dirty Finger Jake":

1857   Following a meeting with Brigham Young and twelve Indian chiefs in Salt Lake City, Hamblin returned to his summer home in Mountain Meadows to find evidence of a terrible massacre. "Oh! horrible! indeed was the sight. . . . The slain, numbering over one hundred men, women and children, had been interred by the inhabitants of Cedar City. At three places the wolves had disinterred the bodies, and stripping the bones of their flesh, had left them strewn in every direction. At one place I noticed nineteen wolves pulling out the bodies, and eating the flesh. . . . This was one of the gloomiest times I ever passed through."

As a prosecution witness, Hamblin earned the animosity of John D. Lee, who was executed for his role in the massacre. To his dying day, Lee referred to Hamblin as "Dirty Finger Jake" or "The Fiend of Hell."

"Apostle to the Lamanites":

1873   When three young Navajos were killed by non-Mormons near Richfield, Utah, Hamblin was invited to meet with the Navajos before they took revenge. After trying to convince the Navajos that Mormons had not been involved, he was told, "You must not think of going home, but your American friends might go if they start immediately after they witness your death."

A tense, night-long council ensued, during which Hamblin's fifteen-year record with Indians was reviewed. After answering their questions and justifying his actions, he was finally released. "Again has the promise been verified, which was given me by the Spirit many years before, *that if I would not thirst for the blood of the Lamanites, I should never die by their hands.*"

1876 Considered by many to have known the Indians of Utah and northern Arizona "better than any one who ever lived," Hamblin was ordained "Apostle to the Lamanites" by Brigham Young. However, he never served as a member of the Quorum of the Twelve.

"Red Men Rules":

"Some of my rules and ways to managing Indians:
"1st. I never talk anything but the truth to them.
"2nd. I think it useless to speak of things they cannot comprehend.
"3rd. I strive by all means to never let them see me in a passion.
"4th. Under no circumstances show fear.
"5th. Never approach them in an austere manner; nor use more words than is necessary to convey my ideas; nor in a higher tone of voice, than to be distinctly heard.
"6th. Always listen to them. . . .
"7th. I never allow them to hear me use any obscene language.
"8th. I never submit to any unjust demands or submit to coercion. . . .
"9th. I have tried to observe the above rules for the past twenty years and it has given me a salutary influence wherever I have met with them. Many times when I have visited isolated bands upon business and have been addressing them in a low tone of voice around their council fires, I have noticed that they have listened with attention and reverence. I believe if the rules that I have

mentioned were observed there would be but little difficulty on our frontier with the Red man."

Death:

1886   Anti-polygamy pressure had forced Jacob and his families into New Mexico. Contracting malaria while living in Pleasanton, the sixty-seven-year-old Hamblin weakened in health and died August 31. Initially buried in Pleasanton, he was re-interred in 1888 in the Alpine, Arizona, Cemetery.

Martin Harris

(1783-1875)

Book of Mormon Scribe
Book of Mormon Witness

Family Background:

1783   May 18: Born in Easttown, New York. In 1808 he married his cousin Lucy Harris; they had three children. She divorced him in 1831 because of his funding of the Book of Mormon. In 1837 he married Brigham Young's niece Caroline Young, by whom he had five children.

Farmer and Community Leader:

1804   Harris's 240 acres of prime land made him one of the most prosperous farmers in the Palmyra, New York, region. He served in the local militia during the War of 1812, and was later elected or appointed to a number of civic posts.

Book of Mormon Scribe:

1827   As a neighbor, Harris was one of the few persons outside the Smith family to know of the existence of the Book of Mormon plates before they were retrieved from the Hill Cumorah.

1828   According to Harris, an angel told the Prophet "to go look in the spectacles, and he would show him the man that would assist him.... He did so, and he saw myself, Martin Harris."
    As a "last precautionary step" to be sure "there was no risk whatever in the matter," Harris took some of the copied characters from the plates to scholars in New York City. Though he did not obtain written certification of their authenticity, he was satisfied, and became the first Book of Mormon scribe.
    To convince his skeptical wife, Harris persuaded the Prophet to let him take the 116 pages of completed manuscript home with him. They were lost or stolen, and as a result, the plates and interpreters were taken "for a season," and Martin was no longer allowed to transcribe.

Book of Mormon Witness and Benefactor:

1830   As one of the Three Witnesses, Harris testified he heard the voice of God declare the Book of Mormon to be authentic as an angel showed him the gold plates.

Harris mortgaged his farm to raise the $3000 needed to print five thousand copies of the Book of Mormon. Lucy, violently opposed to his investment, unsuccessfully sued Joseph Smith for "defrauding Husband." The marital discord increased when Martin testified that "Joseph had never asked him for money that he was not more than willing to give."

Early Church Leader:

1830   Oliver Cowdery baptized Martin Harris shortly after the organization of the Church. The following year, he accompanied Joseph Smith to select the "land of consecration" in Missouri.

1834   Became a member of the first high council in Kirtland.

During Zion's Camp, Harris boasted that he could handle snakes with "perfect safety." While "fooling with a black snake with his bare feet, he received a bite on his left foot."

1835   Harris and the other Book of Mormon Witnesses, David Whitmer and Oliver Cowdery, selected, ordained, and instructed the twelve elders who became the original Quorum of the Twelve.

Dissident:

1834   Tried by the Kirtland High Council for accusing Joseph Smith of not understanding the Book of Mormon, of wrestling too much, and of drinking while translating the Book of Mormon, Martin confessed that his mind had been darkened so that he said things inadvertently.

His discontent mounted with the collapse of the Kirtland Anti-Banking Society, and on September 3, 1837, Harris was dropped from the Kirtland High Council. He and his family remained in Kirtland when most Saints emigrated to Missouri or Nauvoo. "I never did leave the Church," he claimed, "the Church left me."

Kirtland Temple Caretaker:

In later years Harris often conducted tours of the temple. One visitor described him as a "poorly clad, emaciated little man on whom the winter of life was weighing heavily." Harris enjoyed proclaiming his testimony of the Book of Mormon and Joseph Smith:

"Just as surely as the sun is shining on us and gives us light, and the moon and stars give us light by night; just as surely as the breath of life sustains us, so surely do I know that Joseph Smith was a true prophet of God, chosen of God to open the last dispensation of the fullness of times; so surely do I know that the Book of Mormon was divinely translated."

Rebaptism:

On various occasions Harris was reported to be a firm believer in Shakerism, a Strangite, and a member of the Church of Christ. In all, he affiliated with eight different religious groups.

1859   Caroline Harris and their five children emigrated to Utah without him. Though she never divorced Harris, Caroline married John Cathy Davis in 1860.

1870   Harris was persuaded to visit Utah by his son's brother-in-law, William H. Homer. Harris sent a message to Brigham Young through Homer: "Tell him that Martin Harris is an old, old man, living on charity, with his relatives. Tell him I should like to visit Utah, my family and children—I would be glad to accept help from the Church, but I want no personal favor. Wait! Tell him that if he sends money, he must send enough for the round trip. I should not want to remain in Utah."

Brigham Young contributed the first $25, declaring: "Send for him? Yes, even if it were to take the last dollar of my own. Martin Harris spent his time and money freely, when one dollar was worth more than one thousand dollars are now. Send for him? Yes, indeed, I shall send!"

During the trip, Harris was frequently invited to witness to the Book of Mormon. At one of these gatherings, a baptism was performed, and Edward Stevenson explained rebaptism to Harris, who said it was "new doctrine to him." He "had not been cut off from the Church," but if rebaptism were "required of him it would be manifested to him by the spirit."

A short time later, he informed Stevenson that "the Spirit had made known to him that it was his duty to renew his covenant before the Lord." Stevenson rebaptized Harris, and Orson Pratt reconfirmed him. Pratt later explained, "Martin Harris, when he came to this Territory a few years ago, was rebaptized, the same as every member of the Church from distant parts is on arriving here. That seems to be a kind of standing ordinance from all Latter-day Saints who emigrate here, from the First Presidency down; all are rebaptized and set out anew by renewing their covenants."

After visiting friends in Salt Lake, Martin moved to Clarkston, Utah, where he lived with his son, Martin Harris, Jr.

When the Relief Society offered to have a set of false teeth made up for him, Harris replied, "No sisters, I thank you for your kindness but I shall not live long. Take the money and give it to the poor."

Death:

1875   July 10: Died at the age of ninety-two in Clarkston, Utah. Buried in the Clarkston Cemetery with a Book of Mormon in his right hand and a Doctrine and Covenants in his left.

Bill Hickman

(1815-1883)

Lawman
"Lifeguard to Prophets"
Outlaw

Family Background:

1815   April 16: Born William Adams Hickman, eldest of thirteen children, in Warren County, Kentucky. His family moved to Missouri, where he became a skilled woodsman. In 1832 he taught in a small rural school near his home.

1832   Married Bernetta Burckhardt and later Sarah Elizabeth Luce, Minerva Wade, Sarah Basford Meacham, Eliza Virginia Johnson, Margaret Indian, Hanna Dyantha Harr, Martha Diana Case, Mary Lucretia Harr, and Mary Jane Hetherington. Most of his wives divorced him in 1867. "Each [wife] agreed to going, and doing the best we could for our children." Only his first wife remained with him. He was the father of thirty-four children.

Convert:

1839   A Methodist, Hickman "lived a quiet and religious life, making theology my principal study. I investigated every religious belief I had ever heard of, and among the balance, Mormonism, which I had supposed was trivial and trashy, but soon found I was mistaken. I continued to investigate it for two years." Baptized by John D. Lee, he traveled to Nauvoo and was ordained a seventy by Joseph Smith.

"Life Guard":

1840   In Nauvoo, Hickman was one of twelve "life guards" for Joseph Smith.

1846   Fought in the "Battle of Nauvoo:" "How many were killed I never learned. I had been anxious from a boy to be in a battle, but I assure you this fight took a great deal of starch out of me. My appetite for such fun has never been so craving since."

    According to Hickman, a half-breed Indian Church member had a falling-out with Brigham Young in Council Bluffs, Iowa, and threatened to lead Indian attacks against the Mormons.

Brigham Young "sent me word to look out for him. I found him, used him up, scalped him, and took his scalp to Brigham Young, saying: 'Here is the scalp of the man who was going to have a war-dance over your scalp; you may now have one over his, if you wish.' He took it and thanked me very much. He said in all probability I had saved his life, and that some day he would make me a great man in the kingdom."

A short time later, Hickman said, he was "called upon to go for a notorious horse-thief, who had sworn to take the life of Orson Hyde. I socked him away, and made my report, which was very satisfactory. Hyde was well pleased, and said he knew I had saved his life."

Indian Fighter:

1848   At Council Bluffs, Omaha Indians from across the Missouri River were stealing stock from the Saints. Hearing a report of Indians lurking about, "I took my pistol and knife . . . and went in search, crawling through the brush with all the quietness of a cat after a mouse. . . . After watching about an hour, I saw three Indians with ropes and bridle, and armed with bows and arrows. I took deliberate aim, having two in range; one fell, and one ran towards me, the third ran the other way. The one that ran towards me fell about three rods off. The ball had cut the back off his head, and made him crazy; but I was to him as he rose, and shot him dead. I took their bows, arrows, ropes, and bridles, and put them into a pile, went to town, told a few of my friends, who were well pleased, but thought we had best say nothing about it, as there might be some exceptions taken to it by United States agents."

Unfortunately, the Indians were innocent Pawnee. When word of their deaths got around, Hickman was excommunicated for "violating church policy of friendliness towards the Indians."

1849   Called with a group of 150 men to clear out a group of Indians who were harassing settlers on the Provo River. The Indians had called the Mormons "all petticoats and won't fight."

After personally killing the chief, Big Elk, Hickman reported, "I took off his head, for I had heard the old mountaineer, Jim Bridger, say he would give a hundred dollars for it. I tied it in his blanket and laid it on a flat rock; hid his gun and bow and arrows, forty-two number one good arrows, and awaited the arrival of the company.

"I had to laugh. Those rear fellows who had been in the habit of picking up everything, had untied the blanket that was around the chief's head, but on seeing what it contained left it untied with the head sitting in the middle of it, entirely untouched. I took the head, gun, bow and arrows, mounted my horse, took a pretty spuaw [sic] behind me and a sick *pappoose* in front, and was off for our quarters."

Rebaptism:

1850 Rebaptized, Hickman eventually became a member of the West Jordan bishopric.

Lawman:

1854 Brigham Young appointed Hickman sheriff, prosecuting attorney, and assessor for Green River County (later Wyoming). He was also elected a member of the Utah territorial legislature.

1856 Joined businessman Hiram Kimball and frontiersman Orrin Porter Rockwell in a mail-carrying venture. Rockwell carried the mail from Fort Laramie to Salt Lake and back; Hickman carried it from Fort Laramie to Independence, Missouri. The company eventually merged with the Brigham Young Express Company against the advice of Hickman, who knew "I would have to be gone three months or more, suffer many privations, be at a heavy expense, and the way they had things fixed, not make a dollar." When the Utah Expeditionary Force left Fort Leavenworth, the mail contract was suspended, the express company went defunct, and Hickman lost $1000.

Outcast:

1857   A blessing given by Church Patriarch John Young, shortly before Hickman embarked on a mail run, promised, "You shall have power over all your enemies, even to set your feet upon their necks, and no weapon that is formed against you shall prosper.... When danger approaches you the Angel of Life shall be with you to forewarn you of those things. If you are faithful, you shall assist in avenging the blood of the prophets of God.... Not a hair of your head shall fall to the ground by the enemy."

1859   An argument over stolen property between Hickman and Lot Huntington escalated into a wild Christmas Day shootout in Salt Lake City. Forty shots were exchanged, two striking Hickman. This altercation, along with his theft of army horses from the Utah Expeditionary Forces and his association with "bad men," made Hickman a target for Church action. Orson Hyde, a friend since Nauvoo, acknowledged Hickman's guilt but "gave it as the word of the Lord to set him free for the past, and bid him go and sin no more."

1860   According to Brigham Young's office journal, "Mayor Smoot had a conversation with the President about Wm. A. Hickman, observing people see him come in and out the office, and that leads them to suppose he is sanctioned in all he does by the President. He also observed that dogs were necessary to take care of the flock, but if the Shepherd's dogs hurt the sheep it would be time to remove them." Hickman was disfellowshipped by the Third Quorum of Seventy.

1868   Excommunicated for reasons not completely clear. Official Church records cite "apostasy," but Hickman declared it was because he left the territory "without permission."

    When he asked Brigham Young if there were any other charges against him, "He said yes, I had been intimate with the Smith boys, Joseph's sons.... I told him I only went to see them out of respect to their father, and never had a private chat with them. This he was not disposed to believe.... I asked him what more was against me, and he said he did not know, I asked him why I was disfellowshipped. He seemed beat, and was mad, and said, 'If it was not right to have done it, it would not have been done,' and got up and left."

August 15: Hickman wrote Brigham Young, "I feel bad to have so many false charges brought against me. I feel bad when I think you do not feel well towards me. What am I to do when I do not know of wrong I have done? How or of what can I repent? I wish you would point out a course and have it under your immediate notice for me to take, not under [Bishop] Gardner." A postscript added, "I know I was always your friend at home or abroad and true in every sense of the word. I do hope you'll be kind to me—how bad I feel, you do not know."

"Brigham's Destroying Angel":

1871   After killing "Spanish Frank," seducer of his wife, Eliza, Hickman was unable to resolve his difficulties with President Young. He published a sensational autobiography, *Brigham's Destroying Angel: Being the Life, Confession, and Startling Disclosures of the Notorious Bill Hickman,* purporting to give, in vivid detail, an account of his murderous deeds instigated by Brigham Young. Hickman apparently prepared a very rough draft for ghost writer J.H. Beadle, a prominent anti-Mormon journalist intent on implicating Brigham Young in numerous alleged crimes, especially in the 1857 murder of Richard Yates.

Though Hickman testified that "Brigham Young had *ordered* him to kill Yates," he called *Brigham's Destroying Angel* "a lie from the wild boar story onward." Hickman's disclaimer may have been related to his disappointment in not receiving a promised $50,000 for the book—or an honest, albeit belated retraction. In either case, the book is an important document of Mormon folklore.

At the final meeting between the two, Brigham Young asked Hickman if he planned to rejoin the Church. Hickman said that he "had for three years tried to find out what was against me, and could not; consequently, I expected to remain as I was." Later he added, "I had no desire to belong to his Church, but would have accepted a re-union for the purpose of having more peace and a better show to do business and raise my children."

1872 Brigham Young and others were indicted on testimony provided by Hickman. The charges were eventually dropped.

Death:

1883 Seriously wounded in the groin in his 1859 gun battle with Lot Huntington, Hickman recovered only partially and suffered a nearly fatal typhoid infection on two separate occasions. His death on August 21 at the age of sixty-eight was attributed to "diarrhea and old bullet wounds." He was buried in Lander, Wyoming, though rumor "has it that the body was exhumed by a physician from the East and his skull now adorns his private collection."

1934 May 5: As authorized by President Heber J. Grant, all former priesthood and temple blessings were restored.

Orson Hyde

(1805-1878)

Apostle
Dedicator of Palestine for the Return of Jews

Family Background:

1805 January 8: Born in Oxford, Connecticut. Orphaned at the age of twelve, Orson was raised by the Nathan Wheelers, who moved to Kirtland, Ohio, in 1819. There he worked in an iron foundry, carded wool, and clerked in the Gilbert-Whitney store.

In 1834 he married Marinda Nancy Johnson, sister of Apostles Luke and Lyman Johnson. He later married Martha R. Browett (1843), Mary Ann Price (1843), Ann Eliza Vickers (1857), Elizabeth Josephine Gallier (1864), and Sophia Margaret Lyon (1865). Marinda divorced him in 1870. He was the father of thirty-two children, only seventeen of whom lived to adulthood.

Convert:

1827 Joined the Methodist church and later the Campbellite congregation of Sidney Rigdon. For a time he lived with the Rigdons in Mentor, Ohio.

1831 When Sidney Rigdon converted to Mormonism, Hyde studied and prayed for three months. Finally he decided, "I could not be the loser by joining the Mormons and as an honest man, conscientiously bound to walk in the best and clearest light I saw, I resolved to be baptized into the new religion." He was baptized by Rigdon.

Missionary:

1831 Shortly after baptism, Hyde began missionary efforts among his acquaintances in Kirtland. "I felt that all my old friends (not of the 'Mormons') would believe me, and with a warm and affectionate heart, I soon went out among them, and began to talk and testify to them what the Lord had done for me; but the cold indifference with which they received me, and the pity they expressed for my delusion, soon convinced me that it was not wise to give that which is holy unto dogs, neither to cast pearls before swine."

During the next twenty years, Hyde served thirteen missions, including Ohio (1831, 1833), "eastern countries" (1832), Missouri (1833), Pennsylvania (1834), New York (1835), Canada (1836), England (1837, 1846), Indiana (1839), Palestine (1841), and the Eastern United States (1843).

Scholar:

1833   Hyde taught grammar in the Kirtland School of the Prophets and attended Joshua Seixus's school of Hebrew at Kirtland.

1854   Claimed to have memorized the Bible in English, German and Hebrew. Hyde, W. W. Phelps, and Albert Carrington signed the teaching certificates of Utah Territory. In 1855 he taught night classes in English at Salt Lake City.

Apostle:

1835   Called by the Three Witnesses to be a member of the first Quorum of the Twelve. He had served as a member of the first high council and of Zion's Camp. After a six-month excommunication in 1838-1839, he was restored to his former position in the Quorum.

1847   Became president of the Quorum of the Twelve at Council Bluffs, Iowa, a position he held for twenty-eight years. In 1875 Brigham Young reordered the Quorum of the Twelve, giving Hyde and Orson Pratt seniority according to the dates of their return to the Quorum, rather than their original ordinations. Otherwise, at the death of Brigham Young in 1877, Orson Hyde would have been the senior apostle.

Excommunication:

1839   Hyde had been disfellowshipped in 1835 for criticizing Sidney Rigdon's teaching methods. Four years later he was excommunicated with Thomas B. Marsh for "failure to support the Church." The charge stemmed from their sworn affidavit that the Mormons had "among them a company, considered true Mormons, called the Danites ... for the purpose of burning and destroying.... The Prophet inculcates the notion, and it is believed by every true Mormon, that Smith's prophecies are superior to the laws of the land."

Marsh wrote the statement, but Hyde added, "The most of the statements in the foregoing disclosure I know to be true, the others I believe to be true."

Six months after his excommunication, Hyde had a "vision in which it was made known to him that if he did not make immediate restitution to the quorum of the Twelve, he would be cut off and all his posterity, and that the curse of Cain would be upon him." He was reinstated in June, 1839.

John Taylor later explained, "Orson Hyde had been sick with a violent fever for some time, and had not fully recovered therefrom, which with the circumstances with which we were surrounded, and the influence of Thomas B. Marsh, may be offered as a slight palliation for his default."

Dedicator of Palestine for the Return of Jews:

1841 October 24: In fulfillment of a prophecy by Joseph Smith and of his own 1840 vision, Hyde ascended the Mount of Olives in Jerusalem and dedicated Palestine for the future return of the Jews:

"Now, O Lord! Thy servant has been obedient to the heavenly vision which thou gavest him in his native land ... to dedicate and consecrate this land unto thee, for the gathering of Judah's scattered remnants."

In 1979 President Spencer W. Kimball dedicated the Orson Hyde Memorial Garden on the Mount of Olives in Jerusalem.

Utah Politician:

1848 An original member of the Council of Fifty, Hyde was appointed an associate judge of the Utah Supreme Court. He also served in the Utah legislature (1852-53, 1856-59,

1861-73), and was elected president of the upper house in 1870.

Colonizer:

1853   Called by Brigham Young to colonize Fort Supply, Wyoming. Mormon settlers burned Fort Supply and Fort Bridger in 1857 to prevent their falling into the hands of the Utah Expeditionary Force.

1855   Called to settle Carson Valley, Nevada. En route, he was confronted by a soldier whom he had charged with abducting two girls in Salt Lake City. "He slapped me in the face and drew a revolver instantly. My pistols being in the holsters outside on my horse, I was not exactly prepared to measure arms with him at that time. . . . I am resolved to defend myself if I have to shoot him down wherever and whenever I see him." The soldier never arrived for a showdown in Carson Valley.

        Hyde served as probate judge in Carson Valley from 1856-57.

1858   Called by Brigham Young to preside over the Sanpete-Sevier district of south-central Utah. Hyde originally settled in Manti, then moved to Spring City, where his fine old home still stands. In 1860 he was sustained as the first president of the Sanpete Stake.

Death:

1878   November 28: Died in Spring City on Thanksgiving Day at the age of seventy-three. Buried in Spring City Cemetery.

Anthony W. Ivins

(1852-1934)

Juarez Stake President
Officiator for Post-Manifesto Plural Marriages
"Cowboy Apostle"
Member of the First Presidency

Family Background:

1852: September 16: Born Anthony Woodward Ivins in Toms River, New Jersey. First cousin of Heber J. Grant.

The Ivins family arrived in the Salt Lake Valley in 1853 and helped settle Saint George in 1861. In southern Utah Tony developed life-long interests in hunting, fishing, and Indians.

Married Elizabeth Ashby Snow, daughter of Erastus Snow, in 1878; they had nine children.

Explorer and Missionary:

1875 Ordained an elder at the age of thirteen, Ivins was called at the age of twenty-three to help explore Arizona and New Mexico for areas which could be colonized by the Saints.

In 1877-78 he served another mission in New Mexico, and in 1882 he was called to preside over the Mexican Mission in Mexico City. He learned to speak Spanish so fluently that Mexican President Porfirio Diaz described him as "a gentleman who speaks my native tongue as if he were a native born Castilian."

Public Official:

1877 Appointed constable of Saint George.

1882 A self-taught lawyer, Ivins was elected prosecuting attorney for Washington County.

1888 Helped organize the "Sagebrush Democrats," an attempt to move Utah away from the People's (Mormon) and Liberal (non-Mormon) parties toward national parties.

1890 Elected mayor of Saint George, Ivins also served two terms in the Utah legislature.

1896 As a member of the 1894 Utah State Constitutional Convention, Ivins gained widespread popularity among Democratic delegates. Two years later the state Democratic convention telegraphed his cousin Heber J. Grant, "Where can we find Anthony Ivins? We will give him his choice to be nominated for the first Congressman, now that we have statehood, or the first governor."

Grant answered, "He is on the Kaibab Mountain selling the cattle, horses, and property of his company; he has accepted a call of the Church to go to Mexico. Nothing in the world would cause him to fail to fulfill that call."

Presiding Authority in Mexico:

1895   Eight Mormon settlements in Sonora and Chihuahua, Mexico, provided refuge for Saints in danger of prosecution for violating anti-polygamy statutes. When Wilford Woodruff called him to succeed George Teasdale as the presiding officer there, Ivins wrote in his journal, "I answered the letter rec'd from Presidency telling them that I would go to Mexico as soon as possible. I did not want to go to Mexico."

In Juarez, Ivins served as the first stake president, and as vice-president and general manager of the Church's Mexican Colonization and Agricultural Company. For twelve years, his word was final in the ecclesiastical and civic affairs of the colonies.

The Ivins mansion in Juarez was fronted with a heart-shaped lawn bordered by dahlias and imported rose bushes and shrubs. The estate included fruit trees, berries and grape vines. "He built an attractive and spacious barn and outbuildings and filled them with imported purebred horses and cows including Plowboy, an imported stallion. His blooded dogs and registered chickens were in line. From a cement-covered cistern on the west canal he piped water to his home, making inside plumbing possible for the first time in the history of the town."

Officiator for Post-Manifesto Plural Marriages:

1897 Though a monogamist himself, Ivins was authorized by the First Presidency to perform plural marriage sealings, illegal under both U.S. and Mexican laws. A form letter was prepared which, when properly filled out, would indicate to Ivins that the couple presenting the form were authorized to be married. The Anthony W. Ivins collection at the Utah State Historical Society contains a list of more than forty couples so married, and the Joseph F. Smith collection in the LDS Church Archives contains many more signed authorization forms used in Mexico. Additional plural marriages were finally prohibited by Joseph F. Smith's "second manifesto" given at April conference, 1904.

Apostle:

1907 Called to the Quorum of the Twelve by President Joseph F. Smith.

1912 Supervised the evacuation of Mormon colonies during the Mexican Revolution.

1921 Named second counselor to his cousin, President Heber J. Grant. He became first counselor in 1925. As a staunch but discreet Democrat, Ivins was an important political influence, moderating partisan Republican policies whenever they were advocated in Church councils. Ivins aggravated Republican loyalists like Reed Smoot and J. Reuben Clark, inspired Democratic partisans like B.H. Roberts, and amused apolitical gadflies like J. Golden Kimball. As a member of the First Presidency, Ivins also provided tacit encouragement for Mormon modernists.

Businessman:

Ivins had been a prosperous rancher in Saint George, where he was manager of the Mojave Land and Cattle Company and co-owner of the Kaibab Cattle Company. In Salt Lake City he served as vice-president of Utah State National Bank, Zion's Savings Bank and Trust Company, and ZCMI; director of Deseret Savings Bank and United States Fuel Company; and president of Utah Savings and Trust Company.

Death:

1934 September 23: Died of a heart attack at his home at 519 B. Street, Salt Lake City, at the age of eighty-two. Buried in the Salt Lake City Cemetery.

1970 Elected to the National Cowboy Hall of Fame.

Heber C. Kimball

(1810-1868)

Member of the First Presidency
"Brigham's Prophet"

Family Background:

1801   June 14: Born Heber Chase Kimball in Shelton, Vermont. Economic hardships there drove the Kimball family to West Bloomfield, New York, where Heber apprenticed as a blacksmith with his father and as a potter with his brother Charles.

1822   Married Vilate Murray. He later wed forty-two plural wives, including nine widows of Joseph Smith, a widow of Hyrum Smith, the widow of Joseph's counselor, Frederick G. Williams, and the divorced wife of deposed Apostle William Smith. Kimball married many of his wives to provide them a protector and benefactor; he fathered children by only seventeen. Sixteen of his forty-three wives eventually left him.

        Kimball fathered sixty-five children; Christopher Layton, with ten wives, fathered sixty-four; John D. Lee fathered sixty with nineteen wives; and Brigham Young, with fifty-six wives, had fifty-six children.

Heber and Vilate Kimball with children.

Kimball's son J. Golden became a president of the First Council of Seventy; his stepson Joseph F. Smith, sixth president of the Church; and his grandson Spencer W. Kimball, twelfth president of the Church.

To Heber Kimball, his colleagues in the First Presidency were family: "I love these men, God knows I do, better than I ever loved a woman; and I would not give a damn for a man that does not love them better than they love women."

Unwilling to argue with his wives, Kimball declared, "If ever I am so foolish as to quarrel with a woman, I ought to be whipped; for you may always calculate that they will have the last word."

Missionary:

1832   Three weeks after he and Vilate had joined the Baptist church, Kimball read a Book of Mormon left at an inn with Brigham Young's brother Phineas. When Alpheus Gifford mentioned baptism to Kimball the following April, "I jumped up, pulled off my apron, washed my hands and started with him with my sleeves rolled up to my shoulders, and went the distance of one mile where he baptized me in a small stream in the woods." He was sent almost immediately on a local mission with Brigham and Joseph Young. During the next twelve years he served eight missions and converted thousands to the Church.

Apostle:

1835   After serving in Zion's Camp (1834), Kimball was the third elder chosen to be a member of the original Quorum of the Twelve. He and Brigham Young were the only original Quorum members never disfellowshipped or excommunicated, excepting David W. Patten, who was killed in 1838.

1837   In the midst of the Kirtland Safety Society banking crisis, Joseph Smith sent Kimball, Orson Hyde, Willard Richards, and four Canadian converts on a mission to England. It was the first European mission and a phenomenal success. Heber was instrumental in baptizing nearly 1500 people.

1839 He and seven other apostles labored in England, eventually baptizing between seven and eight thousand converts. They "established branches in almost every noted town and city, printed 5,000 copies of the Book of Mormon, 3,000 hymnals, 50,000 tracts, 2,500 of the *Millenial Star*, established a permanent shipping agency, and arranged for the emigration of about 1,000 Saints to Zion."

Mason:

1842 May 4: Kimball and eight others received the "holy order" (later known as the "temple endowment") from Joseph Smith in the Prophet's brick store. He wrote to Parley P. Pratt, "We have received some pressious things through the Prophet on the presthood that would cause your Soul to rejoice. . . . Bro. Joseph Ses Masonry was taken from presthood but has become degenerated. But menny things are perfect." Kimball, who had been a Mason since 1825, was one of the founders of the Nauvoo Lodge.

In 1858 he explained, "We have the true Masonry. The Masonry of today is received from the apostasy which took place in the days of Solomon and David. They have now and then a thing that is correct, but we have the real thing."

Pioneer:

1846 The Nauvoo exodus was particularly hard on Kimball's family, which consisted at the time of at least thirty-eight wives, four of them pregnant.

In Iowa a rattlesnake bit one of his horses. He laid his hands on the animal's head, rebuked the poison, and declared to bystanders, "It is just as proper to lay hands on a horse or an ox and administer to them in the name of the Lord, and of such utility, as it is to a human being, both being creatures of His creations, both consequently having a claim to His attention."

1847 Kimball entered the Salt Lake Valley with the rest of the pioneer company in July; he returned the following month to Winter Quarters. In 1848 he led another wagon train of 66 family members and 556 others to Salt Lake. His company included 226 wagons, "1,253 horses, mules, and cattle, plus sheep, pigs, chickens, cats, dogs, goats, geese, doves, a squirrel, and some beehives."

"Brigham's Prophet":

Throughout their Church careers, Brigham Young and Heber C. Kimball were virtually inseparable, and their close friendship intensified after Joseph Smith's death in 1844.

1847 Brigham Young selected Kimball to be his second counselor in the First Presidency. Ever obedient to his president, Kimball told the Saints, "If brother Brigham tells me to do a thing it is the same as though the Lord told me to do it. This is the course for you and every other Saint to take, and by taking this course, I will tell you, brethren, you are on the top of the heap."

1848 Though not professing to be a prophet, Kimball could not help but notice, he said, that "people all the time are telling me I am." Brigham Young promoted the image: "I am not a visionary man, neither am I given much to prophesying. When I want any of that done I call on brother Heber—he is my prophet, he loves to prophesy, and I love to hear him."

President Spencer W. Kimball described his grandfather as "a prophet perhaps second only to Joseph Smith himself."

Though many of Kimball's dramatic prophecies came to pass, some did not. He predicted, for example, that President Buchanan, who initiated the Utah Expeditionary Force, would die an "untimely death," but the ex-president was ten years older than Kimball when they both died in 1868.

Many of his scriptural quotes could not be found in the scriptures, J. Golden Kimball recalled. But when listeners pointed this out, he countered, "Well, if that isn't in the Bible it ought to be in it."

Entrepreneur:

1850s   Kimball operated large ranches in Cache Valley and Grantsville, and on Antelope Island. On City Creek near Temple Square, he established a gristmill, an oil mill (extracting linseed oil from flax), a sugar cane mill, and a lumber mill.

Kimball's estate was eventually valued at $100,580 (the 1980 equivalent of more than $2,000,000).

Appearance:

"He was erect, portly, full-chested, broad-shouldered, powerfully made, about six feet high, and weighed two hundred pounds. . . . His face was very striking; a compound of keen wit, finesse, insight into character. . . . His form of aldermanic rotundity, his face large, plethoric and lusterous with the stable red of stewed cranberries . . . small, twinkling black beads of eyes. . . . His chin was double and shiny, from the twin effect of good living and close-shaving."

"An Old Horse that Has Lost His Teeth":

1865   Feeling intimidated by those who were better educated, especially Second Counselor Daniel H. Wells, Kimball was afraid of being supplanted. His insecurity was heightened when Brigham Young made important decisions about the First Presidency without consulting him. Heber's son Solomon wrote, "Those were days of sorrow for father, and he became so heart broken towards the last that he prayed to the Lord to shorten his days."

But, Kimball confided in a private memorandum book, "I was told by the Lord that I should not be removed from my place as first counselor to President Young."

Death:

1868   Injured when thrown from a buggy in late May, he apparently recovered, but suffered a stroke on June 11 and died on June 22. Buried in the private cemetery near the rear of his home at 142 North Main Street in Salt Lake City.

J. Golden Kimball

(1835-1938)

President of the First Council of Seventy
"The Mark Twain of Mormonism"

Family Background:

1853   Born Jonathan Golden Kimball in Salt Lake City to Heber C. Kimball and Christeen Golden. His father died when J. Golden was fifteen.

"For twelve years of my life, after my father's death, I was free as the birds that fly in the air! There was no restraint further than the counsel from my mother. I took no active part in the Church. I was just as free as non-members of the Church feel that they are free. . . . I am sorry, oh how sorry! that there was no restraint or responsibility placed upon me, that I was not actively engaged in Church work during those twelve years."

Young Golden set out to be a teamster, becoming "one of the early M.D.'s of the West, for he was as good a mule driver as could be found in these parts." He also worked in logging camps and at other manual labor.

1875   Established a large ranch with eleven of his brothers in Meadowville, Rich County, Utah. He married Jeanette "Jane" Knowlton in 1887; they had six children.

Missionary:

1881   After hearing Karl G. Maeser lecture in Meadowville, Kimball decided to attend the Brigham Young Academy in Provo. But his education was interrupted in 1883 when he was called on a mission to the Southern States under President B.H. Roberts. There he contracted malaria and returned home in 1885.

1891   Kimball invested everything he had in a Canadian land scheme promoted by John W. Taylor. When the project fell through, Kimball was called to be a mission president: "And thus, we were prevented from chasing the golden calf. Moral: Don't set your heart upon riches, don't speculate, and don't go in debt. After this, again the Lord came to my rescue and called me to succeed Elder William Spry as president of the Southern States Mission."

General Authority:

1892   While serving as mission president, he was called to the First Council of Seventy. "The Lord knows I didn't want the position; the Lord knows I balked and bitched when they called me; and I guess he knows I got the job. And now that I got it, he knows I'll work like hell to do it the way he wants it done."

"Some people say a person receives a position in this church through revelation, and others say they get it through inspiration, but I say they get it through relation. If I hadn't been related to Heber C. Kimball, I wouldn't have been a damn thing in this church." In later years, he explained why he had not been advanced to the Quorum of the Twelve: "The main reason was that my father was dead and I was not popular with the brethren."

"The Mark Twain of Mormonism":

When asked about his frequent use of *damn* and *hell*, Kimball responded, "Oh, I never intend to use them when I get up to speak, but they just come to me as naturally as singing to a bird. I'm not thinking about words; I'm concerned about the ideas and how to put them over. But those words you speak of are what's left over from the cowboy days. They used to be my native language and I don't seem to be able to shake them. Really, they come from a much larger vocabulary, only I've gotten rid of the others."

On another occasion a good sister asked Kimball if he ever heard President Grant swear. "Just once," he replied. "He and I were in Saint George together during the depression. It was summer, the crops were dying for want of water, the people were starving. We prayed with them for rain, but our prayers were not answered. I said, 'It's a damned shame!' and President Grant said, 'Yes, it is.'"

When it was suggested that the brethren might consider cutting him off, Kimball responded, "Guess maybe some of them would like to. But they can't cut me off from the church, I repent too damn fast."

Like Mark Twain, J. Golden Kimball was occasionally morose and even bitter. Perhaps he inherited his father's extreme sensitivity to slights from his colleagues. It is a high tribute to J. Golden Kimball that he was able to transcend his own personal struggles, bringing mirth to hundreds of thousands during his lifetime and to millions since.

Appearance:

1933 "Seventy-five inches in height; very slender, somewhat bent by the heavy physical work done in his teens and the burden of his fourscore years; a head unusually large and unlike any other, with a sizeable bump at the back; his complexion sandy; a few lonely hairs on top that have triumphantly weathered the storm; keen and penetrating eyes, black and beautiful, expressive of humor and sympathy; a very long perpendicular face, intensely interesting, with features regular; withal a serious countenance, expressive of sadness rather than of the humor for which he is noted. He seldom laughs, but is often seen to smile dryly as he speaks."

Death:

1938 September 2: As the Kimballs returned from a vacation to California, their car went out of control and crashed into an embankment. Seventy-five-year-old Kimball, asleep in the back seat, was thrown from the car, suffering a fatal skull fracture. Buried in the Salt Lake City Cemetery.

Jesse Knight

(1845-1921)

"Humbug Miner"
Brigham Young University Benefactor

Family Background:

1845   September 6: Born in Nauvoo, Illinois, to Newel Knight and Lydia Goldthwait. His parents' wedding was the first marriage performed by Joseph Smith.

Jesse's father died crossing the plains in 1847. Brigham Young appointed a family to care for one of Lydia's wagons and ox teams, but when they arrived in Utah the family insisted that President Young had given them the wagon and oxen. Despite pleas to the Church president, the property was never returned, and Jesse remained disaffected from the Church for nearly forty years as a result.

The Knight family moved to Provo when Jesse was twelve. At the age of fifteen, he began working as a freighter in Nevada and Montana. In 1867 he fought in the Blackhawk War in Sanpete County, Utah. He married Amanda McEwan in 1869; they had six children.

Conversion:

1891   Amanda was a faithful Latter-day Saint, but Jesse professed to "have no faith in the Church." Then a dead rat contaminated the well at the Knight family home in Payson, Utah. The children became seriously ill, with high fever and chills—probably from typhoid fever. Jennie, the youngest, was given up to death by her attending physician, but the faithful Amanda pleaded with Jesse to call in the elders for administration. When he finally did, the child was healed.

Jesse records: "Soon after the miraculous healing of Jennie, our oldest girl, Minnie, was stricken, and a little later all the other children at once lay very sick. From the time she was taken ill, Minnie felt that she would not recover. When asked why she felt so, she answered that when Jennie was so bad she had asked God to take her if she would do as well as Jennie; so she counted the days, believing she would live but thirty days from the time she took sick.

"Every day she kept the count, and departed as she had said. Her going was peaceful, her breath leaving her as she said the prayer, 'Oh God, bless our household.' I remembered now that when she was a baby she had diphtheria, and that then, almost seventeen years ago, I had promised the Lord that if he would spare her life I would not forget him. I had not kept that promise. How keenly I felt the justice of her being taken from us! I suffered in my feeling. I prayed for forgiveness and help. My prayer was answered and I received a testimony."

"Humbug Miner":

1869 Prospecting on the east side of Godiva Mountain near Eureka, Utah, Knight sat down under a tree to rest. Suddenly he heard a voice: "This country is here for the Mormons." A short time later, he dreamed about a rich vein of ore. The location was indelibly impressed on his mind, and when he went there, it was exactly as he had dreamed.

When he offered Jacob Roundy a partnership in the mine, the experienced Roundy replied, "I do not want an interest in a damed old humbug like this." "Humbug" struck Knight's fancy, and when a 150-foot shaft was completed, he christened it "Humbug Mine."

Two months later Knight and his partners struck a fabulously rich vein of lead and silver ore. Removing the first wheelbarrow of ore himself, Knight declared, "I have done the last day's work that I ever expect to do where I take another man's job from him. I expect to give employment and make labor from now on for other people."

"Uncle Jesse" then proceeded to make good a promise he had made to himself a few years before. He paid his back tithing, with compound interest. President Heber J. Grant later disclosed that Knight paid a lifetime tithe of $680,000—more than the entire Church tithes collected in 1893.

Entrepreneur:

Knight became the largest owner of mining properties in the Intermountain West. In 1901 he purchased 226,000 acres of land and built the second sugar factory in Canada at Raymond, a town named after his son. He also purchased 30,000 acres of land near Spring Coulee, Alberta, where he grazed over 4000 head of cattle.

Other ventures included the Tintic Smelting Company, Knight Consolidated Power, Mapleton Sugar, Layton Sugar, Bonneville Mining, Knight Woolen Mills, Ellison Ranching, Spring Canyon Coal, and Knight Trust and Savings, which eventually merged with the First Security Bank.

Church Benefactor:

1896　The Edmunds-Tucker Act of 1887 stripped the Church of its legal standing and confiscated all Church assets in excess of $50,000. The Church, over $300,000 in debt, found loans next to impossible to obtain. The panic of 1893 compounded financial difficulties: tithing dropped from $879,394 in 1890 to $576,584. Only secured loans from the Eastern financial giant H.B. Claflin Company prevented the Church from bankruptcy.

When the Claflin note came due in 1895, the Church was able to meet only the first principal payment. "Uncle Jesse" loaned $10,000 to save the Church's credit. Eventually the Claflin note was paid off with Church stock in Saltair Beach and the Salt Lake and Los Angeles Railway.

Two years later Knight loaned the Church another $10,000 to protect the reputations of Joseph F. Smith, Francis M. Lyman, and Abraham H. Cannon, who were in an awkward position in the bankruptcy of the Utah Loan and Trust Company of Ogden.

Brigham Young University Benefactor:

1901　After ten years on the board of trustees, Knight became vice-president of Brigham Young University. He donated $65,000 to help construct the Karl G. Maeser Memorial Building, and in 1914 he endowed BYU with an additional $100,000.

Death:

1921   March 14: Jesse Knight died in Provo, Utah, at the age of seventy-six. Buried in the Provo City Cemetery.

1960   The Jesse Knight Building at Brigham Young University was named in his honor.

Harold B. Lee

(1899-1973)

Originator of the Church Welfare Program
Eleventh President of the Church

Family Background:

1899 March 28: Born Harold Bingham Lee in Clifton, Idaho. In 1923 he married Fern Lucinda Tanner; they had two children. She died in 1961, and a year later he married Freda Joan Jensen.

"There came some tests when a loved one was taken from me and my life was crushed. A part of my life was buried in the cemetery, and I wondered, Here I was struggling to help others. Why? Then I theorized that maybe this was a great test, and if I could survive it, maybe there would be no other test that I wouldn't be able to meet. Just as I was recovering from that sorrow a daughter died suddenly, leaving four little children motherless. That was difficult. It is still difficult to understand. But the ways of the Lord are righteous, and sometimes we have to go through experiences like these in order for us to be prepared to face the issues of today's world."

Educator:

1916 At seventeen, he taught at Silver Star School near Weston, Idaho. In 1917 he became the principal of a four-room school at Oxford, Idaho.

1920 Following a mission in Denver, Colorado, he worked as a school principal in Salt Lake City.

Stake President:

1929 Called at the age of thirty to serve as president of Salt Lake City's Pioneer Stake—the youngest stake president in the Church at the time.

Father of the Church Welfare Program:

1932 With nearly half the adult members of his stake unemployed, President Lee instituted programs to provide fuel, bedding, clothes, and food for approximately 2,500 people hardest hit by the Depression. The stake also helped its members find jobs in private enterprise; others were put to work renovating chapels and cutting wood for church stoves.

Goods donated to the stake were stored in the old Bamberger electric train warehouse and then given to the needy or sold to purchase other necessities

Lee's self-sufficiency programs were so successful that the Church allowed tithing revenues to remain within Pioneer Stake. His stake programs provided the first step in the creation of a worldwide Church welfare program.

1935 While serving as a Salt Lake City commissioner, he was called to the first Church Security (Welfare) Committee. In 1937 he became its managing director, traveling with Melvin J. Ballard to institute the new Church welfare program worldwide.

"There I was, just a young man in my thirties. My experience had been limited. I was born in a little country town in Idaho. I had hardly been outside the boundaries of the states of Utah and Idaho. And now to put me in a position where I was to reach out to the entire membership of the Church, worldwide, was one of the most staggering contemplations that I could imagine."

General Authority:

1941 Called to the Quorum of the Twelve by Heber J. Grant after the death of Reed Smoot. An excellent pianist, he often played for Quorum of the Twelve meetings.

In 1960 the First Presidency directed the General Priesthood Committee, which Elder Lee chaired, to provide "more coordination and correlation between the activities and programs of the various priesthood quorums and auxiliary organizations and the educational system of the Church [and] . . . to formulate policy which will govern the planning, the writing, co-ordination, and implementation of the entire Church curriculum." Lee became chairman of the Church Correlation Committee in 1961.

In 1970 he became president of the Quorum of the Twelve and first counselor to President Joseph Fielding Smith.

Eleventh President of the Church:

1972   On the death of President Joseph Fielding Smith, Harold B. Lee became, at age seventy-one, the youngest president of the Church in more than forty years. He selected as counselors N. Eldon Tanner and Marion G. Romney, both cousins of his first wife. He was the only Church president except Heber J. Grant to have served as stake president.

As Church president, he also became chairman of the board for such businesses as Zion's First National Bank, Hotel Utah Corporation, Utah-Idaho Sugar Company, ZCMI, and Bonneville International.

He counseled men against becoming workaholics in their Church assignments: "I find some of our brethren who are engaged in leadership positions justifying their neglect of their families because they say that they are engaged in the Lord's work. I say to them, 'My dear brother, do you realize that the most important part of the Lord's work that you will do is the work that you do within the walls of your own home? That is the most important work of the Lord. Don't get your sense of values mixed up."

His presidency was noted for dramatic changes in Church administration. He emphasized priesthood in youth programs, restructured auxiliary general boards, and created internal and external communication committees for improving the Church's public relations. He is perhaps best remembered for stressing Church programs for the single adult members of the Church: "We are endeavoring to reach those for whom we have had no adequate programs. Man wasn't made for the Church, to paraphrase what the Master said, but the Church was made for man."

Regarding changes in Church policy, he said, "Now brethren of the priesthood, if you knew the processes by which these new programs came into being, you would know that this just didn't come out of a brainstorm, the figment of somebody's imagination; this was done after some of the most soulful praying and discussing that I believe I have ever experienced. We know, and we have announced when it was given that this came from the Lord."

Death:

1973   December 26: His death from a heart ailment at age seventy-four cut short Harold B. Lee's administration to only seventeen months—shortest term of all Church presidents. Buried in the Salt Lake Cemetery.

John D. Lee

(1812-1877)

Danite

Mountain Meadows Massacre Leader

Family Background:

1812   September 12: Born John Doyle Lee in Kaskaskia, Illinois. He married Agatha Woolsey in 1833 and eventually married eighteen plural wives, including three sisters and their widowed mother. Lee fathered sixty children. He gave his youngest wife a divorce so she could marry one of his sons by another wife. Eleven of his nineteen wives left him.

           Lee was Brigham Young's brother-in-law and his "adopted son" by sealing.

Danite:

1838   Lee and his wife were converted by missionaries in Illinois and were baptized in Far West, Missouri, where he joined a paramilitary group called the "Danites." When Lee and other Mormons tried to vote in Gallatin, Missouri, they were prevented by local toughs. After one Mormon was knocked to the ground, Lee saw John L. Butler give the Danite sign of distress ("placing the right hand to the right temple, the thumb behind the ear"), and heard him yell, "Charge, Danites!"

           In the ensuing fight, the eight Danites "knocked down and laid open, in a frightful manner, the skulls of several citizens with a bludgeon."

           William Swartzell, one of the eight, recorded that the Danites began foraging the countryside for "honey which they called sweet oil, hogs which they called bear, and cattle which they called buffalo." Lee admitted looting, but denied killing anyone or burning any buildings.

Missionary:

1839   Ordained a seventy, Lee served a short mission to Tennessee, where he baptized twenty-seven persons, including Bill Hickman. During the next four years he filled four additional short-term missions, including one to his hometown of Kaskaskia, Illinois.

Policeman:

1843　Like many former Danites, Lee served as a city policeman in Nauvoo and guarded Joseph Smith's home. He was also wharfmaster, major in the Nauvoo Legion, and general secretary of Nauvoo seventies.

1844　Campaigning for Joseph Smith's presidential candidacy, Lee said he was told of the Prophet's death by an angelic visitor: "Instead of electing your leader the chief magistrate of this nation—they have Martyrd him in prison—which has hastened his exaltation to the executive chair over this generation."

Council of Fifty Member:

1845　March 1: Became one of the first men admitted to the Council of Fifty following the death of Joseph Smith.

Colonizer:

1848　Settled in Salt Lake City.

1850　Brigham Young called Lee to accompany George A. Smith in colonizing Iron County. Lee offered to donate $2000 instead, but Young insisted, "Bro. George wants you to go with him so do I."

　　　For the next twenty-five years Lee tirelessly "converted the raw wilderness into profitable farms, developed large herds of cattle, sheep, and goats, experimented successfully with many new agricultural products, including silk and cotton, founded settlements, built fences, dug irrigation ditches, erected saw-, grist-, and sugar-cane mills, played the role of explorer, dealt sternly or kindly with the Indians as occasion required, [and] established and operated a ferry across the isolated, silt-laden waters of the Colorado." He served as a Parowan alderman (1851), as Washington County's probate judge (1856), and Utah legislator (1857-58).

Mountain Meadows Massacre Leader:

1857   In the midst of confusion over the advancing Utah Expeditionary Force, a wagon train of approximately 140 California-bound emigrants headed south from Salt Lake City. Some of the men boasted of possessing a gun which had "shot the guts out of Old Joe Smith" and claimed they would return from California with an army to wipe "every damn Mormon off the earth."

Indians accused the emigrants of poisoning springs, causing the death of several Indians and cattle. The emigrants also had the misfortune of being from the state where Apostle Parley P. Pratt had just been murdered—Arkansas.

Sunday, September 6, the train stopped at Mountain Meadows—eighty-five miles west of Cedar City—for a few weeks of rest before crossing the desert westward. Two days later a large band of Indians attacked the company. When word of the attack reached Cedar City, local Church leaders met and asked Lee, who was the Church's liason with the Indians, to "manage" them. A rider was dispatched to Salt Lake City for instructions.

President Young sent the messenger back, "urging him to spare no horse flesh": bloodshed was to be avoided. But before the messenger reached Cedar City, local Church and military leaders held a priesthood prayer circle and ordered the destruction of the emigrant company.

Under a flag of truce, Lee persuaded the emigrants to surrender their weapons. The wounded were loaded into Lee's wagon; their guns were placed in another wagon with the children. Each adult male emigrant was ordered to march single file beside a Mormon militiaman. At a prearranged signal—"Do your duty!"—each Mormon turned and killed the man he was guarding. Indians rushed from their hiding places and fell upon the defenseless women and older children. Lee personally killed the wounded men in his wagon. Accounts of the number of dead vary, but more than a hundred people were killed. Only the eighteen children under age ten survived.

The affair was first reported to Brigham Young as an Indian massacre. When the truth became known, suspected Church leaders in Cedar City were released and advised to remain quiet. Three were excommunicated. Many moved to Arizona under assumed names.

1870 Brigham Young advised Lee to leave his home at Harmony to build a sawmill with Levi Stewart in the pine forests of Lower Kanab. Two weeks after the mill was completed, Lee was astonished to receive a terse notice of his excommunication. When Brigham Young came to Saint George for the winter, Lee "asked him how it was that: I was held in fellowship for 13 years for an act then committed & all of a sudden I must be cut off from this Church. . . . He replied that they had never learned the particulars until lately. . . . I declared my innocence of doeing any thing designedly wrong; what we done was by the mutual consent & council of the high counsellors, Presidents, Bishops & leading men, who Prayed over the Matter & diligently Sought the Mind & will of the Spirit of Truth to direct the affair."

A week later an unsigned letter in the handwriting of Apostle Erastus Snow warned Lee, "If you will consult your own safety & that [of] others, you will not press yourself nor an investigation on others at this time lest you cause others to become accessory with you & thereby force them to inform upon you or suffer. Our advice is, trust no one. Make yourself scarce & keep out of the way."

Scapegoat:

1874 A federal grand jury indicted John D. Lee, former Stake President Isaac Haight, and seven others for complicity in the Mountain Meadows Massacre. When Lee, who had been hiding out at his ferry on the Colorado River, visited one of his families in Panguitch, he was captured and tried. After nine months in the Beaver, Utah, jail, Lee was acquitted. But he was remanded to the territorial penitentiary in Sugarhouse to await yet another trial. In 1875 he wrote:

> Old Mormon Bull, how came you here?
> We have tuged and toiled these many years,
> we have been cuffed and kicked with sore abuse

and now sent here for penetentiary use.
We both are creatures of some Note.
You are food for Prisoners
and I the scap goat.

1876   September: Charges against everyone but Lee were dropped. He was convicted of murder. The verdict was upheld by the Utah Supreme Court.

Execution:

1877   March 23: Returned to Mountain Meadows to be executed, Lee was given a moment to speak: "I have but little to say this morning. Of course I feel that I am on the brink of eternity, and the solemnities of eternity should rest upon my mind.... I am ready to die. I trust in God. I have no fear. Death has no terror.... I ask the Lord, my God, if my labors are done, to receive my spirit."

John D. Lee (with neckscarf) sitting on his coffin, firing squad in the background.

Lee shook hands with those in attendance, had his picture taken sitting on his coffin, gave away articles of his outer clothing, and instructed the firing squad to aim for his heart so as not to mutilate his body. He was shot while sitting on the edge of his casket. He was sixty-five. His body was taken by the family to Panguitch, Utah, for burial.

1961   Reinstated in the Church by authority of the First Presidency and Quorum of the Twelve.

Amasa Lyman

(1813-1877)

Joseph Smith's Special Counselor
Titular President of the Church of Zion
Spiritualist

Family Background:

1813   March 30: Born Amasa ("Amacy") Mason Lyman in Lyman, New Hampshire. He married Louisa Maria Tanner in 1835, Caroline Ely Partridge (1844), Eliza Maria Partridge Smith (1844), Cornelia Eliza Lott (1844), Dionita Walker (1845), Paulina Eliza Phelps (1846), and Lydia Partridge (1853). The three Partridge wives were sisters—daughters of Bishop Edward Partridge. Lyman was the father of thirty-seven children, including Apostle Francis M. Lyman, father of Apostle Richard R. Lyman.

Missionary:

1832   Converted by Lyman Johnson and Orson Pratt, Amasa went to meet Joseph Smith in Kirtland. "Although there was nothing strange or different from other men in his personal appearance," Amasa later said, "yet when he grasped my hand in that cordial way (known to those who have met him in the honest simplicity of truth), I felt as one of the old in the presence of the Lord; my strength seemed to be gone, so that it required an effort on my part to stand on my feet; but in all this there was no fear, but the serenity and peace of heaven pervaded my soul, and the still small voice of the Spirit whispered in its living testimony in the depths of my soul, where it has ever remained, that he was the man of God."

Soon Amasa Lyman and Zerubbabel Snow were sent on a mission to Ohio and Virginia. Lyman later served missions to New York (1836 and 1839), northern Illinois and Wisconsin (1841), Tennessee and southern Illinois (1842), and Mississippi (1847). In 1860 he was named president of the European Mission.

General Authority:

1835   Having served in Zion's Camp, Lyman was called to the First Quorum of Seventy.

1838   Lyman, Joseph Smith, and other leaders were arrested in Far West, Missouri, and charged with "high treason against the state, murder, burglary, arson, robbery, and larceny." Lyman was released six days later.

1842 Called to the Quorum of the Twelve by Brigham Young after the excommunication of Orson Pratt. When Pratt returned to the Quorum in 1843, Lyman was called to be a counselor in the First Presidency, but he was not sustained in a general conference, either as apostle or counselor, during the Prophet's lifetime.

Colonizer:

1847 A member of the Council of Fifty since 1844, Lyman was selected to travel in the Brigham Young pioneer company.

1850 After three years in Salt Lake City, Brigham Young called Lyman and Charles C. Rich to colonize California. They purchased a large ranch and founded San Bernardino, which within four years had a population of 1,400. San Bernardino became a gathering place for California Mormons, a resting and supply station for missionaries, and the disembarking point for immigrants from the Pacific missions. The colony was disbanded in 1857 when the Saints were called to Utah to defend the territory against the federal Expeditionary Force.

1862 Called to colonize Fillmore, Utah: "President Young said he wished me to sell my real estate and settle in Fillmore and gather my family to that place, to make them a home and to educate my children, which I could not do for them in their present scattered condition . . . I have commenced building a home, having been thirty years without one."

Excommunication:

From 1855 to 1859 Lyman denied Christ's special divinity and vicarious blood atonement in several conference sermons. A renowned orator, he told the Saints that Christ "was, simply, a holy man . . . . There was nothing about Jesus but the Priesthood that he held and the

Gospel that he proclaimed that was so very singular."

To counter objections, Lyman argued, "'Well,' says one, 'you do not think much of Jesus.' Yes I do. 'How much?' I think he was a good man." Lyman acknowledged that Jesus "died for the world," but added, "and what man that ever died for the truth that he died for, did not die for the world?... Have we found redemption through them?... We may talk of men being redeemed by the efficacy of [Christ's] blood; but the truth is that that blood had no efficacy to wash away our sins. That must depend upon our own action."

1862 Finally charged with teaching false doctrine while in Scotland, Lyman apologized to the First Presidency, and signed a letter asking the Saints for forgiveness.

1867 Accused again of teaching the same doctrine, Lyman was dropped from the Quorum of the Twelve, disfellowshipped, and advised by President Young to find activities employing his head and hands so "health of mind and body will attend you."

1869 Lyman joined the "New Movement," organized to oppose the political and economic control of Brigham Young in Utah. New Movement leaders, attracted to spiritualism, named Lyman president of their Church of Zion.

1870 Excommunicated. Caroline Lyman left Amasa despite his pleading with her to stay. She was sealed to Joseph Smith. Her youngest daughter recorded that Caroline "felt she must have the protection and the security of the Priesthood in her and her children's lives.... Evidently in her dire circumstances she felt that the Prophet was the only secure anchor to be sealed to."

Spiritualist:

In the 1850s Lyman had secretly participated in seances and automatic writing with like-minded Mormons in San Bernardino. He openly embraced spiritualism during the last years of his life. His daughter Hilda often served as a medium during his seances. "Such deceased relatives as his father, father-in-law, children and aunt delivered comforting messages from beyond the veil. Likewise former Mormon leaders Heber C. Kimball, Hyrum Smith, Jedediah Grant, Newell K. Whitney, and Joseph Smith himself paid occasional visits."

Death:

1877   February 4: Died of pneumonia in Fillmore at the age of sixty-four. Buried in Fillmore Cemetery, wearing a black suit and black boots.

Posthumous Return to the Church:

1898   Martha Lyman Roper, eldest daughter of Amasa and Caroline Lyman, had a "manifestation or dream wherein her father was calling for help. When she heard and saw him she had the impulse to run and embrace him but he warned her to beware and pointed out a great yawning chasm between them, over which she couldn't go to him nor he to her. He requested Martha to appeal to his son, Marion, to help him for he was the only one in a position to do so. He also told her that he was very weary and tired of his black clothes and that he did so want to be with his family, his wives and his children whom he loved and longed for."

1908   May 7: At Caroline's funeral, Francis M. Lyman told "President [Joseph F.] Smith of my desire to do something for father. Told him of my dreams and my Sister Martha's, how father had appeared to us and pled his cause. How President Snow told me that there was no doubt but that he could come out all right in the end."

A short time later Francis M. told his son Richard, "This is one of the most important and happiest days of my life. In the temple today, President Joseph F. Smith placed his hands on my head, and by proxy restored my father to all his former blessings, authority and power."

Amy Brown Lyman

(1872-1959)

Advocate for the Needy
General Relief Society President
Women's Advocate

Family Background:

1872   February 9: Born Amy Cassandra Brown in Pleasant Grove, Utah. Amy's father, John Brown, who had helped lead a group of Mississippi Mormons to Utah, was mayor and bishop of Pleasant Grove.

Of her mother, Margaret Zimmerman Brown, Amy said: "My mother was a partial invalid for a number of years due to childbirth complications, and during that time she directed the affairs of her household and in addition helped solve the social and economic problems of many of her friends.... We had more confidence in her ideas than we had in our own, and usually were willing to accept any plan she had for us without much argument. She was a woman's woman and always maintained that girls should have equal opportunities and privileges with boys."

Student and Teacher:

1888   Amy left Pleasant Grove, where she "had plain living but high thinking," to attend the Brigham Young Academy, where Karl G. Maeser, George H. Brimhall, Alice Louise Reynolds, and Dr. George W. Middleton made lasting impressions.

Graduating in 1890 at the age of eighteen, she immediately took charge of the primary department under Dr. Maeser's supervision.

She boarded with the Maeser family, which had its disadvantages: "One great disappointment that I remember distinctly was when I was advised not to take part in a grand masquerade ball given in the Provo Theater by the society folk of the town. It was really the ball of the season, and all of my girlfriends dressed and masked for the occasion.

"I felt quite rebellious at being advised not to take part and argued the point with Brother Maeser. I told him that I had been held down all my life, and that I was tired of being a bishop's daughter and a Church school teacher. I think I even shed a few tears about it. But I finally gave in, and sat in the front row of the dress circle—we called it bald-head row—with the older people. I watched my friends enjoy all the fun that accompanies those masquerade balls."

She taught elementary school in Salt Lake City from 1894 to 1896, when she married Richard R. Lyman; they had one son and one daughter. Lyman succeeded his father, Francis M. Lyman, as a member of the Quorum of the Twelve in 1918.

Advocate for the Needy:

1901   While Richard pursued a graduate degree in engineering at the University of Chicago, Amy took a course in social work from Dr. George E. Vincent. "It was at this time that I first became interested in social work and social problems. ... Through a former Michigan classmate of my husband, who was then working in the Chicago Charities, I was invited to do volunteer social work in this agency. These experiences ... were all profitable and started me on my way as a social worker."

Eventually Amy Brown Lyman worked actively on behalf of the Salt Lake City Community Clinic, Utah State Welfare Commission, Colorado Conference of Social Work, American Child Hygiene Association, Home Services Institute, National Conference of Social Workers, National Conference of Charities and Correction, National Tuberculosis Association, and the American Association for Mental Deficiency.

Relief Society Leader:

While her husband taught civil engineering at the University of Utah, Lyman took courses in English and history, joined the Author's Club, and read widely in history, American literature, and philosophy.

1909   Called to the general board of the Relief Society. Concerned that she was too young for an "old women's organization," she "shed tears of anxiety because of the responsibility such an appointment involved."

1914   Named assistant business manager of the *Relief Society Magazine*, she became its editor seven years later. After twenty-eight years with the magazine, she said, "It is a dearly-loved child to me."

The Relief Society sent Lyman and four other women to Denver in 1917 for welfare training with the Red Cross and the University of Colorado. Two years later she became director of the Relief Society's social services department.

1928   Named first counselor to newly selected Relief Society President Louise Y. Robinson.

1940   Called as general Relief Society president by Heber J. Grant.

Women's Advocate:

1922   As a Republican member of the Utah House of Representatives, Lyman chaired the Public Health Committee and was a member of the Labor and Appropriations Committees. "I called attention to the fact that since leadership is always scarce and since the supply had been increased by the emancipation of women, we should look among women's groups for new leaders, especially in certain fields; that women are a great asset to any humanitarian cause because they have a special and a different viewpoint which is based on their experience as mothers and homemakers; that their ability as directors and administrators is often apparent when they are left widows and therefore are required to manage their own business and family affairs; that they are especially needed in legislative bodies where the laws are made, because of their special knowledge of human needs and humanistic rights."

A member of the National Council of Women for many years, Lyman became a national executive committee member (1925), recording secretary (1925-1927), auditor (1927-1929), and third vice-president (1929-1934).

Personal Tragedy:

Between 1933 and 1943, Amy Brown Lyman suffered

numerous personal tragedies, ranging from the loss of a kidney and her husband's bout with ulcers, to the death of a daughter-in-law who left an eight-month-old baby, to the suicide of her son.

After five years as general president of the Relief Society, she requested a release due to health problems and personal difficulties related to the 1943 excommunication of her husband, Richard R. Lyman, for "violation of the Christian Law of Chastity."

Death:

1959   December 5: Died at her daughter's home at the age of eighty-seven while recovering from a fall. Her husband, who had been rebaptized in 1954, died in 1963. Both were buried in Wasatch Lawn Memorial Gardens in Salt Lake City.

Francis M. Lyman

(1840-1916)

President of the Quorum of the Twelve

Family Background:

1840   January 12: Born Francis Marion Lyman in Goodhope, Illinois, to future Apostle Amasa Lyman and Louisa Maria Tanner.

At seventeen, he married Rhoda Taylor ("My modesty made me a long time in solving the problem"). He married Clara Caroline Callister in 1869 and her sister Susan in 1884. Father of seventeen children, including Apostle Richard R. Lyman.

Teen-age Freighter:

1855   As a fifteen-year-old freighter, Marion "took to drinking, and found that I really liked it... though it was miserable stuff, and I wonder we were not poisoned by it.... Freighters generally do their praying, if any, before they leave home or after they return, so nothing of that kind takes their attention while on the road."

"I had the pernicious habit of smoking cigarettes fairly well fastened upon me. It gave my father and mother very much concern lest one bad habit should be followed by another. The Mexicans of that [Mojave Desert] region were expert smokers, and would pass volumes of smoke out by the nose which, to such boys as me, appeared to be a very great accomplishment, and I strove to do likewise, or like-*foolish*, and succeeded.... I attempted to break my habit of smoking, and father, to stimulate my undertaking, offered me a number-one horse and saddle and outfit if I would persevere to succeed, but I failed."

Missionary:

1856   Ordained an elder. "I was sixteen years old, six feet one and a half inches high, and weighed 184 pounds. I was notorious for my strength among the boys and small men. I was boisterous but not wicked."

Lyman was called on a mission to Europe with his apostle father, but the approach of the Utah Expeditionary Force cancelled all missions. The following year, he married Rhoda Taylor.

1859 As a nineteen-year-old husband and father, Lyman decided, "I could no longer be a Latter Day Saint in a manner satisfactory to myself without attending to my family and secret prayers." He learned to pray before his mission, and gave up tobacco at age twenty-five and alcohol at twenty-six.

1860 As Amasa Lyman was preparing to leave for another mission, Brigham Young learned that Marion was planning to manage the family farm in his father's absence. President Young declared he "would not leave him home for the price of a farm." As a newly-ordained seventy, Marion Lyman left for Europe with his cousin and close friend, Joseph F. Smith.

Colonizer:

1863 Brigham Young called Marion to assist his father, Amasa, in colonizing Fillmore, Utah, where they jointly built the O.K. Flour Mill.

During his fourteen years in Fillmore, Lyman served as county recorder, superintendent of schools, prosecuting county attorney, officer in the Nauvoo Legion, and member of the Utah legislature.

1874 Joseph F. Smith and Marion Lyman served another mission to Europe. When he returned to Utah, Lyman brought three hundred immigrants with him.

1877 Supervised the colonization of Tooele, Utah, where he served as Tooele Stake president until 1880.

Apostle:

1880 April: Called to the Council of Fifty. "This appears to be one of the greatest steps in my life."

October: Exploring southeastern Utah, New Mexico, and Arizona with Erastus Snow and others, Lyman learned he had been sustained as a member of the Quorum of the Twelve when he read a conference report in the *Deseret News*.

During ordination, the First Presidency and members of the Twelve "told me that Father's robes had fallen on me, and their words so overcame me that I wept." Amasa Lyman had been excommunicated in 1870.

1889   Lyman's two years on the underground in Mexico and Canada produced wild rumors about the apostle. When he heard them, Wilford Woodruff thundered, "I might believe the report of a general earthquake, but the report that Francis M. Lyman is guilty of drunkenness and adultery, never, no never! That is something that can never be truthfully reported in heaven, on earth, or in hell."

Lyman refused to compromise with the government on plural marriage. "How we are to be pitied when we cannot face bonds and imprisonment, persecution or death for our holy religion. Latter-day Saints must be made of better stuff. O that the Lord will let me die before I cower like a whipped cur and yield to the infernal lash. I would a hundred times rather hear of a good man's death than to hear that he has yielded any principle of the gospel."

Following President George Q. Cannon's example, he surrendered to U.S. marshals and was fined $200 and sentenced to eighty-five days in the territorial "Pen."

When a suit of stripes could not be found to accommodate his 280 pounds, Lyman had to settle for a mere "striped hat."

Financial Benefactor:

Lyman served as a director of Zion's Savings Bank and Trust, Consolidated Wagon and Machine, Home Fire Insurance, and the Heber J. Grant Company.

1893   When the federal government confiscated Church assets over $50,000, Lyman and other Church leaders signed personal notes to guarantee the Church's credit:

"The possibility of losing all my earthly possessions by endorsing with the Church, troubles me only so far as it may hurt people I am owing. . . . If it be necessary that I must be sacrificed, I do now and for all time to come acknowledge the hand of the Lord in taking it from me, as freely as I acknowledged His hand in receiving it from Him. 'The Lord giveth and Lord taketh away, blessed be the name of the Lord!'"

A few months later, Lyman exuberantly recorded, "President Cleveland signed the bill to return the personal property of the Church, $300,000. . . . This is a great blessing from the hand of the Lord for He has done it and not men."

President of the Quorum of the Twelve:

1899   When anti-Mormons began disclosing the names of men who had married plural wives after Wilford Woodruff's 1890 Manifesto, Lyman began a private campaign to discourage men from entering plural marriage, despite the encouragement they were receiving from other apostles. He made a public example of a neighbor who unwisely claimed to have entered into an authorized plural marriage: Lyman instigated civil and ecclesiastical actions which resulted in the man's imprisonment and excommunication. As more plural marriages were performed by other apostles in Mexico, Canada, and the United States during the next five years, Lyman quietly tried to counter their influence.

1903   Became president of the Quorum of the Twelve, serving until his death thirteen years later.

1904   The disclosures of the Reed Smoot investigation (1904-07), Joseph F. Smith's "second manifesto" (1904), and the resignation of Apostles John W. Taylor and Matthias F. Cowley (1905) encouraged Lyman to intensify his campaign to stop new plural marriages. As president of the Quorum of the Twelve, he spearheaded numerous investigations and Church court actions against post-manifesto polygamists.

Death:

1916   November 18: Died of pneumonia at the age of seventy-six. Buried in the Tooele, Utah, Cemetery.

Karl G. Maeser

(1828-1901)

Father of Brigham Young University

Family Background:

1828   January 16: Born Karl Gottfried Maeser in Vorbrucke, Meissen, Germany. In 1854 he married Anna Meith in Germany, and twenty-one years later wed plural wife Emilie Damke. He was the father of nine children.

Education:

With private tutoring, Maeser became proficient in French, Italian, and Latin, in addition to his native German. Musically gifted, he played the piano and organ, and conducted choral and orchestral music. He studied two years at the Krenz Schule in Dresden before graduating with honors from the Friederich Stadt normal school. At the age of twenty he taught in the Dresden schools, later serving as a private tutor in Bohemia.

First Mormon Convert in Saxony:

1855   "Scepticism had undermined religious impressions of my childhood days, and infidelity, now known by its modern name of agnosticism, was exercising its disintegrating influence upon me."

Maeser was amused by the "inaccuracies and the poverty of language" he found in Mormon pamphlets. "But as I read on I came to be convinced that 'Mormonism' was a bigger thing than I had anticipated it to be. The humble but straightforward statements of testimony, the mistakes and the meagerness of the language used in the exposition of the wonderful truths that I could see back of it all, brought such uneasiness to me that I could not resist; my soul was on fire, as it were, and I therefore expressed a desire to have an Elder sent to me."

Taught the gospel by William Budge, Franklin D. Richards, and William H. Kimball, Maeser and seven family members and friends were baptized in the Elbe River—the first Mormon converts in Saxony.

Maeser was made president of the small Dresden branch.

Karl G. Maeser 179

1856   The Dresden branch emigrated to Utah, first stopping in England, where Maeser served a short mission to Scotland. When they arrived in America, the Maesers had only enough money to reach Philadelphia. Called on a mission to Virginia, Karl Maeser taught music to the children of ex-President John Tyler and others, earning enough money to complete the trip to Utah.

Teacher:

1860   In Salt Lake City, Maeser announced in the *Deseret News,* "The undersigned begs to inform the Public that he intends opening Evening Classes, both for ladies and gentlemen, for English, German, French, Italian, Latin, Greek, Drawing, Bookkeeping, Mathematics, and all the branches of a sound and practical education." The Fifteenth Ward school was established.

         Brigham Young placed Maeser in charge of Salt Lake's Union Academy in 1861. In 1864 he became the private tutor of Brigham Young's children. He was also organist for the Tabernacle Choir.

Missionary:

1867   At general conference Maeser heard his name announced for a mission to Germany and Switzerland. He gave his last fifty-cent piece to his wife Anna, who said she would return it when he returned.

1870   Anna met him at the door, where Maeser noticed "a new stove, carpet, lace curtains, furniture, all paid for furnished the front room." She gave him his fifty-cent piece and "another one besides."

Father of Brigham Young University:

1870   Maeser opened a teacher training school in the Salt Lake Twentieth Ward.

1876   April 5: A munitions explosion in the hills north of Salt Lake damaged Maeser's schoolhouse. When he complained to Brigham Young that he would be unable to teach until the building was repaired, Young replied, "I want to give you a mission to teach at the Brigham Young Academy in Provo. . . . I want you to remember that you ought not to teach even the alphabet or the multiplication tables without the Spirit of God." Nineteen days later, Maeser began a two-month experimental term of the Brigham Young Academy.

      August 27: Sixty-seven students attended the opening of the Brigham Young Academy on Center Street in Provo, Utah. The school house was "a grim non-descript structure without beauty or grace or any other aesthetic feature calculated to invite a second look. The lower floor was made up of two large rooms at the front, and two small ones at the back. The upper floor had been designed for use as a theater. It consisted of one large room and a stage—both so utterly bare and gloomy as to make inappropriate any form of entertainment except tragedy."

1884   Tragedy struck when the school burned to the ground. Classes reconvened in the ZCMI warehouse, which was used until 1892, when Education Hall was dedicated on University Avenue.

      Among Maeser's students were Reed Smoot, George H. Brimhall, Annie Clark Tanner, Joseph M. Tanner, James E. Talmage, and Susa Young Gates.

      He guided the lives of his students by memorable sermonettes:

      "Everyone's life is an object lesson to others."

      "There is a Mount Sinai for every child of God, if he only knows how to climb it."

      "Every one of us sooner or later must stand at the forks of the road and choose between personal interest and some principle of right."

      "The truly educated man will always speak to the understanding of the most unlearned of his audience."

      "Whatever you do, don't do nothing. Whatever you be, don't be a scrub."

Church Educator:

1888 Wilford Woodruff called Maeser to be the first general superintendent of Church schools. In 1889 the Church Board of Education conferred on him the degree of doctor of letters and didactics, and one year later released him from his Brigham Young Academy responsibilities so that he could devote more time to establishing Church schools in Utah, Idaho, Arizona, Colorado, New Mexico, Canada, and Mexico.

1894 Appointed second assistant to George Q. Cannon in the superintendency of the Deseret Sunday School Union. In 1899 he was ordained a patriarch.

Author:

1898 To express his philosophy of education, Maeser wrote *School and Fireside.* "Discover and evaluate the worth of each individual," he advised. "Teacher's plans should be varied and flexible to allow for student differences. . . . Discover the sphere of action for which any given child is adapted and turn its thoughts and energies in that direction. . . . Teachers and parents should be living examples of what they teach."

Death:

1901 February 14: Died of cardiac insufficiency in Salt Lake City. Buried in the Salt Lake City Cemetery.

1912 The Maeser Memorial Building was erected at Brigham Young University.

Thomas B. Marsh

No Known Photograph

(1799-1868)

First President of the Quorum of the Twelve

Family Background:

1799   November 1: Born Thomas Baldwin Marsh in Acton, Massachusetts. He married Elizabeth Godkin on his twenty-seventh birthday in 1826.

First President of the Quorum of the Twelve:

1830   Marsh was baptized by David Whitmer and appointed by revelation to be a "physician to the Church" (D&C 31:10). Sections 31 and 112 of the Doctrine and Covenants are addressed to him, and he is mentioned in sections 52 and 56.

1835   Called to be a member of the original Quorum of the Twelve by the Three Witnesses. Seniority was determined by age; Marsh at thirty-six was the eldest, and therefore became the first Quorum president.

Dissident:

1838   After David Whitmer, Church leader in Far West, Missouri, was deposed, Marsh became "President Pro Tem of the Church in Missouri" with Brigham Young and David Patten as counselors.

    Later that year, a Church court ruled against his wife in a dispute over milk strippings. According to George A. Smith, "The wife of Marsh and Sister Harris [wife of George Washington Harris] agreed to exchange milk, in order to enable each of them to make a larger cheese than they could do separately. Each was to take the other the 'strippings' as well as the rest of the milk. Mrs. Harris performed her part of the agreement, but Mrs. Marsh kept a pint of 'strippings' from each cow. When this became known the matter was brought before the Teachers, and these decided against Mrs. Marsh. . . . [Marsh] appealed to the Bishop. He sustained the Teachers. . . . [Marsh] appealed to the High Council . . . that body confirmed the Bishop's decision. . . . [Marsh] appealed to the First Presidency. . . . They approved the finding of the High

Council. Was Marsh satisfied then? No. With the persistency of Lucifer himself, he declared that he would uphold the character of his wife, 'even if he had to go to hell for it.'"

Excommunication:

1839   Marsh and Orson Hyde were excommunicated for signing an affidavit that the Mormons "had a company called 'Danites' organized for the purpose of murdering 'enemies.' . . . [They] have taken an oath to support the heads of the Church in all things that they say or do, *whether right or wrong*. . . . They appointed a company of twelve, by the name of the 'Destruction Company,' for the purpose of burning and destroying."

Marsh went into hiding in Howard County, Missouri, "afraid the 'Mormons' would kill him; and he durst not let them know where he was."

"Chief of the Twelve":

1856   During six weeks of paralysis from a massive stroke, Marsh experienced a change of heart and sent a "revelation" to President Brigham Young:

"Behold I say unto thee Brigham Young! Where is the servant of the Lord, Thomas Marsh, Chief of the 12 to whom the Lord gave the keys of the kingdom? from whom they have not been taken, who was driven out from among you because of the iniquity of his brethren who hunted for his blood. . . . Now if ye would prosper in the land which the Lord, thy god hath given thee ye shale spedily take with thee two wise & faithful servants of the Lord and go to the land of Missouri and inquire in the County Howard for his son Edward Marsh, who will, if ye are prudent direct you to his father; but if ye act not discretely he will fear lest ye seek the life of his father, and withhold from thee the desired information. Behold ye shale take with you means for his conveyance . . . confer with him in a kind and friendly manner and he shall rejoice and be glad to see you . . . he will accompany you and ye shale bring him to this land even to your chief City."

"The Fruits of Apostasy":

1856   After his wife died, Marsh traveled through Missouri teaching biblical geography to raise money for a trip to Council Bluffs, Iowa. On the day of his arrival he suffered another stroke.

"Look at me," he said to the Saints in Winter Quarters, "and see the result of apostasy; had I been faithful to my calling as the President of the Twelve, I would now occupy the position that Brigham Young does, as President of the Church."

Marsh was rebaptized in Papyo Creek on the journey west.

"Decrepid, Broken Down Old Man":

1857   Standing before the Saints in Salt Lake City, Marsh must have been an impressive sight to those who believed his broken condition was the result of divine chastisement. John Taylor described him as "a poor decrepid, broken down old man . . . one of his arms hangs down."

Brigham Young could not resist the opportunity to compare himself physically with Marsh: "He has told you that he is an old man. Do you think I am an old man? I could prove to this congregation that I am young; for I could find more girls who would choose me for a husband than any of the young men. . . . What do you think the difference is between his age and mine? One year and seven months to a day."

Marsh pleaded with the Saints for acceptance and fellowship. Brigham Young was skeptical: "A man that will be fooled by the Devil—a man that has not sense to discern between steel grey mixed and iron grey mixed, when one is dyed with logwood and the other with indigo, may be deceived again."

"T.B.M.":

1858   After visiting Salt Lake, Marsh moved to Springville, Utah, then to Spanish Fork, where he taught history and geography. His contact with Brigham Young was minimal, but occasionally he asked the president for shirts, summer pants, a coat, and white flannel for his temple garments.

In 1863 he moved to Ogden, Utah. He died in 1868, at the age of sixty-three. For many years the only grave marker of the first president of the Quorum of the Twelve in the Ogden City Cemetery was a weatherbeaten board marked: "T.B.M."

David O. McKay

(1873-1970)

Teacher
Ninth President of the Church

Family Background:

1873   September 8: Born David Oman McKay in Huntsville, Utah. In 1901 he married Emma Ray Riggs; they had seven children.

Educator:

1893   Principal of the Huntsville schools at the age of twenty.

1897   Graduated from the University of Utah and went on a mission to Scotland. At the university McKay played guard on the school's first football team, played the piano at dances, was student body president and valedictorian of his class.

1899   Taught at the Church-owned Weber Academy in Ogden, Utah.

1901   Called to the Weber Stake Sunday School Superintendency, where he introduced course outlines and preparation meetings—innovations later adopted churchwide.

General Authority:

1906   Called to the Quorum of the Twelve by Joseph F. Smith after the resignations of John W. Taylor and Matthias Cowley. During the next forty-five years, he served as a counselor and as superintendent of the general Sunday Schools.

         Served as Church commissioner of education for ten years, then as president of the European Mission (1922-24).

         He was second counselor to Presidents Heber J. Grant (1934-45) and George Albert Smith (1945-51), and became president of the Quorum of the Twelve in 1950.

Outdoorsman:

A lover of the outdoors, President McKay frequently

returned to his boyhood home. "The air is better at Huntsville," he often commented; "That's what keeps me young."

Ninth President of the Church:

1951   April 9: Set apart as the ninth president of the Church, with Stephen L. Richards and J. Reuben Clark as counselors. Other counselors in his administration were Henry D. Moyle (1959-63), Hugh B. Brown (1961-70), and N. Eldon Tanner (1963-70). Four others were called as additional counselors to the First Presidency: Hugh B. Brown (June-October 1961), Thorpe B. Isaacson (1965-70), Joseph Fielding Smith (1965-70), and Alvin R. Dyer (1968-70). The precedent for additional counselors in the First Presidency was set in 1843 when Joseph Smith moved Amasa Lyman into the First Presidency and reinstated Orson Pratt in the Quorum of the Twelve.

Only Brigham Young and Heber J. Grant served as president of the Church longer than his nearly nineteen years. His service of sixty-four years as a general authority is longest in the history of the Church, his thirty-six years in the First Presidency second only to the thirty-eight served by Joseph F. Smith.

At 6'1", President McKay was the tallest Church president and the first since Joseph Smith not to wear a beard. His ninety-six years overlapped the lives of every Church president preceding him except Joseph Smith. The transcontinental railroad was completed shortly after his birth; man reached the moon shortly before his death.

During his life David O. McKay journeyed more than two million miles, making him the most-traveled general authority in the history of the Church.

Church Growth:

During President McKay's administration, Mormonism became recognized as an international religion rather than merely a western United States church. Asked to describe his greatest accomplishment in life when he was nearly eighty years old, he responded: "Making the church a worldwide organization."

Between 1951 and 1971 the number of missionaries grew from 2,000 to 13,000, and the number of missions doubled. His vision of missionary work was far-reaching: "It is generally understood that every member of the Church should be a missionary."

The number of stakes increased from 184 to 500 on the day of his death in 1970. Church membership in the period expanded from 1,111,000 to 2,931,000. At his death, more than half the Church members had never known another Church president.

Under his leadership, the Church completed more than 3,700 buildings, including the Swiss, Los Angeles, New Zealand, London, and Oakland temples.

Administrative Changes:

The Church president became chairman of the boards of all Church businesses and full time management personnel were assigned to the presidency of each business. Supportive departments, such as legal services, building, communications, and accounting departments saw unprecedented growth.

Love and Home:

Mormons remember President McKay most for his emphasis on family. In a 1964 conference he declared: "No other success can compensate for failure in the home. . . . I know of no other place where happiness abides more securely than in the home. It is possible to make home a bit of heaven. Indeed, I picture heaven as a continuation of the ideal home."

His "love affair" with Emma, became legendary. To David O. McKay love was a "tender flower, the roots of which are in the human heart. It thrives in the element of confidence and trust, as the rose thrives in the sunshine and morning dew. . . . Fidelity and constancy are to that little flower of the soul what the sun is to the rose."

Author:

More than a dozen books have been compiled from his sermons, including *Stepping Stones to an Abundant Life, Treasures of Life, Secrets to a Happy Life, True to the Faith, Man May Know for Himself, Highlights in the Life of David O. McKay, Ancient Apostles, Gospel Ideals, Cherished Experiences,* and *Home Memories of President David O. McKay.*

His writings reflect his love for mankind and his positive outlook: "Every noble impulse, every unselfish expression of love, every brave suffering for the right, every surrender of self to something higher than self, every loyalty to an ideal, every unselfish devotion to principle, every helpfulness to humanity, every act of self-control, every fine courage of the soul, undefeated by pretense or policy, but by being, doing, and living the good for the very good's sake—that is spirituality."

Death:

Despite his age, President McKay remained remarkably vigorous. On one occasion, climbing a platform to speak, he tripped on the stairs. Waving help aside, he quipped, "It's awful to grow old, but I prefer it to the alternative."

1970   Died at the age of ninety-six in Salt Lake City of congestive heart failure; buried in the Salt Lake City Cemetery.

Edward Partridge

(1793-1840)

First Bishop of the Church

Family Background:

1793   August 27: Born in Pittsfield, Massachusetts. He became a hatter, following the waterways to obtain the beaver pelts necessary to his work. He later moved to Painsville, Ohio, where his business prospered.

In 1819 he married Lydia Clisbee; they had seven children. Two daughters, Eliza Marie and Emily Dow, married Joseph Smith on the same day in 1843. After the Prophet's death, Eliza married Amasa Lyman, and Emily married Brigham Young. Two other daughters, Caroline Ely and Lydia, also married Amasa Lyman.

Convert:

1830   Edward Partridge had been a member of Sidney Rigdon's Campbellite congregation for two years when the Mormon missionaries visited his hatter's shop. He quickly sent the "imposters" packing, but then had a change of heart and sent an employee after them to bring back a Book of Mormon.

He read it, was converted, and went to New York to meet Joseph Smith. The Prophet baptized him in the Seneca River on December 11.

First Bishop of the Church:

1831   Partridge is mentioned in twelve sections of the Doctrine and Covenants, including section 41: "He should be appointed by the voice of the Church and ordained a Bishop unto the Church, to leave his merchandise and to spend all his time in the labors of the Church. And this is because his heart is pure before me, for he is like unto Nathaniel of old, in whom there is no guile."

Anxious about leaving a flourishing business, Partridge wrote Lydia, "I must not fail, pray for me that I will not fail." The prayers were answered; his financial competence was soon appreciated in the Church.

1831   August 3: Partridge attended the dedication of the temple site at Independence, Missouri, and eventually became "head of the Church in Zion."

For ten months, Partridge was the only bishop in the Church. Then Newel K. Whitney was appointed in Ohio.

1832   For a time, Joseph Smith thought Partridge was usurping authority. Doctrine and Covenants 85:8 warned, "that man, who was called of God and appointed, that putteth forth his hand to steady the ark of God, shall fall by the shaft of death, like as a tree that is smitten by the vivid shaft of lightning." But Partridge and the Prophet reconciled, and the bishop continued to preside over the Church in Zion.

Tar-and-Feather Martyr:

1833   July 20: A mob attacked the home of W.W. Phelps and destroyed the print shop of the *Evening and Morning Star*. Partridge was dragged from his home and taken to the public square. The mob demanded that the Mormons leave Jackson County. "I told them that the Saints had suffered persecution in all ages of the world; that I had done nothing which ought to offend anyone; that if they abused me, they would abuse an innocent person; that I was willing to suffer for the sake of Christ; but, to leave the country, I was not then willing to consent to it."

Having made his speech, Partridge was daubed with tar "from the crown of my head to my feet, after which feathers were thrown over me.... I bore my abuse with so much resignation and meekness, that it appeared to astound the multitude, who permitted me to retire in silence, many looking very solemn, their sympathies having been touched as I thought; and as to myself, I was so filled with the Spirit and love of God, that I had no hatred towards my persecutors or anyone else."

Partridge, John Corrill, John Whitmer, W.W. Phelps, Algernon S. Gilbert, and Isaac Morley offered themselves as hostages if the Missourians would leave the rest of the Saints alone, but their offer was rejected; every Mormon would have to leave Jackson County. As presiding authority, Partridge signed an agreement to remove the Saints by January 1, 1834. In return, Missourians were not to interfere with their preparations.

November 5: Mobs destroyed more than two hundred Mormon homes in Jackson County. "Gangs of men, sixty or more, went from house to house, whipping the men, driving the women and children at the point of their guns from their homes, and then setting fire to the houses." With hundreds of others, the Partridge family was driven across the Missouri River into Clay County.

1838   November: After five more years of mounting hostility and violence, Partridge, Joseph Smith, and other leaders were arrested and charged with "high treason against the state, murder, burglary, arson, robbery, and larceny." Scores of Mormons were rounded up and "confined in a large open room, where the cold northern blast penetrated freely. Our fires were small and our allowance for wood and food was scanty; they gave us not even a blanket to lie upon; our beds were the cold floors." Three weeks later Partridge and most of the other prisoners were released and ordered from the state. Joseph Smith and several others were remanded to the jail at Liberty. Leaving his family in the care of King Follett, Partridge fled to Quincy, Illinois, where his family later joined him.

Death:

1840   While the family remained in Quincy, Partridge made preparations to relocate in Nauvoo. He built a stable and was working on the house when word arrived that his daughter Harriet had died in Quincy. After her funeral, he moved the rest of the family into the stable. But the burdens proved too great; he succumbed to exhaustion and exposure on May 27, at the age of forty-seven.

"No man had the confidence of the Church more than he," the *Times and Seasons* reported. "His station was highly responsible.... Deeds and conveyances of land to a large amount were put into his hands for the benefit of the poor and for the church's purpose; for all of which the directest account was rendered, to the fullest satisfaction of all concerned."

Partridge was buried on the family property in Nauvoo.

David W. Patten

No Known Photograph

(1800-1838)

Apostle
"Captain Fearnaught"
Missouri Martyr

Family Background:

1800   Born David Wyman Patten in Theresa (near Indian Falls), New York. He married Phoebe Ann Babcock in 1828.

Missionary:

1832   Baptized by his brother John, David Patten immediately left on a mission to Michigan, Ohio, and Pennsylvania.

1834   Began a mission to Tennessee, where he served with Abraham O. Smoot and Wilford Woodruff. One day, "riding along the road on my mule, I suddenly noticed a very strange personage walking beside me. He walked along beside me for about two miles. His head was about even with my shoulders as I sat in the saddle. He wore no clothing, but was covered with hair. His skin was very dark. I asked him where he dwelt and he replied that he had no home, that he was a wanderer in the earth, but that he could not die, and his mission was to destroy the souls of men. About the time he expressed himself thus, I rebuked him in the name of the Lord Jesus Christ and by virtue of the Holy Priesthood, and commanded him to go hence, and he immediately departed out of my sight."

Patten also rebuked the disease of a woman who had been seriously ill for several years, commanding, "In the name of Jesus Christ, arise!" Arising from her bed, she walked a mile to a stream, where Patten baptized her. Remembering her seven years of childless marriage, he promised children. Within a year she gave birth to a son, whom she named David Patten.

Wilford Woodruff told Abraham H. Cannon that one day Patten found his mule "on the ground nearly dead with the colic. Brother Patten said: 'See here, old fellow, this won't do! You have got to carry me 40 miles today,' and with these words he stepped up to the animal, laid his hands on the animal, and blessed him. The mule immediately arose, and made the journey. Pres. Woodruff said that was the only time in his life when his faith had been tried, but he thought it strange for an Elder to administer to a mule, and thus do what seemed sacrilege in his mind at that time."

Member of the Original Quorum of the Twelve:

1835　Called to the original Quorum of the Twelve by the Three Witnesses—Oliver Cowdery, Martin Harris, and David Whitmer. Patten, Brigham Young, and Heber C. Kimball were the only members of the original Quorum never disfellowshipped or excommunicated.

1836　Patten filled a second mission to Tennessee.

1837　July: During a disagreement, the Prophet "kicked him out of the yard." Whatever the cause of this fracas, Joseph "later forgave him."

1838　As general authorities acting in a local capacity, Patten, Brigham Young, and Thomas B. Marsh were called "Presidents Pro Tem" of the Church in Missouri.

"Captain Fearnaught":

1838　Clashes with Missourians had been common since 1833, when the Saints were driven from Jackson County. Caldwell County provided safety for a short time, but as opposition rose, Mormon men formed a secret, quasi-military band commonly known as "Danites."

Death:

1838　October 24: Captain Samuel Bogard of the Caldwell County militia ordered a number of Mormon families to leave the state and took three men into custody. When word reached Far West, "Captain Fearnaught" Patten rallied seventy-five Mormons and set out to rescue the prisoners. Under cover of darkness, they attacked the encamped militia at Crooked River. In his white duster, Patten was an easy target. He was wounded in the bowels and died the next day at the age of thirty-eight.

　　　Patten's comrade-in-arms John D. Lee later wrote, "I admit up to this time that I frankly believed what the Prophet and his apostles had said on the subject. I had considered that I was bullet proof, that no Gentile ball could ever harm me, or any Saint, and I had believed that a Danite could not be killed by Gentile hands. I thought that one Danite could chase a thousand Gentiles, and two could put ten thousand to flight. Alas! my dreams of security were over. One of our mighty men had fallen, and that by Gentile hands!"

Erroneous intelligence communications, coupled with a Thomas B. Marsh-Orson Hyde affidavit confirming the existence of the Danites, led Governor Lilburn W. Boggs to believe reports that Patten's company had "massacred Captain Bogard and all his company," and that Richmond was "laid in ashes this morning." The governor issued his infamous "Mormon Extermination Order" on October 27: "The Mormons must be treated as enemies, and must be exterminated or driven from the state if necessary for the public peace—their outrages are beyond all description."

Burial in Far West:

1838   At Patten's funeral, Joseph Smith said, "There lies a man who had done just as he said he would: he had laid down his life for his friends." Patten was buried in Far West, Missouri.

Romania Pratt Penrose

(1839-1932)

Pioneer Physician
Women's Advocate

Family Background:

1839   August 8: Born Romania Bunnell in Indiana. She moved with her newly-converted Mormon family to Nauvoo in 1846. Lacking provisions, they were unable to travel west with the main body of Saints and returned to Indiana. Her father joined the gold rush to California, hoping to raise enough money to move the family to Utah. But he contracted typhoid fever in 1849 and died in a mining camp.

        In 1859 she married Parley P. Pratt, Jr.; they had seven children.

Pioneer:

1855   Romania's mother took her four children to Omaha, Nebraska, where they joined a wagon train for Utah. Romania later recalled, "The journey across the plains with ox teams was a summer full of pleasure to me; the early morning walks gathering wild flowers, climbing the rugged and oftimes forbidding hills— the pleasant evening gatherings of the young folks by the bright camp fire while sweet songs floated forth on the evening air to gladden the wild and savage ear of the red men or wild beasts as well as our own young hearts."

Student:

    Romania had attended the Female Seminary in Crawfordsville, Indiana, before moving to Utah. The death of a friend may have determined the course of her future career. "I saw her lying on her bed, her life slowly ebbing away, and no one near knew how to ease her pain or prevent her death; it was a natural enough case, and a little knowledge might have saved her. Oh, how I longed to know something to do, and at that moment I solemnly vowed to myself never to be found in such a position again, and it was my aim ever afterward to arrange my life work that I might study the science which would relieve suffering, appease pain, prevent death."

1873   When Brigham Young called for women to study medicine, Romania sold her home and piano, arranged for her mother to care for her five surviving children (ages one to fourteen), and went to medical school in New York City.

       While waiting for the term to begin at Women's Medical College, Romania helped her husband Parley edit *The Autobiography of Parley P. Pratt.*

1874   Medical school was difficult. Long hours of study made the days seem "so much alike that it was as one long day." After her first year, Romania returned home to a destitute family. She called on President Young for assistance; he told Eliza R. Snow, "She must continue her studies in the East. We need her here, and her talents will be of great use to this people. Take this upon yourself, Sister Eliza, to see to it that the Relief Societies furnish Sister Pratt with the necessary money to complete her studies."

       The next fall Romania returned to the Women's Medical College; she graduated March 15, 1877. Her thesis was, "Puerperal Hemorrhage, Its Cause and Cure." She remained in Philadelphia for two more years, specializing in diseases of the eye and ear.

Plural Marriage, Divorce, and Plural Marriage:

> Returning to Salt Lake, she learned that her husband had married a plural wife. "The principle of plural marriage seemed a most rational and eternal truth. I never opposed the principle when practiced with singleness of heart as commanded. See it lived according to the great and grand aim of its author, though it be a fiery furnace at some period of our life, it will prove the one thing needful to cleanse and purify our inmost soul of selfishness, jealousy, and other mundane attributes which seem to lie closest to the citadel of life."
>
> She divorced Pratt in 1881 and became the third plural wife of Charles Penrose in 1886. Penrose became an apostle in 1904, and counselor in the First Presidency in 1911.

Physician:

1879   Dr. Romania B. Pratt established a medical practice in Salt Lake City. She also taught classes in anatomy, physiology, and obstetrics, and wrote hygiene articles for the *Woman's Exponent* and *Young Woman's Journal*.

1883   As a visiting professor at the Deseret Hospital, she performed the first cataract operation in Utah. She continued her medical practice until 1912.

Women's Advocate:

1882   Dr. Pratt accompanied Zina D.H. Young and Ellen B. Ferguson, another Mormon physician, to the Woman's Suffrage Convention in New York. As an advocate of woman's suffrage, she espoused the philosophy that it was each woman's "duty and privilege to do whatever she can that will promote the advancement and evolution of her own sex."

1908   While her husband, Charles W. Penrose, served as president of the European Mission, Romania Pratt Penrose represented Utah at the Woman's International Suffrage Alliance in Amsterdam, speaking to the convention on women's suffrage in the western United States.

Death:

1932   November 9: Died in Salt Lake City at the age of ninety-three. Buried in the Salt Lake City Cemetery.

W. W. Phelps

(1792-1872)

Publisher
Pioneer

Family Background:

1792   February 17: Born William Wines Phelps in Hanover, New Jersey. His complicated marital history began in 1815, when he married Sally Waterman; they had ten children.

1847   Married three women while on a trip to Saint Louis, but the marriages were later annulled by Brigham Young.

1848   Married a twenty-one-year-old "Sarah," thirty-five years his junior. Brigham Young refused to grant her request for a divorce in 1849, and after a stormy period of adjustment, the couple apparently worked out their differences; Sarah gave birth to a son in 1861.

        Phelps married a third wife, "Harriet H." of Philadelphia, about 1855.

First Mormon Publisher:

1830   Phelps was a prominent New York editor of several anti-Mason newspapers, including the *Western Courier, Lake Light,* and *Ontario Phoenix.* Three days after the organization of the Church, he bought a copy of the Book of Mormon from Parley P. Pratt and read all night. "I always believed the scriptures, and believed that there was such a sacred thing as pure religion; but I never believed that any of the sects of the day had it.... I rejoiced that there was something coming to point the right way to heaven."

1831   Phelps moved his family to Kirtland, Ohio, where he was baptized June 16. Three days later he left for Missouri with Joseph Smith, Sidney Rigdon, Martin Harris, Edward Partridge, and others "to seek the land of Zion.... When that goodly land was consecrated, we kneeled together; when the first house was raised I helped carry the first log."

        Joseph Smith called Phelps to be the Church printer in Independence, Missouri, authorizing him to "review and prepare such revelations as shall be deemed proper for publication" in the Book of Commandments. Phelps was also directed to correct and print the hymns selected by Emma Smith, and publish the Church newspaper, the *Evening and Morning Star.*

1833 July: A Phelps editorial in the *Star,* intended "to prevent any misunderstanding among the churches abroad respecting free people of color," was viewed by Missourians as an "invitation to free people of color to settle in Jackson County!"

Phelps tried to placate slaveholders in a special edition of the *Star:* "Our intention was not only to stop free people of color from emigrating to this state, but to prevent them from being admitted as members of the church."

The clarification was too late. The Missourians demanded that Mormons stop publishing the *Star* and leave "within a reasonable time." When Church leaders, including Phelps, refused, the "old settlers" stormed the printing office, threw Sally Phelps and her children into the street, destroyed the press, scattered pages of the uncompleted Book of Commandments, and pulled down the walls of the building.

George A. Smith could not recommend Phelps to the Prophet as editor to reissue the *Star:* "I told him that I considered Phelps the sixth part of an editor, and that was the satirist. When it came to the cool direction necessarily entrusted to an editor in the control of public opinion—the soothing of enmity, he was deficient, and would always make more enemies than friends; but for my part, if I were able, I would be willing to pay Phelps for editing a paper, providing no body else should have the privilege of reading it but myself. Joseph laughed heartily—said I had the thing just right. Said he, 'Brother Phelps makes such a severe use of language as to make enemies all the time.'" Oliver Cowdery was chosen editor.

Poet:

1836 Phelps's "The Spirit of God Like a Fire is Burning," written for the dedication of the Kirtland Temple, so impressed Joseph Smith that he asked for it to be printed "on white satin" for the event. In all, Phelps penned lyrics for twenty-nine of the ninety-one hymns Emma Smith selected for the Church's first hymn book. His lyrics include: "Gently Raise the Sacred Strain," "Redeemer of Israel," "O God, the Eternal Father," "Earth with Her Ten Thousand Flowers," and "Praise to the Man" (written after Joseph Smith's death).

Excommunication and Readmission:

1838 When Zion's Camp, of which Phelps was a member, failed to "redeem Zion" in 1834, the Prophet advised, "the land should not be sold, but be held by the Saints, until the Lord in His wisdom shall open a way for your return."

But the presidency of the "Church of Christ in Missouri"—W. W. Phelps and John and David Whitmer—ignored the counsel and tried to sell their abandoned lands. In February, 1838, a stake conference rejected their presidency, and when they refused to attend a March 10 hearing before the high council, they were excommunicated for "wickedness by endeavoring to palm themselves off upon the Church as her Presidents."

Two months later the excommunicated dissidents received a long letter from Sidney Rigdon and eighty-three other Mormons, advising that "there is but one decree for you, which is depart, depart, or else a more fatal calamity shall befall you." Phelps, who had intended to stay in Far West, departed.

July 8: Joseph Smith received a revelation respecting Phelps and former First Presidency member Frederick G. Williams: "If they will be saved, let them be ordained as Elders." Phelps ignored the invitation, making no overtures to the Prophet for nearly two years.

1840 When Phelps finally requested readmission to the Church, Joseph Smith responded:
Come on, dear brother, since the war is past,
For friends at first, are friends again at last.

1847 Phelps married three women in Saint Louis without Church permission. On December 6 the Twelve voted that "W. W. Phelps be cut off from the Church for violating the laws of the priesthood in having women that do not belong to him & committing adultery with them."

Pioneer Judge Hosea Stout noted, "It appeared that Phelps had while East last summer got some new ideas into three young women & they had consented to become his wives & got Jacobs [Henry B.] to marry them to him in St. Louis and he lived with them as such all the way to this place. After a long and tedious hearing of the matter which was altogether their own admissions, President Young decided that Phelps had committed adultery every time that he had laid with one of them." He was rebaptized in 1848.

Toastmaster:

1844   While living in Nauvoo, W. W. Phelps came to be recognized as a supreme toastmaster. New Years Day, 1845, he made a memorable toasting of the Twelve by giving each a descriptive sobriquet:
Brigham Young—"Lion of the Lord"
Heber C. Kimball—"Herald of Grace"
Parley P. Pratt—"Archer of Paradise"
Orson Hyde—"Olive Branch of Israel"
Willard Richards—"Keeper of Rolls"
John Taylor—"Champion of Right"
William Smith—"Patriarchal Jacob Staff"
Wilford Woodruff—"Banner of the Gospel"
George A. Smith—"Entablature of Truth"
Orson Pratt—"Gauge of Philosophy"
John E. Page—"Sundial"
Lyman Wight—"Wild Ram of the Mountain"

Eulogizer of Joseph Smith:

1844   June 29: W. W. Phelps addressed the nearly ten thousand persons gathered to pay final respects to Joseph and Hyrum Smith two days after their murder. In his lengthy sermon at this memorial service, Phelps predicted: "Be assured, brethren and sisters, this desperate 'smite' of our foes to stop the onward cause of Mormonism, will increase its spread and prosperity an hundred fold.... The priesthood remains unharmed.... The 'Twelve' (most now absent) ... when they return will turn the 'mantle' and step into the 'shoes' of the 'Prophet, priest and King' of Israel." Phelps's hymn, "Praise to the Man," is a eulogy of continuing popularity in the Church.

Versatile Pioneer:

A charter member of the Council of Fifty in 1844, Phelps served as a Nauvoo city councilman, assisted in drafting the constitution of the "State of Deseret" in 1849, and worked in the Utah legislature as Speaker of the House. In 1851 he served as "topographic engineer" with Parley P. Pratt's exploring expedition to the south to "study the land for the site of possible settlements and for a road toward the sea." That same year, he was sworn into office as "counsillor and attorney at law and solicitor in chauncery," and became superintendent of metereological observations of the Territory of Deseret, furnishing the *Deseret News* with weather and astronomical observations. But he was perhaps most noted in Utah for his convincing portrayal of Satan in the endowment ceremony in the Salt Lake Endowment House on Temple Square.

Death:

1872 March 6: W. W. Phelps died at the age of eighty. Oliver B. Huntington recorded, "Before Brother Phelps died he lost all his judgment, lost all his mind, reason, consciousness and all sense. He knew nothing, not even his name, nor how to eat, thus being unable to taste of anything, not even death. His mind gradually dwindled, withered and dried up."

Phelps was buried in the Salt Lake City Cemetery. His epitaph, a poem called "Eternalism," had been written by him for Brigham Young:

There is no end to matter
There is no end to space
There is no end to spirit
There is no end to race
There is no end to glory
There is no end to love
There is no end to being
There is no death above.

Orson Pratt

(1811-1881)

Apostle
Scholar
Defender of Plural Marriage

Family Background:

1811   September 19: Born in Hartford, New York. Orson attended a few classes in bookkeeping, mathematics, geography, grammar, and surveying, but was basically self-educated.

He married Sarah Marinda Bates in 1836, and later Charlotte Bishop (1844), Adelia Ann Bishop (1844), Mary Ann Merrill (1845), Sarah Louisa Chandler (1846), Marion Ross (1852), and Juliette Ann Phelps (1855). He was the father of forty-five children.

Missionary:

1830   Baptized on his nineteenth birthday by his older brother, Parley. A short time later he was ordained an elder by Joseph Smith and sent on a mission to the Eastern States. Between 1830 and 1869 he served ten additional missions to the Eastern States, plus seven missions to Great Britain.

He was the first Mormon missionary to Canada (1832), and also the first to Scotland (1840), where in nine months he established an Edinburgh branch of more than two hundred members.

Member of the Original Quorum of the Twelve:

Pratt attended the School of the Prophets in Kirtland (1833), participated in Zion's Camp (1834), and at the age of twenty-four was called to the first Quorum of the Twelve by the Three Witnesses (1835).

Excommunication:

1841   July: When Pratt returned from a mission to Great Britain, he found that Church leaders had withdrawn his wife's food allotment and were accusing her of adultery with John C. Bennett. She countered that Joseph Smith had proposed she become one of his "celestial wives," and that Brigham Young had urged her to say nothing, but "do as Joseph wished."

1842   May: Pratt did not join the other apostles in withdrawing "the hand of fellowship" from John C. Bennett.

July 15: According to the Prophet, Pratt attempted to commit suicide "and caused almost all the city to go in search of him."

July 22: Pratt refused to endorse a resolution affirming Joseph Smith's moral character. Brigham Young wrote Parley P. Pratt that "Br. Orson Pratt is in trouble in consequence of his wife. His feelings are so wrought up that he does not know whether his wife is wrong, or whether Joseph's testimony and others are wrong, and do lie, and he deceived for 12 years or not; he is all but crazy about the matters. . . . We will not let Br. Orson go away from us. He is too good a man to have a woman destroy him."

Church leaders tried in vain to get Pratt to "recall his sayings against Joseph and the Twelve," Wilford Woodruff recorded, "but he persisted in his wicked course and would not recall any of his sayings which were unjust and untrue."

August 20: After four days of fruitless efforts at reconciliation, the Twelve excommunicated Pratt for "insubordination." and Sarah for "adultery."

Within three months Pratt publicly "confessed his error and his sin in criticizing Joseph." In 1878 he said that he had "got his information from a wicked source, from those disaffected, but as soon as he learned the truth he was satisfied." Joseph Smith rebaptized Orson and Sarah Pratt in January, 1843, and Orson was reinstated in the Quorum of the Twelve.

Sarah never admitted error. After Orson's death she related details of the incident in a vituperative attack on Joseph Smith in "Workings of Mormonism" (unpublished), and in an 1886 interview in *Mormon Portraits*.

Brother Against Brother:

1846   Parley P. Pratt, in the midst of severe marital problems with his wife Mary Ann, accused Sarah of "influencing his wife against him, and of ruining and breaking up his family," of "being an apostate, and of speaking against the head of the church and against him." In the Nauvoo

Temple on January 11 he accused her of "whispering against him all over the temple." Orson exploded, defending Sarah so vehemently that they were both "voted" out of the temple, and Orson disfellowshipped. In an explanatory letter to Brigham Young, Orson argued, "If I had . . . insulted any of your families in so disgraceful a manner I should have been very thankful if I escaped without getting my head broke." Orson "made satisfaction" a few days later and was readmitted to fellowship.

Pioneer:

1847   July 13: Eleven days before the main party of pioneers entered the Salt Lake Valley, Pratt led an advance company of twenty-two wagons to "proceed to the Weber River canyon and ascertain if we can pass through safely, if not to find a pass over the mountains."

July 21: Pratt and Erastus Snow were the first pioneers to enter the Salt Lake Valley.

During the trek Pratt had invented an odometer to measure the distance traveled each day. He also directed the surveying of Salt Lake City.

1851 Between 1851 and 1881, in addition to several missions, Pratt served seven terms in the Utah legislature, where he was elected Speaker of the House.

Defender of Plural Marriage:

1852 August: Brigham Young selected Pratt to introduce the doctrine of plural marriage officially to the Saints at a special conference in Salt Lake City. He was also called to begin a new magazine, *The Seer,* in Washington, D.C. The publication would expound "the views of the Saints in regard to the *Ancient Patriarchal* Order of Matrimony, or Plurality of Wives, as developed in a Revelation, given through JOSEPH THE SEER."

1870 Dr. John P. Newman, chaplain of the U.S. Senate and President Ulysses S. Grant's personal pastor, delivered a strong anti-polygamy sermon in his Metropolitan Methodist Church in Washington, D.C. *Salt Lake Daily Telegraph* editor Edward Sloan proposed Newman debate polygamy in Salt Lake. Newman accepted and, when Brigham Young declined to be his opponent, settled for Orson Pratt. The extended debate was reported daily in the *New York Herald.* Mormon writer Edward Tullidge declared that "millions of readers followed the arguments of Dr. Newman and Orson Pratt and it is safe to estimate that quite two-thirds of them yielded the palm to the Mormon apostle."

Scholar:

Pratt was "Professor of Mathematics and English Literature" at the University of Nauvoo. He taught mathematics at the University of Deseret, served as Church recorder and historian (1874-81), and prepared the 1878 editions of the Book of Mormon and Doctrine and Covenants, arranging both books into chapters and verses, with footnotes and references.

His philosophical bent conflicted with Brigham Young's practical posture. They publicly disagreed on everything from the nature of God to the propriety of publishing Joseph's "inspired version" of the Bible. President Young said Pratt didn't know enough to keep his foot out of it [his mouth], but drowns himself in his philosophy."

1860 Wilford Woodruff told the Saint George High Council of Pratt's "unyielding stubbornes, and of upbraiding the Twelve for not being manly, for not declaring their views the way he looked at it, and branding them as cowards &c &c. Spoke of the firmnes of Pres Young in correcting Orson Pratt and setting him aright; of Orson wishing to resign his position in the Quorum; of Pres. Young saying 'No you wont Orson, I'll rub your ears until I get you right.'"

Although Pratt apologized publicly, his popular philosophical writings continued to irritate the president so much that the First Presidency and apostles published point-by-point condemnations of Pratt's views in 1865.

Following the death of Brigham Young, George Q. Cannon learned that Pratt found so little support in the presiding quorums because of the president's dominating manner: "Some of my brethren . . . did have feelings concerning his course. They did not approve of it, and felt oppressed, and yet they dared not exhibit their feelings to him, he ruled with so strong and stiff a hand, and they felt that it would be of no use."

Quorum Seniority Adjusted:

1875 Two years prior to his death, Brigham Young readjusted the seniority of the members of the Quorum of the Twelve. Orson Pratt and Orson Hyde, both of whom had been ordained before John Taylor, were placed behind him, according to the dates of their reinstatement in the Quorum.

Death:

1881   October 3: Died of diabetes at the age of seventy-seven in the home of his wife Marion Ross at 300 North 300 West in Salt Lake City. Shortly before his death, he dictated his epitaph to Joseph F. Smith: "My body sleeps for a moment, but my testimony lives and shall endure forever." Buried in the Salt Lake City Cemetery.

Parley P. Pratt

(1807-1857)

Apostle
"Martyr"

Family Background:

1807   April 12: Born Parley Parker Pratt in Burlington, New York. He married Thankful Halsey in 1827, and, six weeks after her death in 1837, married Mary Ann Frost. In 1843 he wed his first plural wife, Elizabeth Brotherton, and over the next twelve years married nine additional wives: Mary Wood (1844), Hannahette Snively (1844), Belinda Marden (1844), Sarah Huston (1845), Phoebe Sopher (1846), Martha Monks (1847), Ann Agatha Walker (1847), Keziah Downes (1853), and Eleanor J. McComb McLean (1855). He was the father of thirty children.

Parley P. Pratt and wife Elizabeth Brotherton.

Convert:

1830   Pratt was a member of Sidney Rigdon's Campbellite congregation in Ohio when he learned of the Book of Mormon. "I opened it with eagerness, and read its title page. I then read the testimony of several witnesses in relation to the manner of its being found and translated. After this I commenced its contents by course. I read all day; eating was a burden, I had no desire for food; sleep was a burden when the night came, for I preferred reading to sleep."

He traveled to Palmyra, New York, to meet Joseph Smith, only to discover the Prophet had moved to Pennsylvania. After discussing the Book of Mormon with Hyrum Smith, Pratt requested baptism. The next day they walked to the Peter Whitmer home, twenty-five miles away, and on September 1, 1830, Oliver Cowdery baptized Parley P. Pratt in Seneca Lake. Except for Joseph Smith's younger brother William, Pratt was the first of the original Quorum of the Twelve to be baptized.

Missionary:

1830   One month after his baptism, Pratt was called with Oliver Cowdery, Peter Whitmer, and Ziba Peterson on a mission "into the wilderness among the Lamanites" (D&C 32), some 1500 miles away in western Missouri. In Kirtland, Ohio, they gave a Book of Mormon to Pratt's former minister, Sidney Rigdon. Within three weeks they baptized Rigdon, Edward Partridge, and one hundred twenty-five more converts. Eventually, the number baptized in Kirtland reached a thousand.

The missionaries preached and distributed the Book of Mormon to the Catteraugua Indians near Buffalo, the Wyandots of Ohio, and the Shawnee and Delaware in western Missouri. "We traveled on foot for three hundred miles through vast prairies and through trackless wilds of snow—no beaten road; houses few and far between; and the bleak northwest wind always blowing in our faces with a keenness which would almost take the skin off the face. We traveled for whole days from morning till night without a house or fire, wading in snow to the knees at every step.... We often ate our frozen bread and pork by the way, when the bread would be so frozen that we could not bite or penetrate any part of it but the outside crust."

Missouri Persecutions:

1833   Pratt and his family were among 1200 Saints driven from Jackson County into Clay County, Missouri. He later returned to Kirtland and served in Zion's Camp (1834).

1838   April: Pratt moved his family from Ohio to Far West, Missouri. In October he was imprisoned with other Mormon leaders on charges of "treason, murder, burglary, arson, robbery, and larceny," but was never brought to trial. After eight months of imprisonment, he was allowed to escape. In 1843 he "confessed he was wrong in one thing in Missouri; that is, he left alive, and left them alive; and asked forgiveness, and promised never to do so again."

Member of the Original Quorum of the Twelve:

1835   Called to the original Quorum of the Twelve by the Three Witnesses, Pratt was ordained an apostle by Joseph Smith.

1837   Returning from a mission to Canada, Pratt was swept up in the "jarrings and discords" over the collapse of the Kirtland Safety Society. Charging that the "spirit of speculation" was "of the devil," he demanded Joseph Smith refund the $2000 he had paid for three lots that had not cost the Prophet more than $200. A Church court convened to excommunicate Pratt and several others, but the dissenters successfully challenged the jurisdiction of the court. Before another court could try them, Pratt had a change of heart and obtained Joseph Smith's forgiveness. His former companions were all excommunicated.

1840   While serving a mission in Great Britain with the Quorum of the Twelve, Pratt published the *Millennial Star* and in 1841 presided over all British conferences.

1845   Presided over the Church in New England and the Atlantic States.

Family Problems:

1846   Pratt exchanged strong words in the Nauvoo Temple with his brother Orson over Parley's accusations that Orson's wife Sarah was "ruining and breaking up his family." Orson, expelled from the temple, complained to Brigham Young about Parley's alleged immorality: "If he feels at liberty to go into the city of New York or elsewhere and seduce girls or females and sleep and have connexion [sic] with them contrary to the law of God, and the sacred counsels of his brethren, it is something that does not concern me."

Orson was referring to Parley's relations with Belinda Marden, to whom he had been secretly sealed on November 20, 1844. At the time Belinda accompanied Pratt on a mission to New York, not even his wife, Mary Ann, was aware of the marriage. When Belinda gave birth to a son (1846), Mary Ann asked Belinda if the child were illegitimate. Told the truth, Mary Ann immediately severed her marital relationship with Pratt, though she did not divorce him until 1853, after coming to Utah.

July: Brigham Young sent Parley Pratt, Orson Hyde, and John Taylor to investigate the embezzlement of emigration funds in England.

Pioneer:

1847   Pratt entered the Salt Lake Valley in September.

1849   Helped formulate a constitution for the provisional government of Deseret. When Utah became a territory in 1850, Pratt was elected to the territorial senate.

Author:

Parley P. Pratt's *Voice of Warning* (1837) was the first published defense of Mormon doctrine. He also wrote *Key* to *Theology, History of Missouri Persecutions,* and his *Autobiography,* published posthumously in 1873.

The lyrics of many popular Mormon hymns were written by Parley P. Pratt, including "The Morning Breaks," "Come, O Thou King of Kings," "An Angel from on High," and "Jesus, Once of Humble Birth."

Two Left Feet:

Orson Hyde related, "When dancing was first introduced in Nauvoo among the Saints, I observed Brother Parley standing in the figure and he was making no motion particularly, only up and down. Says I, 'Brother Parley, why don't you move forward?' Says he, 'When I think which way I am going, I forget the step and when I think of the step I forget which way to go.'"

"Martyr":

1857 May 13: Parley P. Pratt was murdered near Van Buren, Arkansas, at the age of fifty, by the legal husband of his twelfth wife, Elenore McComb McLean.

Pratt had met the McLeans in San Francisco. Her Church activity and Mr. McLean's alcoholism led to separation, she moving to Salt Lake City. Though she and McLean were never divorced, Elenore married Pratt November 14, 1855.

Mrs. McLean, who declared that a marriage performed by "sectarian priests... is no marriage at all," lost custody of her children to their father, who took them to Arkansas. When Pratt went to help her recover the children, he was arrested on a complaint sworn out by McLean for "alienating the affections of his wife and attempting to abduct the children." Both Pratt and Mrs. McLean—who had been arrested on grounds of stealing her children's clothes—were acquitted in Van Buren.

Immediately after the trial, Pratt headed for Missouri, where he planned to join an immigrant train west. A short distance out of town, he was overtaken by McLean, who, after missing with six pistol shots at the unarmed apostle, plunged a Bowie knife into his left side twice, then shot him in the neck after he had fallen from his horse. Pratt survived for nearly three hours, long enough to tell passersby his name and the name of his assailant, and give instructions as to the disposition of his body and personal effects. Asked if he wanted a doctor, he replied, "I want no doctors for I will be dead in a few minutes."

Pratt was buried a mile from the murder site in the cemetery at Sterman (also known as Fine's Springs), near Van Buren, Arkansas. The first stanza of his hymn "The Morning Breaks, the Shadows Flee" is his epitaph.

Alice Louise Reynolds

(1873-1938)

"Seeker After Knowledge"
Professor

Family Background:

1873   April 1: Born in Salt Lake City to Mary Ann Tuddenham and George Reynolds, secretary to Brigham Young, John Taylor, Wilford Woodruff, Lorenzo Snow, and Joseph F. Smith. Alice described her father as a man who "loved knowledge and it certainly was a dreadful thing in [his] eyes to be unnecessarily ignorant."

Alice Louise Reynolds never married. "To some of you," she said, "the sweetest word in the English language is 'husband,' to some of you, 'child,' but to me the sweetest word in the English language is 'friend.'"

1877   When she was four, Alice was wheeled by her mother's maid to her first day at school in a baby buggy. Thereafter family and friends referred to her as "Princess Alice."

"Seeker After Knowledge":

Extremely absentminded, she "carried her teakettle to school, thinking it to be her purse, she wore a dress the wrong side out to a play, she slid through a window to a classroom, bloomers first, and once she walked while reading a book through a herd of cows, absently swatting them with her purse."

1890   Having begun her studies with Karl G. Maeser at thirteen, she graduated from the Brigham Young Academy and began teaching there.

Professor:

1894   Completing a B.A. in two years at the University of Michigan, she returned to Brigham Young Academy, where she taught until her death forty-four years later.

She taught theology, organized a literature department, and established the first library collection at the school. Much of her time was spent helping students edit their compositions; she felt "tough criticism would help them to grow." She was the second woman in Utah to attain full professorship.

Her sabbaticals were spent at the University of Chicago, Columbia, Queens College in London, Berkeley, and Cornell.

Book Lover:

1933   She encouraged women's clubs to donate books to the Brigham Young University library and in 1933 helped former students and friends organize the Alice Louise Reynolds Club, which promoted libraries and the study of literature throughout the country. "Members found in her a champion of their sex, a custodian of their cultural and spiritual values, and an exponent of friendship. They continued to send back books and money, and to sponsor an English student scholarship. Their meetings became spontaneous centers of continuing education." Thirteen chapters of the club were organized in Provo, Springville, Salt Lake City, Hurricane, Saint George, and New York City.

Reynolds wrote extensively for the *Young Woman's Journal,* the *Improvement Era,* the *Instructor,* and the *Relief Society Magazine.* She also wrote many lessons for Church auxiliaries, including ten years of literature courses for the Relief Society.

Popular Speaker:

During a single six-month period in 1934 Reynolds lectured to sixteen different groups. She was a leader in the Federation of Women's Clubs and the National Education Association, and represented the Relief Society General Board in the National Council of Women in the years just prior to World War I.

Death:

1938   December 6: Died of cancer at the age of sixty-five in Salt Lake City's LDS Hospital. Shortly before her death, she commented to her sister Polly, "Well, I am not afraid to die. I have lived the best I could, and I am sure no girl or woman ever had a more wonderful life, with more opportunities, more privileges, and more friends. I have been most fortunate and for all these blessings, I am sincerely grateful." Buried in the Salt Lake City Cemetery.

Willard Richards

(1804-1854)

"Thompsonian Botanical Physician"
Member of the First Presidency

Family Background:

1804   June 24: Born in Hopkinton, Massachusetts. Brigham Young was his first cousin, and Joseph Smith his fourth cousin. In 1838, while serving a mission in England, he married Jennette Richards, one of the first English converts. Many English Saints opposed the marriage, feeling that Richards should devote himself "wholly to the ministry."

Jennette died at Nauvoo in 1845. After her death, Richards married Nanny Longstroth (1843), and later Sara Longstroth (1843), Susannah Lee Liptrot Walker (1843), Amelia Perrson (1845), Alice Longstroth (1845), Mary Thompson (1846), Ann Rees Babcock (1846), Jane Hall (1846), Susannah Bayless (1847), and Rhoda Harriet Foss (1851).

"Physician":

1830s   While traveling with his "electro-chemistry" show, Richards became interested in herbal medicine and joined the Friendly Botanic Society in 1833. The following year, he paid $20 to attend the six-week course of Samuel Thompson, founder of the Thompsonian method of herbal medicine. Completion of the course earned him the title used throughout his life—"Dr. Willard Richards."

Parley P. Pratt's wife, Mary Ann Frost, described Dr. Richards's treatment for measles: "We were liberally dosed with composition, lobelia, etc. To me the red pepper was something dreadful, and taking the composition through straws did not help the matter much—and oh, how I did long for a drink of cold water. But we got well . . . and I will not condemn the bridge that brought us safely over."

Three of Richards's sons became prominent Utah physicians, and more than thirty of his grandsons and great-grandsons earned M.D.s or Ph.D.s.

Convert:

1835   While practicing medicine in Boston, Richards read the

Book of Mormon his cousin Brigham Young had left with Lucius Parker. After reading half a page, he concluded, "God or the Devil has had a hand in that Book, for man never wrote it."

He read the book through twice in ten days, then "commenced settling his accounts, selling his medicine, and freeing himself from every incumbrance, that he might go to Kirtland 700 miles west, the nearest point he could hear of a Saint, and give the work a thorough investigation: firmly believing, that if the doctrine was true, God had some greater work for him to do than peddle pills."

Richards was baptized "on the 31st of December, at the setting of the sun . . . under the hands of President Brigham Young, in the presence of Heber C. Kimball, and others, who had spent the afternoon in cutting ice to prepare for the baptism."

Apostle:

1837   Richards was in the first group of missionaries sent to England.

1840   While on a second mission to England, he was one of six called to fill vacancies in the Quorum of the Twelve. He was ordained in England by Brigham Young.

Near Martyr:

1844   June 27: Richards was with Joseph Smith, Hyrum Smith, and John Taylor in Carthage Jail when a group of armed men broke in, killing Joseph and Hyrum, and seriously wounding Taylor. Richards escaped with a slight wound on one ear lobe.

A few hours after the murders, Richards sent the first message to Nauvoo: "CARTHAGE JAIL, 8:05 o'clock, p.m., June 27th, 1844: Joseph and Hyrum are dead. Taylor wounded, not very badly. I am well. Our guard was forced, as we believe, by a band of Missourians from 100 to 200. The job was done in an instant, and the party fled towards Nauvoo instantly. This is as I believe it. The citizens here are afraid of the Mormons attacking them. I promise them no!"

"Keeper of Rolls":

1845   Willard Richards was toasted by W. W. Phelps as "Keeper of Rolls"—not a pun on his nearly-three-hundred-pound physique. Richards had been appointed Church historian and general clerk in 1842 and had served as Joseph Smith's private secretary, recorder of the Nauvoo City Council and clerk of the municipal court, and recorder of the Council of Fifty.

    He was the first postmaster of "Great Salt Lake City of the Great Basin Kingdom," and the editor and proprietor of the *Deseret News* from 1849 to 1854.

Member of the First Presidency:

1847   Called to be Brigham Young's first counselor in the newly reorganized First Presidency.

Death:

1854   March 11: Died in Salt Lake City at the age of fifty from "the Palsy," an ailment which had afflicted him since before joining the Church. Shortly before his death he told the Deseret territorial legislature, "Death stares me in the face, waiting for its prey." Buried in the Salt Lake City Cemetery.

Sidney Rigdon

(1793-1876)

Baptist and Campbellite Minister
Prophet's Spokesman
Founder of "The Children of Zion"

Family Background:

1793   February 19: Born in Saint Clair Township, Pennsylvania. In 1820 he married Phebe Brooks; they had twelve children.

Baptist and Campbellite Minister:

1824   A prominent Regular Baptist minister, Rigdon joined Alexander Campbell and Walter Scott in the "Disciples"—the Campbellite movement. He built up large congregations in Mantua and Mentor, Ohio.

1830   Rejecting Rigdon's proposal for an experimental economic community at the annual meeting of the Mahoning Baptist Association, Campbell delivered a "bitter, scathing attack" on Rigdon, who grumbled, "I have done as much in this reformation as Campbell or Scott, and yet they get all the honor."

Convert:

Parley P. Pratt, Oliver Cowdery, Ziba Peterson, and Peter Whitmer, Jr., on their way to an Indian mission in Missouri, visited Rigdon. Believing the Book of Mormon, he asked Phebe, "My dear, you have followed me once into poverty, are you willing to do the same again?" Mrs. Rigdon replied, "I have weighed the matter, I have contemplated on the circumstances in which we may be placed. I have counted the cost, and I am perfectly satisfied to follow you; it is my desire to do the will of God, come life or come death." They were baptized November 30 by Oliver Cowdery.

Immediately after his baptism, Rigdon visited Joseph Smith in New York and convinced him that the Church should remove to Ohio's "Western Reserve"—Kirtland. Sidney Rigdon and Joseph Smith were never thereafter more than a few miles apart until just before the Prophet's death.

Prophet's Counselor and Spokesman:

Nine sections of the Doctrine and Covenants were revealed to Joseph Smith and Sidney Rigdon.

1832 February 16: They envisioned "the glory of the Son, on the right hand of the Father, and received of his fullness.... This is the testimony . . . which we give of him: That he lives!"

March 8: Joseph Smith ordained Rigdon a counselor in the Presidency of the Church.

March 24: In the middle of the night, a mob seized Rigdon in Hiram, Ohio, dragged him by the heels across the frozen ground, and tarred and feathered him. In the morning, Joseph Smith, who had also been assaulted, found Rigdon out of his mind, asking his wife to bring a razor so he could kill the Prophet. When she refused, he asked Joseph for a razor so he could kill her. Church leaders later speculated that the Hiram mobbing caused Rigdon's periodic instability.

July: Rigdon apparently resented his subordinate position to the Prophet's other counselor, Jesse Gause. While Joseph Smith was out of Kirtland, Rigdon announced to a stunned congregation that God had taken "the kingdom" from Joseph and had given it to him.

The Prophet later told Rigdon, "You had better give up your license and divest yourself of all the authority you can, for you will go into the hands of Satan, and he will handle you as one man handleth another, and the less authority you have the better for you." But Joseph restored Sidney to fellowship three weeks later.

1833 March 18: Chosen first counselor to Joseph Smith in the First Presidency.

October 12: A revelation given to Joseph Smith and Sidney Rigdon announced that Rigdon should be "a spokesman unto this people; yea, verily, I will ordain you unto this calling, even to be a spokesman unto my servant Joseph" (D&C 100:9).

A contemporary, Amos S. Hayden, described Rigdon as an "orator of no inconsiderable abilities, his personal influence with an audience was very great. . . . While speaking, open and winning, with a little case of melancholy... his language copious, fluent in utterance, with articulation clear and musical."

1834   Rigdon was a member of the committee charged to "arrange the items of the doctrine of Jesus Christ for the Government of the Church." The result is now known as the Doctrine and Covenants. Rigdon was also a trustee of the "Kirtland School," where he taught penmanship, arithmetic, English grammar, and geography.

Firebrand:

1838   July 4: Visiting the beleaguered Saints in Missouri, Rigdon delivered an Independence Day "Call to Liberty" oration. "From this hour, we will bear it no more," he declared. "Our rights shall no more be trampled on with impunity; the man, or the set of men, who attempts it, does it at the expense of their lives. And that mob that comes on us to disturb us, it shall be between us and them a war of extermination; for we will follow them till the last drop of their blood is spilled, or else they will have to exterminate us." The oration helped precipitate Governor Boggs's "extermination order" and the expulsion of Mormons from the state.

October 31: Among eighty Mormons arrested on charges ranging from treason to murder, Rigdon was incarcerated for several months in the Richmond and Liberty jails. In Richmond he was "compelled to sleep on the floor with a chain and padlock around his ankle, fastened to six others." The abuse drove Rigdon beyond the breaking point, resulting in fits of uncontrollable laughter and incoherent speech.

1839   February: After pleading his own case before the court, Rigdon was discharged from custody. He was afraid the "mob was watching, and would most certainly take my life," and remained in protective custody ten more days. The sheriff then secretly led him to the place where his family was waiting, "telling me to make my escape, which I did with all possible speed."

Controversial Leader:

1839 May: Appointed to petition the federal government for $1,381,044 in compensation for Church losses suffered in Missouri. Deteriorating health prevented him from completing the October trip with Joseph Smith and Elias Higbee. Sick and discouraged, Rigdon returned to Nauvoo and declared "he never would follow Brother Joseph's revelations any more, contrary to his own convenience."

1841 April: Joseph Smith effectively replaced Rigdon in the First Presidency by calling John C. Bennett as an added counselor because of Rigdon's "poor health."

  October: Ordained a "Prophet and a Seer and Revelator, and to be equal with him [Joseph Smith] in holding the Keys and authority of this kingdom."

1842 May: Lasting difficulties were created between Joseph Smith and Sidney Rigdon when Rigdon's daughter Nancy, her brother John, and her brother-in-law George W. Robinson testified that the Prophet had proposed "spiritual marriage" to her. Joseph publicly denied the accusations.

  Rigdon wished to keep the problems private: "On my part they were never mentioned to any person, nor a subject of discourse at any time or place." He wrote the Prophet, "I had hoped that all former difficulties had ceased forever."

1843 March 27: Joseph Smith accused Rigdon of "seeking to destroy me and this people" by attempting to turn the Prophet over to Missouri lawmen who sought his extradition.

  August 13: Joseph Smith accused Rigdon of conspiring with John C. Bennett and other anti-Mormons, and a Church conference temporarily disfellowshipped him.

  October 7: The Prophet proposed that Rigdon be dropped from the First Presidency because he had not fulfilled his Church responsibilities since their arrival in Nauvoo. But Stake President William Marks moved that Rigdon be sustained in his position, and the Church conference voted to retain him. "I have thrown him off my shoulders," Joseph declared, "and you have put him on me; you may carry him, but I will not."

Joseph Smith's Vice-Presidential Running Mate:

1844   Spring: Joseph Smith again extended a forgiving hand, admitting Rigdon to the Council of Fifty and to the endowment ceremonies of the Holy Order. He also selected him as his vice-presidential running mate, but this choice was apparently made only after other options had failed.

Just before leaving for Pittsburgh, Rigdon allegedly prophesied the death of Joseph Smith and the destruction of Nauvoo. "Poor Rigdon," the Prophet reportedly said, "I am glad he is gone to Pittsburgh, out of the way; were he to preside, he would lead the Church to destruction in less than five years."

Excommunication:

1844   After the death of Joseph Smith, Rigdon presented himself to the Church as its "guardian." He was rejected in favor of the leadership of the Quorum of the Twelve under Quorum President Brigham Young. Rigdon's continued efforts to make himself a rallying standard for the Church resulted in his excommunication in September.

The next thirty-two years of his life were erratic and pathetic. With great enthusiasm and a significant following, he organized a new Church of Christ in Pittsburgh in April, 1845. But the death of his daughter Eliza shortly thereafter seems to have affected his emotional balance. Prophesying that Cincinnati would soon be destroyed by an earthquake, and New Orleans and London "sink to the bottom of the sea," Rigdon proclaimed that he would soon "sit on the throne of England and lead 'little Vic' [Queen Victoria] by the nose."

Insisting his followers establish a communitarian society on Pennsylvania farmland, Rigdon threatened to wreak blood and vengeance upon opposing local residents. Despite his long opposition to polygamy and his published condemnations of its practice, Rigdon introduced a form of polygamy within his declining commune, which totally disintegrated by 1847.

Founder of the Children of Zion:

Rigdon retired to Friendship, New York, with his family. Aside from a single episode of preaching in 1859, he had ended his public ministry. But in 1856 he began a strange absentee leadership of a new religious organization. After corresponding with former followers of James J. Strang, Rigdon appointed Stephen Post to be his spokesman, writing him lengthy instructions, revelations, and sermons that were to be read on Rigdon's behalf at meetings of "The Church of Jesus Christ of the Children of Zion." A small group of followers perpetuated the organization for a few years after Rigdon's death.

1871   Rigdon wrote Brigham Young that he would like to visit Utah if the Church would pay for the trip. Brigham Young was agreeable, commenting that "if it were possible to do the old man any good by him coming here, he should be glad." But before arrangements could be completed, Rigdon wrote again, asking for $100,000 in gold coin in return for spiritual counsel. Counselor George A. Smith's feelings expressed the sentiments of the Church leadership: "He pitied the old gentleman, as he thought he was crazy, and if he had kept faithful, he might have accomplished a great deal of good."

Death:

1876   July 14: Died at the age of eighty-three in Friendship, New York; buried in Friendship's Maple Grove Cemetery.

B. H. Roberts

(1857-1933)

President of the First Council of Seventy
Historian and Theologian
Democrat

Family Background:

1857   March 13: Brigham Henry Roberts, named after Brigham Young, was born in Warrington, England. His mother emigrated to Centerville, Utah, after separating from her husband, leaving five-year-old Henry in England in the care of friends. Four years later, he emigrated to Utah with his sister Polly. As an adult, Roberts summed up his youth: "My childhood was a nightmare; my boyhood was a tragedy."

Roberts married Sarah Louisa Smith in 1878, and later married Celia Ann Dibble (1884) and Dr. Margaret Curtis Shipp (1890). He was the father of fifteen children.

Miner:

1871   Young Roberts worked for Centerville farmers, made bricks for construction of the Salt Lake ZCMI, and drove an ox-team grader for the Utah Central Railway. At fourteen, he prospected in the Utah mining districts of Ophir, Jacob City, and Mercur. His evenings were spent in gambling houses, where he "manipulated the jack of hearts and spades; learned to drink his coffee black and his liquor straight; learned to bet and bluff and cajole."

Bishop Edwin D. Woolley, disapproving Roberts's mining activities, disfellowshipped him. A short time later George A. Smith met Roberts on a Salt Lake street and remarked, "Henry, I understand you've been cut off from the Church."

"So?"

"Well, what are you going to do about it?"

"Nothing! If Bishop Woolley wants me out of the Church, then I'm out of the Church."

"Well, then, you're on your way to hell," retorted Smith. Roberts appealed his case and was restored to fellowship.

At seventeen, he put his mining camp life behind him and returned to Centerville, where he apprenticed as a blacksmith. The transition was not easy—"The good boys didn't want me; I did not want the bad ones, so I stayed to myself."

Valedictorian of the University of Deseret:

1878   Respectably married and ordained a seventy, Roberts attended the University of Deseret, at the time scarcely more than a high school. He was so destitute that he wore the same "brown-sack-suit" every day of the school year. And when he delivered the valedictory speech he wore a secondhand suit made over by his sister.

Missionary:

1880s   Roberts spent most of the decade as a missionary in the Midwest, the Southern States, and Great Britain. He worked first in Iowa and Nebraska, then Tennessee (1880-1882).

B. H. Roberts in disguise (1884).

A few months later, he returned as assistant president of the Southern States Mission. Violence against his missionaries was commonplace. When Elders John H. Gibbs and William S. Berry were murdered in Cane Creek, Tennessee, Roberts shaved his beard and mustache, dressed in old, mismatched clothes, and rubbed soot grease from the smokehouse walls over his face. So disguised, he entered the hostile region and recovered the temporarily buried bodies for return to Salt Lake.

Exile:

1886 December 5: As associate editor of the *Salt Lake Herald,* Roberts was preparing the daily dispatches when deputy marshals arrested him for "unlawful cohabitation." By six o'clock he was called on a mission to Great Britain, jumped his $2000 bail, and left for Liverpool.

1888 October 7: Soon after his return from England, he was called to the First Council of Seventy.

1889 April: Tiring of life on the underground, Roberts gave himself up. "I preferred to spare these women all the publicity, all the court inquiry that it was in my power to spare them. So I ended matters by pleading guilty." The customary sentence for "Mormon Cohabs" was "6 by 3"—six months in jail and a fine of $300. Roberts was forced to take a "pauper's oath," becoming, in his words, "an inferior hero," because his sentence was only "4 by 2."

During the 1900 Congressional hearings on his right to be seated as a U. S. Representative, he was again charged with "unlawful cohabitation," having fathered polygamous children after 1890. He argued that polygamists "have found it necessary to regard their moral obligations as more binding upon their consciences than their technical obedience to statutory law."

Democrat:

1891 When the Church disbanded the People's Party and encouraged the Saints to divide along national party lines, Roberts became an ardent Democrat.

1894   Drafting Utah's proposed constitution, Roberts argued that woman's suffrage was a privilege rather than a right, and he observed that in his own home he preferred "some asylum, some refuge from the storms and cares of life," not "political argument." His position was widely criticized. One editorial cartoon pictured him as a bull braced on a railroad track to contend with an approaching train. The caption was supplied by Orson F. Whitney: "We can admire your courage, but damn your judgment."

1895   June: Utah Democrats nominated Moses Thatcher for the U. S. Senate and B. H. Roberts for the House of Representatives.

October: At conference Joseph F. Smith of the First Presidency remarked that Roberts and Thatcher were out of harmony with the brethren because they had not cleared their political activities in advance. Five weeks later, both Democrats were defeated. Roberts later wrote that "unquestionably... the defeat of Mr. Roberts and the Democratic party in general was more or less influenced by the criticism."

1896   February: Roberts and Thatcher refused to sign a Church "political manifesto" which stipulated that before a general authority could seek political office he must "apply to the proper authorities and learn from them whether he can, consistently with the obligations already entered into with the Church upon assuming his office, take upon himself the added duties and labors and responsibilities of the new position."

March 5: The First Presidency, the Twelve, and Seven Presidents of Seventy continued to labor with the Democrat leader. "We spent the whole day here until six o'clock laboring with B. H. Roberts," Wilford Woodruff wrote. "He stood like Adamant and he is going to destruction." Roberts felt that the political manifesto constituted an infringement on basic civil liberties. He was suspended from ecclesiastical duties and given three weeks to recant. Two weeks later Heber J. Grant recorded that Roberts "held all the brethren at bay."

March 24: He walked the streets all night, wrestling with the dilemma of sacrificing principle or being stripped of his Church blessings. Just hours before the deadline,

1898   he decided to sign and was accepted back into fellowship.

1898   With approval from Quorum of the Twelve President Lorenzo Snow, Roberts ran for the House of Representatives and won by a plurality of 7000 votes.

1900   After a lengthy debate the U. S. House of Representatives refused to seat him because of his plural marriages. "Gentleman," he responded, "I have lived with a good conscience until this very day and am sensible of no act of shame upon my part; you can brand me with shame and send me forth, but I shall leave here with head erect and brow undaunted, and walk the earth as angels walk the clouds. If you violate the Constitution of these United States all the shame will be with you."

Utah Democratic Chairman:

1902   Utah Democratic Chairman B. H. Roberts wrote a letter criticizing Senator Reed Smoot for seeking re-election instead of magnifying his office as an apostle. The letter was published and caused an uproar. Fellow Democrat Heber J. Grant recorded that in a meeting of the First Presidency and the Quorum of the Twelve, "the general feeling was that after having run for Congress himself twice, that it came with very poor grace for [Roberts] to take the position that no high church official should hold any high office politically."

1910   Roberts stunned the Mormon community during the 1910 campaign when he accused Smoot of being "content to be the tool of the trusts and a trickster in the politics of his own state." Smoot did not publicly reply to his political and ecclesiastical subordinate, but in private he observed that B. H. Roberts "is a very contemptible man and dishonest in his life and utterances."

        Roberts continued to advocate causes not favored by Republican general authorities, notably the League of Nations and Roosevelt's "New Deal."

Orator:

Roberts was recognized as the greatest Mormon orator

since Sidney Rigdon. Preston Nibley described his style: "How often have we seen him arise and face an audience, beginning at first to talk in a modulated tone, so low that he could scarcely be heard, increasing gradually in volume, making a point here and there, and then approaching his climax with a perfect Niagara of words, that left us almost breathless, and ending finally in a voice that was scarcely audible. There is power in oratory, and nature never lavished this gift more freely than she did on B. H. Roberts."

Sixty-Year-Old Chaplain:

1917   During World War I Roberts served, at the age of sixty, as chaplain of the 145th Utah Light Field Artillery in France.

B. H. Roberts—World War I.

During an influenza epidemic near Bordeaux, "he was unafraid of the vicious malady. He never hesitated to go into the sick rooms and never seemed to worry about the risk of getting the disease himself. Many times, especially when visiting the Latter-day Saint men, he would administer to them and the blessings Brother Roberts would give were tremendous and would kindle encouragement and hope to the men."

President of the First Council of Seventy:

Roberts's non-ecclesiastical activities created friction between himself and other members of the First Council of Seventy. In 1899, commenting on Roberts's lack of Church involvement, J. Golden Kimball commented, "No man can be inactive in the Church and have much faith." And even Kimball cringed when Roberts referred to a political opponent as a "son of a bitch."

In 1901 another member of the Council, Joseph W. McMurrin, "took Bro. Roberts to task for not doing his part in filling appointments," and the senior president of the Council, Seymour B. Young, noted that when "Bro. Roberts was asked if he could find time to devote a little more time to his Seventies duties, he said no and seemed offended that such a question should be asked."

Roberts's weakness for alcohol seems to have put another barrier between him and other members of the Council. In 1908 Seymour B. Young recorded that Roberts "has been many times much worse for liquor in so much that his brethren of the council have had to take up a labor with him."

1924   Became senior president of the First Council of Seventy. From 1922 to 1927 he served as president of the Eastern States Mission.

Historian:

Although he had no professional training in history, Roberts ranks among the most productive historians of

Mormonism. Appointed assistant Church historian in 1901, he was author of many historical works, including *The Life of John Taylor, Outlines of Ecclesiastical History, Succession in the Presidency, New Witnesses for God, Missouri Persecutions, The Rise and Fall of Nauvoo, Joseph Smith—Prophet, Teacher,* and the six-volume *Comprehensive History of the Church.* He also edited the *History of the Church* in seven volumes.

Theologian:

His numerous theological works include *Defense of the Faith and the Saints, Seventys' Course in Theology,* "Man's Relationship to Deity," "Man's Need of God," and "The Immortality of Man."

When, in 1921, James E. Talmage forwarded several pointed questions about the Book of Mormon, Roberts prepared for the Quorum of the Twelve "Book of Mormon Difficulties" and "A Book of Mormon Study."

"I am thoroughly convinced of the necessity of all the brethren herein addressed becoming familiar with these Book of Mormon problems, and finding the answer for them, as it is a matter that will concern the faith of the Youth of the Church now as also in the future, as well as such casual inquiries that may come to us from the outside world."

Released from the presidency of the Eastern States Mission in 1927, Roberts devoted his full efforts to "The Truth, the Way, the Life"—a systematic theology of Mormonism. He had worked intermittently on the project for more than thirty years. But when the manuscript was completed in 1928, objections from Joseph Fielding Smith and others prevented Church publication. Opposition centered around Roberts's contention that a race of men existed before Adam. Additional concerns were expressed over his attempts to reconcile the "scientific theory of catastrophism" with the scriptures. Roberts's observation in 1931 that "Doctrinal questions before the Twelve and the First Presidency in connection with my book... [have] little prospect of settlement," proved correct. "The Truth, the Way, the Life" has never been published.

Death:

1933   September 27: Died in Salt Lake City from complications of diabetes at the age of seventy-six. Buried in Centerville, Utah.

Porter Rockwell

(1813-1878)

Joseph Smith's Bodyguard
"The Destroying Angel"
Folk Hero

Family Background:

1813   June 28: Orrin Porter Rockwell was born in Belcher, Massachusetts. By 1830 the Rockwells were living one mile from Joseph Smith's family in Manchester, New York. Porter was baptized shortly after the Church was organized. His 1832 marriage to Luana Beebe ended in separation ten years later, and he married Mary Ann Neff, Christine Olsen, and a Mrs. Davis. He was the father of fourteen children.

Joseph Smith's Bodyguard:

1840   Joseph Smith asked Rockwell to be one of his Nauvoo bodyguards. Porter replied, "Your enemies are my enemies, Joseph." The Prophet felt more threat "from some little doughhead of a fool in this city than from all my numerous and inveterate enemies abroad. I am exposed to far greater danger from traitors among ourselves than from enemies without, although my life has been sought for many years by civil and military authorities, priests, and people of Missouri."

"The Destroying Angel":

1842   Rockwell was arrested in Saint Louis and charged with the attempted murder of Missouri Governor Lilburn Boggs. Ex-Mormon John C. Bennett claimed, "In the spring of the year Smith offered a reward of five hundred dollars to any man who would secretly assassinate Governor Boggs." After the attempt on Boggs's life, according to Bennett, "Smith said to me, speaking of Boggs, 'The Destroying Angel' had done the work, as I predicted, but Rockwell was not the man who shot; the Angel did it.'"

    Rockwell never denied shooting Boggs. General Patrick E. Conner reported that Rockwell told him, "I shot through the window and thought I had killed him, but I had only wounded him; I was damned sorry that I had not killed the son of a bitch!"

    Joseph Smith prophesied, "Orrin Porter Rockwell will

get away honorably from the Missourians." Eight months later, Rockwell was released.

When he arrived at the Nauvoo Mansion House on Christmas Day, Joseph prophesied, "Orrin Porter Rockwell, so long as ye shall remain loyal and true to thy faith, [you] need fear no enemy. Cut not thy hair and no bullet or blade can harm thee." Rockwell did not cut his hair until 1855.

1845   Fifteen months after Joseph and Hyrum were murdered, Rockwell was watering his horse on the outskirts of Nauvoo when Sheriff Jacob Bakenstos rode his lathered horse onto the scene. Hot on his trail was a group of Carthage Greys, a paramilitary group responsible for Joseph Smith's security in the Carthage Jail. Bakenstos ordered Rockwell and another man to protect him "in the name of the State of Illinois, County of Hancock." Rockwell took aim at the lead rider's belt buckle and fired. Franklin A. Worrell "jumped four feet in the air and rolled away from his horse dead." He was the first of forty to one hundred men reportedly killed by Orrin Porter Rockwell throughout his life.

Pioneer:

1847   A member of the Council of Fifty since 1844, Rockwell was guide and chief hunter for the Brigham Young pioneer company. When camp hunters argued about whether a buffalo could be dropped with a frontal shot to the head, Rockwell deftly maneuvered his mount ahead of a large bull and fired point-blank into the shaggy forehead. "The ball just stirred up a little dust is all. That old bull shook his head like he was brushing off a fly and kept right on coming. I had to move pretty fast to get out of his way."

1849   Elected deputy marshall of Salt Lake City. One year later he was appointed "Deputy Sheriff for Life."

1855   The widow of the Prophet's brother, Don Carlos Smith, had lost her hair from typhoid fever. Rockwell cut his hair to provide her with a wig—and claimed that henceforth he could no longer control his drinking and swearing.

Folk Hero:

Porter Rockwell could not read nor write. Like his friend Joseph Smith, he suffered a life-long limp because of a childhood injury. Rockwell's voice was high-pitched, and when he became emotional, it raised to a high falsetto. But to the Eastern Press, he was "The Destroying Angel of Mormondom," "Chief of the Danites," "one of the pleasantest murderers I ever met."

Stories about Rockwell's "immortality" and "quick trigger" spice Mormon history. Once he reportedly dodged the rapid fire of several outlaws, then routed them with deadly accuracy. "When the smoke cleared, he shook himself like a great shaggy bear and several pistol balls of various calibers fell from the folds of his ill-fitting homespun coat, thus offering witnesses additional evidence of the fulfillment of Joseph Smith's prophecy protecting Rockwell from harm."

Another time a young gunslinger got the drop on Rockwell. "Say your prayers," he demanded. Rockwell replied, "You wouldn't try and shoot a man without a cap on your pistol, would you?" The instant the man glanced at his gun, he was blown from his saddle by Rockwell, who had a gun hidden in his pocket.

Rockwell was the object of several ballads:
> Old Port Rockwell looks like a man,
> With a beard on his face and his hair in a braid,
> But there's none in the West but Brigham who can
> Look in his eyes and not be afraid.
> For Port is a devil in a human shape,
> Though he calls himself 'Angel,'
> say vengeance is sweet;
> But he's black, bitter death, and there's no escape,
> When he wails through the night his dread war cry,
> 'Wheat! Wheat!'
> Somewhere a wife with babes kneels to pray,
> For she knows she's a widow and orphans are they.

In his later years Rockwell raised horses in Skull Valley, fought Indians, continued as a lawman, carried mail across the plains, worked as a scout and guide, and established the Hot Springs Brewery Hotel near the present site of the Utah State Penitentiary in Draper, where he also operated a Pony Express station.

Arrest:

1877   September 30: The *Salt Lake Tribune* reported, "Another one of 'our best society', O. P. Rockwell, was jugged yesterday. This man has been one of the chief murderers of the Mormon Church, opening his career of blood in Nauvoo, under the regime of the Prophet. He was indicted a day or two ago by the grand jury of the First District Court, for participation in the horrible atrocious murder of the Aiken party, in 1858, on the Sevier."

After a week in jail he was released on $15,000 bail posted by friends. Trial date was set for October, 1878. Lawyers attempting to prepare his defense met with frustration; his answer to every question they asked him was, "Wheat! Wheat!"

Death:

1878   June 8: Rockwell died at the age of sixty-five, before he was brought to trial. He had attended the theater the previous evening with his daughter, and after the performance walked the few blocks to the Colorado Stables, where he often slept to be close to his animals. After a fretful night of chills and nausea he vomited violently and frequently. Recovering, he rose up in his bed and attempted to put on his boots, then fell suddenly back on his bed, dead.

At the time of his death, Rockwell had been a member of the Church longer than any other Mormon. Joseph F. Smith eulogized, "He had his little faults, but Rockwell's life on earth, taken altogether, was one worthy of example, and reflected honor upon the Church. Through all his trials he had never once forgotten his obligations to his brethren and his God." The anti-Mormon *Salt Lake Tribune* dryly commented that this eulogy was "fitting tribute of one outlaw to the memory of another."

Rockwell's epitaph in the Salt Lake City Cemetery reads, "He was brave & loyal to his faith, true to the prophet Jos. Smith, a promise made him by the prophet thro obedience it was fulfilled."

Aurelia S. Rogers

(1834-1922)

"Mother of the Primary Association"

Family Background:

1834   October 4: Aurelia Read Spencer was born in Deep River, Connecticut, to Catherine Curtis and Orson Spencer. Her father was a charter member of the Council of Fifty, Saint Louis Stake president, president of the British Mission, and president of the University of Deseret.

Her family joined the Church and moved to Nauvoo when she was seven. Aurelia learned to smoke a pipe at her grandmother's knee, but finally responded to a "monitor within that told me it was wrong, and what it would lead to if persisted in: I should be, if I lived, an old lady smoker. This thought disgusted me, for I never did like to see women smoke."

Aurelia was only thirteen when her mother died during the Nauvoo exodus. Orson Spencer related the last days of his wife's life: "Under the influence of a severe cold, she gradually wasted away, telling her children, from time to time, how she wanted them to live and conduct themselves, when they should become motherless and pilgrims in a strange land."

Aurelia and her older sister Ellen cared for the other four children in Winter Quarters while their father filled a mission to England.

Mother:

1851   Three years after arriving in the Salt Lake Valley with Brigham Young's 1848 company, Aurelia married Thomas Rogers and moved to Farmington, Utah. They had twelve children, only seven of whom lived to maturity. After the death of one, Aurelia wrote: "I almost lost faith in God; for once in my life, I even doubted the existence of a Supreme Being.

"One day while reflecting on these things, one of my father's letters came to my mind, wherein he said, 'Trust in God though he slay you!' I caught at the suggestion, which had surely been given by the Spirit of the Lord, and went to Him in prayer, asking Him to forgive me for my lack of faith, and to grant me strength to endure, feeling that I would put my trust in Him henceforth and forever."

"Mother of the Primary Association":

1878   March: When Relief Society President Eliza R. Snow visited Farmington, Aurelia expressed concern about rowdy boys. "What will our girls do for good husbands, if this state of things continues? Could there not be an organization for little boys, and have them trained to make better men?"

         Farmington Bishop John W. Hess received a letter from John Taylor authorizing a new organization in the ward. August 11, 1878, Bishop Hess set Aurelia Rogers apart as president of the Church's first Primary Association. Though she felt "willing, but very incompetent," she taught her charges "obedience, faith in God, prayer, punctuality, and good manners."

         Rogers also served as secretary of the Farmington Relief Society for twenty-two years.

Women's Advocate:

1893   Called to the Primary General Board. One year later she was a Utah delegate to the Women's Suffrage Convention in Atlanta, Georgia. In 1895 she was elected a delegate to the National Council of Women in Washington, D.C.

Death:

1922   August 19: Died in Farmington, Utah. Shortly before her death, she told family members: "I would like just a few simple blossoms from my own garden . . . if any one has money to spend for flowers for me, it would make me happier to have it given to comfort someone in need." Buried in the Salt Lake City Cemetery.

Ellis Shipp

(1847-1939)

Pioneer Obstetrician

Family Background:

1847   January 20: Ellis Reynolds was born in Davis County, Iowa. Soon after her birth, the family converted to Mormonism. They moved to Utah in 1852 and settled in Pleasant Grove.

In 1865 Ellis was "adopted" into the home of Brigham Young. Educated in the Young family school taught by Karl G. Maeser, she later attended the University of Deseret.

Plural Wife:

1866   May 5: Married Milford B. Shipp: "He was to me all that the enlivened fancy of girlhood or the matured judgment of woman could picture in her imagination. So kind and affectionate, so faithful to the cause of Mormonism.... He was ambitious, ardent and energetic in all that was noble and laudable. Enthusiastic and spirited in conversation. In truth, I never saw a person who could so enchant and fascinate by the power of language." The Shipps had ten children, five of whom died in infancy.

Milford Shipp operated a hat and shoe store in Fillmore, Utah, for several years. When the store failed, the family returned to Salt Lake. Milford later married three plural wives.

Student:

Eliza R. Snow began urging women in the late 1860s to become physicians in order to keep men out of the delivery room. In 1873 Brigham Young added, "The time has come for women to come forth as doctors in these valleys of the mountains."

Determined to care for her children *and* prepare for medical school, Ellis Shipp established a rigorous schedule. "Last night I wrote down my work for today which is as follows: rise at four in the morning, dress, make a fire, sweep, wash in cold water, comb my hair, clean my teeth. Write a few lines in my journal. Write a letter to Grandmother. Read a chapter in Dr. Bunn on health. Read a few extracts from Johnson. Dress the

Dr. Shipp (center row on right) and nursing students.

children, make bed, sweep, dust and prepare my room for the breakfast table. Breakfast at nine. Sew on the machine until three—dinner hour. After dinner call on Sister Jones, who is sick. Wash and prepare the children for bed; from six till eight, knit or do some other light work. Review my actions for the day—offer my devotions to heaven and retire at nine."

Four years later, in 1872, medical school still seemed a remote possibility: "I know that I am tired of this life of uselessness and unaccomplished desires, only so far as cooking, washing dishes and doing general housework goes. I believe that woman's life should not consist wholly and solely of routine duties."

Milford provided little help, but with supplements from her sister-wives, Ellis worked her way as a seamstress through the Women's Medical College of Pennsylvania. "How pure and heavenly is the relationship of sisters in the holy order of polygamy," she wrote. "How beautiful to contemplate the picture of a family where one works for the interest, advancement, and well-being of all."

Physician:

1878   Shipp received an M.D. in March. Returning to Utah, she and sister-wife Maggie Shipp, with Romania Pratt and Martha Paul, were set apart to the "ecclesiastical calling" of administering medicine to the Saints. (Maggie and Milford Shipp received their M.D.s in 1883.)

Dr. Shipp advertised herself as a "Physician and Surgeon; Special attention given to Obstetrics, diseases of women and minor surgery," and opened a school of obstetrics and nursing "with the object of qualifying women for the important offices of nurse and accoucheur." During the school's first four years, she delivered over a thousand lectures while continuing her own practice.

Supportive of Dr. Shipp and other female doctors, the *Deseret News* urged "that the competent and educated doctors of our community . . . be patronized when necessary, by those of their own sex and faith, in preference to others. This is one of the occupations in which qualified women can act to advantage, and is a gesture of the woman's rights question we can endorse and support."

By 1893 Dr. Shipp had attended to 1,543 obstetrical and 2,350 gynecological cases. She delivered more than five thousand babies during her career, including N. Eldon Tanner.

One of the most highly trained physicians in Utah, Dr. Shipp did postgraduate work at the University of Michigan and at New York and Philadelphia hospitals. Despite her training as a general practitioner, she preferred to deal with female patients: "Let men care for their own sex and do the major operations. I have never had an ambition to take such responsibilities, for even men have fatal cases and, if a woman should have them, [she] would always be condemned because she was a woman."

She was the personal physician of Emmeline B. Wells, Eliza R. Snow, and Zina D. H. Young. She served as staff physician at Deseret Hospital, specializing in "care of women and children."

Women's Advocate:

1898 Shipp was called to the Relief Society General Board, where she served for nine years. A personal friend of women's rights leaders Susan B. Anthony, Elizabeth Stanton, and Clara Barton, she was also an officer in two Salt Lake cultural societies—the Reapers' Club and the Utah Women's Press Club.

Concerned that so few Utah women were going to medical school, she observed, "In a land renowned for its equal opportunities for women, it's simply amazing such a few follow a profession so befitting them."

Death:

In her later years, she reflected, "I do not feel my spirit Great. But oh, I have suffered and pray it has never been in vain."

1939 January 31: Died of neck cancer at her home at 1320 Michigan Avenue in Salt Lake City at the age of ninety-two. Buried in the Salt Lake City Cemetery.

Emma Smith

(1804-1879)

"Elect Lady"
First Relief Society President

Family Background:

1804   July 10: Born in Harmony, Pennsylvania.

1827   January 18: Eloped with Joseph Smith, Jr.; they had eleven children:
    Alva (born and died June 15, 1828)
    Louisa and Thaddeus (twins born and died April 30, 1831)
    Joseph and Julia (adopted twin son and daughter of John and Julia Clapp Murdock born April 30, 1831; Joseph died March 29, 1832, and Julia in 1880)
    Joseph III (born November 6, 1832; died November 10, 1914)
    Frederick Granger Williams (born June 20, 1836; died April 13, 1862)
    Alexander Hale (born June 2, 1838; died August 12, 1909)
    Don Carlos (born June 13, 1840; died August 15, 1841)
    Unnamed son (born and died December 26, 1842)
    David Hyrum (born November 17, 1844; died August 29, 1904)

"Elect Lady":

1829   Assisted the Prophet for a short time as a Book of Mormon scribe after Martin Harris lost the 116 pages of manuscript.

1830   June 20 Baptized by Oliver Cowdery.
    July: A revelation designated Emma "an elect lady whom I have called . . . . And the office of thy calling shall be for a comfort unto my servant Joseph Smith, Jun., thy husband, in his affliction, with consoling words, in the spirit of meekness. . . . And thou shalt be ordained under his hand to expound scriptures, and to exhort the church according as it shall be given thee by my Spirit " (D&C 25:3, 5, 7).

First Relief Society President:

In response to an 1835 commandment, Emma selected hymns to be published in the first hymnbook, *A Collection of Sacred Hymns.* She also worked on revisions in 1839 and 1842 and, later, on a Reorganized LDS hymnbook.

1842 March 17: Called to be the first president of the Relief Society.

Wife and Homemaker:

An efficient businesswoman, Emma often helped Joseph with tithing appraisals and the operation of his boardinghouses. She was also an accomplished hostess. On their fifteenth wedding anniversary she and Joseph served seventy-four guests at four tables. An immaculate housekeeper, she redressed her hair every day after completing her afternoon work.

1842 August: After three weeks of hiding from Missouri lawmen, Joseph returned to Nauvoo, where he described his feelings for Emma: "With what unspeakable delight, and transports of joy swelled my bosom, when I took by the hand, on that night, my beloved Emma—she that was my wife, even the wife of my youth, the choice of my heart. Many were the reverberations of my mind when I contemplated for a moment the many scenes we had been called to pass through, the fatigues and the toils, the sorrows and sufferings, and the joys and consolations, from time to time, which had strewed our paths and crowned our board. Oh what a commingling of thought filled my mind for the moment, again she is here, even in the seventh trouble—undaunted, firm, and unwavering—unchangeable, affectionate Emma!"

First Woman to Receive Fullness of Priesthood with Husband:

1843 September 28: A year after Joseph Smith introduced the Holy Order (endowment) to eight men, Emma Smith was sealed to him for time and eternity. According to the manuscript "Meetings of the anointed Quorum," the Prophet was "anointed & ordained to the highest order of the priesthood (& Companion-d[itt]o.)"

As an anointed prophetess, queen, and priestess, Emma Smith often performed the anointing and endowment ceremonies for other women introduced into the Holy Order during the next six months. Joseph Smith asked her, Bathsheba W. Smith, and Eliza R. Snow to design the garment for the actual endowment ceremonies. "They were too poor to buy buttons, so they tore strips of the cloth for strings ... in making the garment they did not know just how to finish them at the top. Emma suggested that a small collar be put on which was done." The basic garment worn by endowed persons when not participating in temple ordinances was the two-piece undergarment in common use at the time, with the addition of specified markings.

Prophet's Widow:

1844 June: Emma has often been blamed for causing Joseph's return across the Mississippi River to Nauvoo by accusing him of cowardice. Actually, businessmen Reynolds Cahoon and Hiram Kimball, worried that the city business district would be adversely affected if the governor were to declare martial law, wrote to the Prophet demanding he return. Emma's letter apparently described the difficulties in Nauvoo and the possible consequences of his leaving or returning.

When Joseph requested advice from Porter Rockwell and Hyrum Smith, Hyrum replied, "Let us go back and give ourselves up and see the thing out." Joseph then said, "If you go back I will go with you, but we shall be butchered." Hyrum, anxious to attend his daughter's wedding in Nauvoo, replied: "No, no: Let us go back and put our trust in God, and we shall not be harmed. The Lord is in it. If we live or have to die, we will be reconciled to our fate."

Contrary to popular belief, Joseph seems not to have been planning to go west. On June 23 he wrote Emma, "You may sell the Quincy property or any property that belongs to me that you can find anything about, for your support and children and Mother. Do not despair. If God ever opens a door that is possible for me I will see you again. I do not know where I shall go or what I shall do, but shall if possible endeavor to get to the city of Washington."

Emma Smith was widowed June 27, 1844, when Joseph and Hyrum were killed in Carthage Jail. Eliza R. Snow wrote of her at this time:

> I knew her ere she had been left
> In her heart's loneliness—
> Before her prospects were bereft
> Of all its happiness.
> I've seen the willow bending low,
> And 'tis unbroken still.

"Excommunication":

Less than enthusiastic about the ascendency of the Quorum of the Twelve and Brigham Young to the leadership of the Church, Emma Smith became suspect because of her closeness to Joseph's erratic brother William and his succession claims. She and Brigham Young also disagreed over the disposition of Joseph's estate.

Disfavor with Brigham Young, Heber C. Kimball, and others prompted rumors that she had been excommunicated. The September 11, 1844, *Warsaw Signal* reported, "It is rumored that on Sunday, nineteen of the leading Mormons were ejected from the church at Nauvoo, among whom were . . . Emma Smith, the prophet's widow." Such rumors, however, were unfounded.

Emma Bidamon:

1846   Two years after Joseph's death, Emma moved to Fulton, Illinois, to be closer to her family. One year later, however, she moved back to the Nauvoo Mansion House, declaring, "I have no place to go but home, and no friend but God."

1847   December 23: Married non-Mormon businessman Lewis C. Bidamon—an attentive husband and father, although he had a drinking problem and fathered an illegitimate child whom Emma raised as her own.

She also cared for the Prophet's mother, who, like Emma, did not go west with the Saints. Lucy Smith wrote of her, "I have never seen a woman in my life, who would endure every species of fatigue and hardship, from month to month, and from year to year, with that unflinching courage, zeal, and patience, which she has ever done; for I know that which she has had to endure—she has been tossed upon the ocean of uncertainty—she has breasted the storms of persecution, and buffeted the rage of men and devils, which would have borne down almost any other woman."

1860   Emma Smith affiliated with the Reorganized Church of Jesus Christ of Latter Day Saints after Joseph Smith III became its first president. She had not raised her son to become president of the RLDS Church. Reluctant at first, he only decided to accept the presidency after persuasion from the church's founders.

Standing, L-R: David Hyrum Smith, Alexander Hale Smith.
Sitting, L-R: Major Lewis Bidamon, Frederick Smith, Joseph Smith, III.

1869 Emma Smith's opposition to polygamy and her refusal to go west prompted much bitterness against her on the part of Utah Mormons, especially Brigham Young. Angered by the 1869 RLDS mission of Alexander and David Hyrum Smith to Utah, President Young said, "The sympathies of the Latter-day Saints are with the family of the martyred prophet. I never see a day in the world that I would not almost worship that woman, Emma Smith, if she would be a Saint instead of being a devil. . . . To my certain knowledge Emma Smith is one of the damnedest liars I know of on this earth; yet there is no good thing I would refuse to do for her, if she would only be a righteous woman."

By this time Emma Smith cared no more for Brigham Young than he cared for her: "I tried before they [her sons] left here to give them an idea of what they might expect of Brigham and all his ites, but I suppose the impression was hardly sufficient to guard their feelings from such unexpected falsehoods and impious profanity as Brigham is capable of. . . . I do not like to have my children's feelings abused, but I do like that Brigham shows to all, both Saint and Sinner, that there is not the least particle of friendship existing between him and myself."

1879 "I have been called apostate," she acknowledged, "but I have never apostatized, nor forsaken the faith I at first accepted; but was called so because I would not accept their newfangled notion [plural marriage]."

Death:

1879 April 30: Died in Nauvoo, Illinois, at the age of seventy-five; buried near Joseph and Hyrum Smith behind the Smith family homestead.

George A. Smith

(1817-1875)

"Potato Saint"
Member of the First Presidency

Family Background:

1817   June 26: Born George Albert Smith in Potsdam, New York, to Clarissa Lyman and future Church Patriarch John Smith. First cousin to Joseph Smith, Hyrum Smith, and Church Patriarch John Smith, and second cousin to President Joseph F. Smith and Apostle Amasa M. Lyman.

          In 1841 he married Bathsheba W. Bigler; one year later he married Lucy Meserve, Zilpha Stark, Sarah Ann Libby, Hannah Marie Libby, and Nancy Clement, and, in 1857, Susan Elizabeth West. He was the father of twenty children, including Apostle John Henry Smith, and the grandfather of President George Albert Smith.

Convert:

1832   A strict Congregationalist, Smith was converted through a Book of Mormon left at his home by his uncle Joseph Smith, Sr., and cousin Don Carlos Smith.

1833   He moved to Kirtland, Ohio, where he met Joseph Smith for the first time. Large for his sixteen years, he became a bodyguard for the Prophet. He hauled the first two loads of stone for the Kirtland Temple.

1834   A huge, clumsy seventeen-year-old, Smith joined Zion's Camp, outfitted in striped pantaloons made of feather ticking and awkward boots that wore blisters on his feet.

Missionary:

1835   Ordained a seventy by Joseph Smith, Joseph Smith, Sr., and Sidney Rigdon. In the next nine years he served seven missions: Ohio-Pennsylvania-New York (1835), Ohio (1836), Virginia (1837), Kentucky-Tennessee (1838), England (1840), Middle and Eastern States (1843), and Michigan (1844).

          During his 1838 mission he committed "the meanest act of my life." Delayed for several days on the Mississippi River below Saint Louis, the always hungry Smith observed a black servant baking potatoes in a stove. He offered to buy some, but was refused. When the servant left the stove unattended, Smith helped himself to some of the potatoes, carefully replacing each one with a piece of coal. The potatoes and "a little parched corn" were all he ate in three days.

Apostle:

1839   At twenty-two, having previously served on the high council of the Adam-Ondi-Ahman Stake in Missouri, George A. Smith was called to the Quorum of the Twelve after the deposing of Apostles Orson Hyde and Thomas B. Marsh.

"Potato Saint":

1846   After his wife Nancy and four children died of scurvy in Winter Quarters, he began advocating use of the potato to prevent the disease.

1847   July: Arriving in the Salt Lake Valley with the pioneer company, Smith soon wrote in his journal, "Potatoes all planted. I planted first." His interest in the vegetable won him the affectionate nickname, "The Potato Saint."

         Exploring the Salt Lake City Valley, he discovered the warm springs at the base of Ensign Peak. Impressed by the temperature of the water, he commented that "hell was not one mile from the place."

         After a few weeks in the valley, Smith returned to Council Bluffs, where he and Orson Hyde presided over the Saints for several years.

"A Man Who Had No Quarrel With His Cook":

Five feet, ten inches tall, Smith weighed 250 pounds. An English traveler described him as "a huge, burly man, with a Friar Tuck joviality of paunch and visage, and a roll in his bright eye which, in some odd, undefined sort of way, suggested cakes and ale. He talked well, in a deep rolling voice, and with a dash of humour in his words and tone—he it was who irreverently but accurately likened the Tabernacle to a land turtle."

Lawyer:

A member of the Council of Fifty, Smith was "elected" lieutenant governor of the "ghost state" of Deseret in 1849, became a member of the Utah territorial legislature (1850-1870), and served as president of the upper house (1864-1870). He also represented Utah in the 1856 statehood bid.

1851   A self-taught lawyer, Smith argued his first and most notorious case just weeks after being admitted to the Utah bar. Howard Egan, a Mormon school teacher, had joined the California gold rush in 1849. While he was away, James Monroe seduced one of his wives, who gave birth to an illegitimate child. Egan returned to Utah and killed Monroe "in the name of the Lord" because his "peace on earth" had been destroyed.

Smith argued that "in this territory it is a principle of mountain common law, that no man can seduce the wife of another without endangering his own life.... The man who seduces his neighbor's wife must die, and her nearest relative must kill him!" The jury declared Egan not guilty.

Colonizer:

1851   Called to settle Parowan, Utah, and develop an iron works. En route, three of his oxen disappeared; one was found dead and another mortally wounded by eleven arrows. Seeing the oxen, "which had been in our service ever since we left Nauvoo," Smith and his wife shed tears. But when two starving Indian boys accused of the crime were brought to Smith, he fed them and persuaded the older boy to trade his twelve-year-old companion for the dead oxen.

Smith was the commanding military officer during the Walker and Black Hawk Indian wars in southern Utah. During the 1857 advance of the Utah Expeditionary Forces he warned that "the first man that ravishes or seduces a wife or daughter of mine, I fully intend to blow out his brains."

Historian:

1854   Called to be Church historian and recorder at the death of Willard Richards. His grandfather described fourteen-year-old George as "a rather singular boy. When he comes here, instead of going to play as the rest of my grandchildren do, he comes into my room and asks me questions about what occurred seventy or eighty years ago."

Smith's memory was legendary. Brigham Young referred to him as a "cabinet of history," and Orson F. Whitney described him as "a walking encyclopedia of general information." His greatest contribution to Mormon history was completing the multi-volume *History of the Church* begun by Joseph Smith.

"Man-Who-Takes-Himself-Apart":

Describing himself to a New York cousin, Smith wrote, "When my wig is off there is scarcely a hair between me and heaven." He also wore glasses and false teeth. An acquaintance noted that Smith "sometimes astounded the Indians by slowly removing all these appendages before them, and he came to be called by the natives, 'Non-choko-wicher,' which means, takes himself apart."

Dixie Mission:

1861   Accompanied Brigham Young, Erastus Snow, and others to establish the new "Dixie Mission" in southern Utah. Nearly 800 families—approximately 3,000 persons—were called to this mission over the next three or four years. The primary purpose of the mission was to produce indigo, madder, fruit, wine, tobacco, and especially cotton—a commodity in great demand since the outbreak of the Civil War. The first year 100,000 pounds of seed cotton were produced, and, in 1863, 56,094 pounds of ginned cotton. A factory was built in 1870 for cotton processing, but poor soil, unstable water supplies, and the completion of the transcontinental railroad in 1869 made Utah cotton production unprofitable. Brigham

Young named the principal settlement "Saint George" in honor of George A. Smith.

Member of the First Presidency

1868   October 7: Sustained as first counselor to President Brigham Young after the death of Heber C. Kimball. President Young described Smith as a "devoted friend, a wise counselor, and a life-long companion."

1870   During the first thirty-eight years of his ministry, George A. Smith delivered 3800 discourses. "No one ever wearied of his preaching. He was brief and interspersed his doctrinal and historical remarks with anecdotes most appropriate and timely in their application. Short prayers, short blessings, short sermons, full of spirit, was a happy distinction in the ministry of Geo. A. Smith."

On one occasion after a full day of conference meetings in Parowan, Smith reportedly prayed: "Heavenly Father bless all good people, Thy servant George A. is tired. In the name of Jesus Christ, Amen."

Death:

1875   September 1: Following a long illness which deprived Smith of his speaking voice and prevented sleep except in an upright position, he died of "lung disease" at the age of fifty-eight. His wife Bathsheba wrote, "He had a restless night, the following morning he walked into the front parlor twice. The last time he sat down in his chair and expired in about five minutes.... He was now through; all was quiet; his head lay against my bosom; good angels had come to receive his precious spirit. Perhaps our sons, prophets, patriarchs, saints beloved were there, but he was gone my light, my Sun, my life, my joy, my Lord, yea, almost my God; but I must not morn but prepare myself to meet him; but my hart sinks within my bosom nearly."

Joseph F. Smith, to whom George A. had been a surrogate father, was nearly overcome with grief. Presiding over the European Mission, he wrote from England, "At first I could not weep. Words seemed like mockery. My soul revolts at them, and would bury itself for a while in the grave with 'Uncle George.' . . . Oh! Why should he go! Who needed him so much as bleeding, persecuted Israel? . . . Israel needed him! The world needed him! and yet God has taken him, and the world is emptier than it was by one who was a prophet, seer and revelator and a King and Priest unto the Most High God." Buried in the Salt Lake City Cemetery.

George Albert Smith

(1870-1951)

Eighth President of the Church

Family Background:

1870   April 4: George Albert Smith was born in Salt Lake City to Susan Farr and John Henry Smith. He was a great-grandnephew of Joseph Smith, Sr., and a grandson of George A. Smith.

At twelve, George attended the Brigham Young Academy for a year under Karl G. Maeser, returning home when his father left on a mission to England. At eighteen, he attended the University of Utah, but left after a year to work as a salesclerk at ZCMI.

In 1892 he married Lucy Emily Woodruff, a granddaughter of Wilford Woodruff; they had three children. She died in 1937. He never remarried.

Missionary:

1891   Filled a two-month mission promoting the MIA in central Utah.

1892   One week after their wedding, Lucy and George Albert Smith were called on a mission to the Southern States.

While serving as president of the European Mission in 1919, he took his first airplane ride—from Brussels to London—in a two-passenger open-cockpit plane. This resulted in his life-long passion for flying.

Federal Official:

1898   An enthusiastic supporter of William McKinley, Smith was appointed receiver in the U.S. Land Office when McKinley was elected president.

Apostle:

1903   Called to the Quorum of the Twelve by Joseph F. Smith after the death of Brigham Young, Jr., fulfilling an 1882 promise by Patriarch Zebedee Coltrin that Smith would "become a mighty prophet in the midst of the sons of Zion."

When President Smith sought the approval of George Albert's father for his choice, Apostle John Henry was hesitant: "I told him if it was a political office I would advise against it but I could not stand in the way of the suggestions of the spirit to him." They were the only father and son combination to serve in the same Quorum of the Twelve.

Just after ordination, Elder Smith listed the guidelines by which he intended to live his life: "I would not seek to force people to live up to my ideals, but rather love them into doing the thing that is right. . . . I would not be an enemy to any living soul."

Prolonged Nervous Breakdown:

1909 From 1909 until 1913 George Albert Smith suffered what Reed Smoot called "mental trouble," and a recent biographer termed "mental collapse." He seemed to recover until the 1930s, when further complications developed. Throughout his service as a general authority after 1909, particularly as Church president, his associates did their best to limit demands upon him that might trigger a relapse.

Recovering in the winter of 1909-10, he "became so weak as to be scarcely able to move. It was a slow and exhausting effort for me even to turn over in bed. One day under these conditions, I lost consciousness of my surroundings and thought I had passed to the Other Side. I found myself standing with my back to a large and beautiful lake, facing a great forest of trees. . . .

"Through the forest, I saw a man coming towards me. . . . I recognized him as my grandfather [George A. Smith]. . . . He looked at me very earnestly and said: 'I would like to know what you have done with my name.' Everything I had ever done passed before me as though it were a flying picture on a screen—everything I had done. . . . I smiled and looked at my grandfather and said: 'I have never done anything with your name of which you need be ashamed.'"

Scouter:

1932   A long-time advocate of the Boy Scout movement in the Church, Smith was awarded the Silver Buffalo—the highest award in American Scouting. His citation read, "George Albert Smith: Business executive, religious leader, former President of the International Irrigation Congress and International Farm Congress, Federal Receiver of Public Moneys and Special Disbursing Agent for the State of Utah. Member of the Quorum of Twelve Apostles of the Church of Jesus Christ of Latter-day Saints and General Superintendent of the Young Men's Mutual Improvement Association of the Church. Organizer and President of the Utah Pioneer Trails and Land-Marks Association. Member of the National Executive Board of the Boy Scouts of America, Program Divisional Committee on Relationships and of its Region Twelve Executive Committee, and identified with its local activities since its organization. He has been indefatigable in serving the cause of scouting and to his enthusiasm for its program must be largely traced the fact that Utah stands above all other states in the percentage of boys who are Scouts."

Advocate for the Visually Impaired:

Smith was a long-time supporter of visual-handicap societies, serving as president of the Society for the Aid of the Sightless for sixteen years. As a teenager his own sight was permanently impaired while working in the desert glare near Green River, Utah, with a railroad surveying crew.

His own words best sum up his philosophy of benevolent Christianity: "I plead with you, my brothers and sisters, let us be generous with one another. Let us be as patient with one another as we would like others to be with us. Let us see the virtues, not find fault and criticize. If we will do that, we will radiate sunshine, and those who know us best will love us."

Eighth President of the Church:

1945   May 14: After two years as president of the Quorum of the Twelve, George Albert Smith, upon the death of Heber J. Grant, became the eighth President of the Church, with J. Reuben Clark and David O. McKay as counselors. He was the first Church president who did not have plural wives.

He dedicated the Idaho Falls Temple (1945), and was the first Church president to tour Mexico (1946) and to appear on a telecast of general conference (1949).

Shortly after World War II, President Smith visited Harry Truman to "'ascertain from you, Mr. President, what your attitude will be if the Latter-day Saints are prepared to ship food and clothing and bedding to Europe.' He smiled and looked at me, and said: 'Well, what do you want to ship it over there for? Their money isn't any good....' 'We would give it to them. They are our brothers and sisters and are in distress. God has blessed us with a surplus, and we will be glad to send it if we can have the cooperation of the government.' 'How long will it take you to get this ready?' I said: 'It's all ready.'"

President Smith served as a director of Utah Savings and Trust, Utah-Idaho Sugar, ZCMI, Heber J. Grant Company, Mutual Creamery, Utah National Bank, Salt Lake Theatre, and Decker Wholesale Jewelry Company. He was also president of Libby Investment Company.

Death:

1951   April 4: George Albert Smith died on his eighty-first birthday at his Yale Avenue home in Salt Lake City of lupuserythematosus disseminatus, a disease of the connective tissue which may have contributed to his mental collapse. Buried in the Salt Lake City Cemetery.

Hyrum Smith

(1800-1844)

Church Patriarch and Associate President
Martyr

Family Background:

1800   February 9: Born in Tunbridge, Vermont, he was an older brother of Joseph Smith, Jr., and Apostle William Smith, first cousin to Apostle George A. Smith, and third cousin to Oliver Cowdery.

When he was eleven and Joseph seven, Joseph suffered a serious leg infection. "Hyrum," recalled his mother, "sat beside him almost day and night, for some considerable length of time, holding the affected part of Joseph's leg in his hands and pressing it between them, so that his afflicted brother might be enabled to endure the pain which was so excruciating that he was scarcely able to bear it."

He married Jerusha Barden in 1826; they had six children. Jerusha died October 13, 1837, eleven days after giving birth.

Two months later, Hyrum married Mary Fielding, by whom he had two children, Joseph Fielding and Martha Ann. In 1843 he married Mary's sister Mercy Fielding Thompson, Catherine Phillips, and Lydia Dibble Granger.

Promised by his brother Joseph that "his children shall be many and his posterity numerous, and they will rise up and call him blessed," Hyrum had a son (John) who became patriarch to the Church, another (Joseph F.) who became sixth president of the Church, and a grandson (Joseph Fielding) who became tenth president of the Church. All patriarchs of the Church since 1855 have been descendants of Hyrum Smith.

Early Church Leader:

1829   June 29: Baptized by Joseph Smith in Seneca Lake, New York. He later became one of the Eight Witnesses to the Book of Mormon.

1830   April 6: At thirty, Hyrum was the oldest of the original six members of the Church. David Whitmer was twenty-five; Joseph Smith, twenty-four; Oliver Cowdery, twenty-three; Samuel H. Smith, twenty-two; and Peter Whitmer, Jr., twenty.

1831   Shortly after arriving in Kirtland, Hyrum Smith was called on a mission to Independence, Missouri, where he attended the dedication of the temple site August 9.

1833   June 5: Following two short missions to Ohio with Orson Hyde and Reynolds Cahoon, Smith, as chairman of the building committee, dug a foundation trench for the Kirtland Temple. He acted as foreman in the temple stone quarry and later served as chairman of the Nauvoo Temple building committee.

1834   Served as Joseph Smith's bodyguard in Zion's Camp, where both were struck by cholera which "seized us like the talons of a hawk." Fourteen men died of the malady.

Counselor to the Prophet:

1834   December 6: Hyrum and Joseph Smith, Sr., were ordained assistant presidents to the Prophet Joseph Smith.

1835   In Kirtland Joseph and William Smith debated the question, "Was it necessary for God to reveal Himself to mankind in order for their happiness?" When the debate was awarded to Joseph, six-foot-six William attacked the Prophet and Jared Carter. The following Saturday, Hyrum delivered a letter of apology for William. "I pray in my heart," wrote Joseph, "that all brethren were like unto my beloved Hyrum, who possesses the mildness of a lamb, and the integrity of a Job, and in short, the meekness and humility of Christ; and I love him with that love that is stronger than death."

1837   November 7: Sustained as second counselor in the First Presidency after the excommunication of Frederick G. Williams. The Prophet would often ask, "What shall we do, Hyrum?" After obtaining his brother's judgment, Joseph usually concurred: "That is good enough."

Prisoner:

1838   October 31: Joseph and Hyrum Smith and other leaders were arrested in Far West, Missouri, for "treason, murder, arson, larceny, theft, and stealing." They were taken to Independence for trial while the rest of the Saints were driven from the state under the threat of Governor Lilburn W. Boggs's extermination order.

November 28: After three weeks chained in a Richmond, Missouri, log cabin, the Smiths and five other prisoners were taken to the jail in Liberty. "Poison was administered to us three or four times. The effect it had upon our system was that it vomited us almost to death, and then we would lie some two or three days in a torpid stupid state, not even caring or wishing for life."

1839   April 16: The prisoners were allowed to escape en route to Boone County on a change of venue. Hyrum's seven-year-old son John later recalled his father returned with "a full beard, his hair was long, and he was riding a small bay horse."

Church Patriarch and Associate President:

1840   September 14: On his deathbed, presiding Patriarch Joseph Smith, Sr., ordained Hyrum his successor.

1841   January 19: A revelation confirmed Smith's appointment as patriarch to the Church and appointed him a "prophet, seer, and revelator unto my church, as well as my servant Joseph; that he may act in concert also with my servant who shall show unto him the keys whereby he may ask and receive, and be crowned with the same blessings and glory, and honour, and priesthood, and gifts of the priesthood, that once were put upon him that was my servant Oliver Cowdery."

In a public meeting, July 16, 1843, the Prophet "said I would not prophesy any more, and proposed Hyrum to hold the office of prophet to the Church, as it was his by birthright. I am going to have a reformation, and the Saints must regard Hyrum, for he has the authority, that I might be Priest of the Most High God."

Plural Marriage Opponent:

1843   In the controversy over John C. Bennett's lurid allegations of spiritual wifery at Nauvoo and the denials of Joseph Smith and others, Hyrum condemned polygamy and declared he would never believe in plural marriage unless God gave a revelation sanctioning it.

July 12: Joseph Smith dictated the revelation now known as section 132 of the Doctrine and Covenants. Converted, Hyrum presented the revelation to the Nauvoo high council in August, performed plural marriages for the Prophet and others, and married plural wives himself.

Hyrum, Joseph, and Emma Smith grave from
the Smith family homestead window.

Martyr:

1844 June 23: Hyrum, Joseph, Willard Richards, and Porter Rockwell rowed across the Mississippi River into Iowa to escape lawmen trying to arrest the Prophet for ordering the destruction of the *Nauvoo Expositor*. "I advised my brother Hyrum to take his family on the next steamboat and go to Cincinnati. Hyrum replied, 'Joseph, I can't leave you.' Whereupon I said to the company present, 'I wish I could get Hyrum out of the way, so that he may live to avenge my blood.'"

Entreated to return to Nauvoo, Hyrum, who wished to attend his daughter's wedding, responded, "Let us go back and put our trust in God and we shall not be harmed. The Lord is in it. If we have to die, we will be reconciled to our fate."

June 27: Martyred at forty-four with his brother the Prophet in Carthage Jail. Four bullets struck Hyrum; as he fell to the floor, he exclaimed, "I am a dead man."

October: Brigham Young told the April conference of the Church, "Did Joseph ordain any man to take his place? He did. Who was it? It was Hyrum. But Hyrum fell a martyr before Joseph did."

Joseph and Hyrum, who had never been separated for more than six months during their lives, were buried together in the unfinished basement of the Nauvoo House. Later they were moved across the street behind the Smith family homestead. The Reorganized Church located and verified the gravesites in 1928.

Joseph Smith

(1805-1844)

Prophet
First President of the Church
Martyr

Family Background:

1805   December 23: Born in Sharon, Vermont, to Joseph Smith, Sr., and Lucy Mack. He was a brother of Hyrum Smith and William Smith, a first cousin to George A. Smith, third cousin to Oliver Cowdery, fourth cousin to Willard Richards, fifth cousin to Heber C. Kimball, and sixth cousin to Brigham Young, Parley P. Pratt, and Orson Pratt.

1827   January 18: Eloped with Emma Hale. They had eleven children, including adopted twins. Only five of the children reached adulthood, and one of them, David Hyrum, was born shortly after his father's death. Joseph Smith, III, became the first president of the Reorganized Church of Jesus Christ of Latter Day Saints.

Although some evidence indicates Joseph Smith may have been involved in polygamy as early as Kirtland, Erastus Snow testified that Louisa Beaman became the Prophet's first plural wife in 1841. The total number of Joseph Smith's wives is unknown. Some accounts list eighty. Fawn Brodie's *No Man Knows My History* names forty-eight, including widows of Bishop Vincent Knight and Seventies President Lyman R. Sherman, daughters of Heber C. Kimball, Edward Partridge, and Newell K. Whitney, sisters of Brigham Young and Willard Richards, the sister-in-law of Parley P. Pratt, and two stepdaughters of Seventies President Josiah Butterfield.

Prophet:

Joseph Smith reported a boyhood vision of God and Jesus Christ in Palmyra, New York. Though several accounts of this vision exist, the first known record was not made until 1831-32, and no account was published until Orson Pratt's 1840 missionary tract, *Interesting Account of Several Remarkable Visions and of the Late Discovery of Ancient American Records*. The best-known version, published by the Prophet in the 1842 *Times and Seasons*, is included in the Pearl of Great Price.

Angelic visitations resulted in the young Prophet's obtaining the Book of Mormon plates September 22, 1827.

Joseph Smith and Oliver Cowdery later reported they had been baptized and ordained to the Aaronic Priesthood by John the Baptist on May 15, 1829, and ordained one month later to the Melchizedek Priesthood by Peter, James, and John. In 1832 Joseph and Sidney Rigdon had a vision of God, Christ, and the eternal worlds, and in 1836, the Prophet and Oliver Cowdery had a vision of Christ, Moses, Elias, and Elijah in the Kirtland Temple.

Joseph Smith recorded more than a hundred revelations, including the Book of Moses (1830), the Law of Consecration (1831), a revelation prophesying the Civil War (1832), the Word of Wisdom (1833), and the revelation on plural marriage (1843).

"When did I ever teach anything wrong from this stand?" he asked. "When was I ever confounded. . . ? I never told you I was perfect: but there is no error in the revelations which I have taught."

Translator:

He began the translation of the Book of Mormon on April 28, 1828, publishing it in March, 1830. In 1833 he said he had completed his "translation of the Bible," but periodically made additional changes until his death. In March, 1842, he published the Book of Abraham—"a translation of some ancient Records, that have fallen into our hands, from the catacombs of Egypt." He had worked on this translation since 1835, also developing "an alphabet to the Book of Abraham," and arranging "a grammar of the Egyptian language as practiced by the ancients."

Although the Prophet translated "through the Gift and Power of God," he also acquired rudimentary reading skills in Hebrew, Latin, and German.

Kirtland:

During the nearly seven years that he lived in Ohio, Joseph Smith organized the First Presidency (1832), prepared an "inspired version" of the Bible (1833), organized the first high council (1834), led Zion's Camp to

Missouri (1834), conducted the School of the Prophets (1834), and dedicated the Kirtland Temple (1835).

While living with the John Johnson family in Hiram, Ohio, Joseph Smith and Sidney Rigdon were beaten, tarred, and feathered. A "doctor" intent on emasculating the two lost heart when he saw their naked bodies stretched out on the ground. But a vial of acid forced into the Prophet's mouth injured a tooth and his palate, causing a whistle in his speech. Joseph also had a permanent limp from a childhood operation for osteomyelitis, a complication of typhoid fever.

First President of the Church:

1830   Joseph Smith and Oliver Cowdery, each designated as "an apostle of Jesus Christ, an elder of this church," organized the "church of Christ" on April 6, 1830 (Book of Commandments 24:1-4). Joseph became "President of the High Priesthood" on January 25, 1832. The first First Presidency, which included counselors Sidney Rigdon and Jesse Gause, was organized in March, 1832.

Missouri:

1831   June: Joseph Smith first visited Missouri with Sidney Rigdon, Martin Harris, Edward Partridge, W. W. Phelps, and others. There the temple site was revealed (D&C 57) and the Colesville, New York, Branch began the Mormon settlement of Jackson County.

1838   January 12: Following the collapse of the Kirtland Safety Society, Joseph and Sidney Rigdon fled to Far West, Missouri. They were arrested there in October on charges of "treason, murder, arson, larceny, theft, and stealing." They spent the following six months in the Richmond and Liberty jails, "within the walls, grates, and screeking of iron doors, of a lonesome, dark, dirty prison."

Joseph had forty-eight lawsuits brought against him during his lifetime. He prevailed in forty-seven. The sole exception was an 1826 indictment for fraudulent "glass looking" brought by Peter G. Bridgeman. *Fraser's Magazine* of February, 1873, claimed Smith was convicted of a misdemeanor in the case. George A. Smith may have been referring to this case when he told a Salt Lake City congregation in 1855 that Joseph Smith "was never found guilty but once."

Nauvoo:

1840s During the Prophet's five years in Illinois, he served as trustee-in-trust for the Church, receiving, managing, and conveying Church property; married several plural wives; edited the *Times and Seasons* (1842); received a Master Mason Degree "on sight" from Illinois Grand Master Abraham Jonas (1842); organized the Relief Society (1842); organized the Council of Fifty (1842); instituted the full endowment ceremony in the second story of his "red brick store" (1842); became mayor of Nauvoo (1842); dictated the revelation on plural marriage (1843); and became a U. S. presidential candidate: "When I get hold of the Eastern papers, and see how popular I am, I am afraid myself that I shall be elected" (1844).

"Strong and Active":

Joseph Smith was six feet tall and weighed two hundred pounds. Parley P. Pratt described him as "tall and well built, strong and active, of light complexion, light hair, blue eyes, very little beard, and of an expression peculiar to himself, on which the eye naturally rested with interest and was never weary of beholding. His countenance was ever mild, affable, beaming with intelligence and benevolence; mingled with a look of interest and an unconscious smile, or cheerfulness, and entirely free from all restraint or affectation of gravity; and there was something connected with the serene and steady penetrating glance of his eye, as if he would penetrate the deepest abyss of the human heart, gaze into eternity, penetrate the heavens and comprehend all worlds."

Aroet Hale, a Nauvoo acquaintance, wrote, "Joseph was always goodnatured and full of fun. I have seen him

sit down on the carpet in his office in the Mansion and pull sticks with the Nauvoo Police.... The Prophet would ... pull the stoutest man up with one hand."

Martyr:

1844 During his last days the Prophet reported a revelation which instructed him to leave Nauvoo and promised his life would be preserved. He planned a trip to Washington, D.C., to seek federal aid for the Saints. But nervous followers in Nauvoo accused him of cowardice, begging him to return to Nauvoo from his haven across the Mississippi. Despite the revelation, he returned, declaring shortly before his death, "I have heard to [sic] the brethren, & gone to Carthage contrary to the council of the spirit & I am now no more than another man."

Submitting to arrest for ordering the destruction of the *Nauvoo Expositor*, Joseph Smith was incarcerated in Carthage Jail. On the morning of June 27, he wrote Emma, "I am very much resigned to my lot, knowing I am justified, and have done the best that could be done. Give my love to the children and all my friends."

He was shot to death that evening, at the age of thirty-nine, by a mob which stormed the jail.

Two years before his death, Joseph had built a family tomb near the Nauvoo Temple. He wanted the tomb to be called the tomb of Joseph, a descendant of Jacob. "And when I die," he said, "let me be gathered to the tomb of my Father." Emma, fearful the bodies would be disinterred by enemies, secretly buried the brothers in the unfinished basement of the Nauvoo House. They were later moved across the street behind the Smith family homestead.

Joseph F. Smith

(1838-1918)

Sixth President of the Church

Family Background:

1838   November 13: Born Joseph Fielding Smith at Far West, Missouri, to Hyrum Smith and Mary Fielding. He was a stepson of Heber C. Kimball, nephew of Joseph Smith, and half-brother of Church Patriarch John Smith.

         Joseph F. Smith married Levira Annette Clark Smith April 5, 1859, and later Julina Lambson, niece of George A. Smith (1866); Sarah Ellen Richards, daughter of Willard Richards (1868); Edna Lambson (1871); Alice Ann Kimball, daughter of Heber C. Kimball (1883); and Mary Taylor Schwartz, niece of John Taylor (1884). He had forty-eight children, including five adopted children.

         His father was in the Richmond, Missouri, jail when Joseph F. was born. As a mob ransacked their Far West home looking for papers, a mattress was thrown over the infant and he nearly suffocated. Young Joseph was not seen by his father until several months later, when Hyrum was transferred to Liberty Jail.

1844   June 27: When Joseph F. was five years old, he heard a man knock on his mother's window and announce that his father had been killed. Memories of his grieving mother's moans remained with him throughout his life.

1848:   When he was nine, Joseph F. drove a team of oxen from Winter Quarters to the Salt Lake Valley, arriving in September. From 1846 to 1854 he was a "teamster, herd boy, plowboy, irrigator, harvester, with 'scythe or cradle,' operator of a fanning mill, logger, and 'general roustabout'—and always penniless."

         Orphaned in 1852, Joseph F. was persuaded by his surrogate father, George A. Smith, to attend school in Sugarhouse. When the teacher tried to "put the strap" to Joseph F.'s younger sister, the hot-tempered youth intervened. The teacher turned on Joseph F., but "instead of him whipping me, I licked him good and plenty."

Missionary:

1854   Expelled from school, Joseph F. was sent on a mission to the Sandwich Isles (Hawaii) at fifteen years of age. The mission had been opened in 1850 and under George Q. Cannon had experienced phenomenal growth.

Smith, who remained in Hawaii for four years, learned the language in three months. Receiving no support from home, he lived in poverty with the natives. For weeks the missionaries had little to eat, and for a while Smith and his companion had only one suit of clothes between them; one stayed home while the other wore the suit to meetings.

Joseph F. Smith served three missions to England (1860-1863, and, as president of the European Mission, 1874-1875 and 1877), a second mission to Hawaii (1864), and a historical research mission to the Eastern States with Orson Pratt (1878).

Husband and Father:

1858   Returning from Hawaii, Joseph F. served briefly in the militia called out to oppose the federal Expeditionary Force. He courted his sixteen-year-old cousin, Levira Annette Clark Smith, daughter of Samuel Smith. "I am aware that our acquaintance has been short," he wrote. "To you, I do not know how pleasant. But allow me to say that since I saw you first, the admiration and respect I first conceived for you have daily grown, till they have changed to something stronger and more fervent." They were married April 5, 1859. He served briefly on the Salt Lake Stake High Council, then left on a mission to England in April, 1860.

Joseph F. was absent on missions nearly five of their first six years of married life. He wrote often, sometimes bouyantly: "Wake up snakes! and come to Judgment! for Mormonism is destined to rule the warts!" sometimes good-naturedly: "What would you think of me for a rational sensible 'Lord' and husband if my every sentence was "'Sugar, Honey, Cherub, Duckey, Darling, Precious, and Bewildering Beauty.' Bah! Soft-soap, vinegar, crab-apple, and sauerkraut."

But his letters failed to console his depressed, childless, impoverished wife. The news that he had adopted a four-year-old boy without consulting her did little to improve their relationship. By the time he returned in the fall of 1863, she was suffering from a nervous breakdown. Joseph F. remained with her constantly for six weeks, occasionally restraining her physically.

In January, 1864, he left on another mission to Hawaii. Levira sought medical treatment in San Francisco, where relatives cared for her. When Joseph returned in November, they fought often.

1866   May 5: After a brief acquaintance, Joseph F. Smith married seventeen-year-old Julina Lambson, who had been living with her uncle George A. Smith while Joseph F. worked for him in the Church historian's office.

1867   June 10: Levira and Julina apparently got along well personally, but Levira ultimately could not accept plural marriage. After a separation of eight months she obtained permission from Brigham Young to have their marriage dissolved. Levira asked Joseph F.'s permission to keep one letter and picture of him: "They will awaken saddest, sweetest, memories of the past tho the life history of one of earth's poor daughters had been burned to ashes. And why? Because one of earth's brave and noble sons could not appreciate or stoop to the musings of a gentle girlish heart."

In 1868 Levira obtained a divorce in California, charging that her husband had "been guilty of the crime of Adultery with several different women." Joseph F. Smith was the last divorced president of the Church.

He did not hesitate to scold his wives or children for violating his standards. After one Christmas, he wrote to his wife Edna, accusing her of being extravagant with the children's gifts. She fired back his letter with a post-scripted note: "How kind, how loving! This is from your heart and it has sunk deep in mine. But it is cruel and unjust. How can I be so horribly extravagant on $25 per month?"

Hugh B. Brown recalled Joseph F. Smith as "a very rugged man who had been raised in the school of hard knocks. . . . In some ways Joseph F. Smith seemed to me to be the man that I would like to have for my father, but I know if I had, that his severe discipline would have been hard on me." But Joseph Fielding Smith recalled his father as "the most tenderhearted man I ever knew."

Counselor to Four Prophets:

1866   July 1: Following the regular Sunday prayer circle of the First Presidency and the Quorum of the Twelve, Brigham Young suddenly said, "Hold on. Shall I do as I feel led? I always feel well to do as the spirit constrains me. It is my mind to ordain bro. Joseph F. Smith to the Apostleship, and to be one of my Councilors."

Though an apostle, Joseph F. Smith was not admitted to the Quorum of the Twelve until 1867, replacing Amasa Lyman. Knowledge of the secret ordination was kept even from Heber C. Kimball, Brigham Young's first counselor—and Joseph F. Smith's stepfather.

Joseph F. Smith served in the First Presidency for thirty-eight years, longer than any other man. He was counselor to Brigham Young, John Taylor, Wilford Woodruff, and Lorenzo Snow.

"Hawaiian Exile":

Between 1884 and 1891 President Smith spent five years in exile to escape arrest for polygamy. Most of the time was spent in Hawaii. To his wife Sarah he wrote, "I cannot see the use of mothers with whole flocks of little helpless children being driven about the country for fear of a mob of deputy marshals. If they call on you, my darling, to go before the Grand inquisition or court—I want you, and I mean it too, to tell the God damned fiends that you are my wife now and forever, and they may help themselves."

Republican Partisan:

1867   January 25: Admitted to the Council of Fifty.

Joseph F. Smith served as Salt Lake City councilman (1866-84), Provo City councilman (1868-69), Utah territorial legislator (1865-74, 1880-82), and member of the Utah Constitutional Convention (1882). According to the 1882 Edmunds Act he should have been disqualified from holding public office because of his plural marriages, but he continued to maintain a low profile as Salt Lake City councilman for two more years.

Although most Utah Mormons in the 1860s were sympathetic to the Democratic Party, Joseph F. Smith voted for Republican Abraham Lincoln in 1864. When the Church disbanded its People's Party in 1891 and urged the Saints to join either of the two national parties, Smith declared himself a Republican. For the next twenty-eight years he ardently defended Republican causes and candidates, put administrative hobbles on Democratic general authorities, and urged Latter-day Saints to vote straight Republican.

Sixth President of the Church:

1901   October 17: Set apart as president of the Church, with John R. Winder and Anthon H. Lund as counselors.

Joseph F. Smith was the first president born in the Church, the only president, excepting Joseph Smith, not previously sustained as president of the Quorum of the Twelve, and the only president to have a son who also became president of the Church.

In addition to serving as Church president, he also became general superintendent of the Deseret Sunday School Union, a position he held until his death. Church auxiliaries under his leadership established the *Improvement Era*, the *Children's Friend*, and the *Relief Society Magazine*.

Thanks largely to the efforts of his predecessor, Lorenzo Snow, the Church's heavy financial debts were paid by 1906. The new solvency paved the way for an expanded Church building program including construction of the Church Administration Building and Hawaii and Alberta temples. Historic sites were purchased, including Joseph Smith's birthplace in Vermont, the Smith home and Sacred Grove near Palmyra, New York, the Carthage Jail in Illinois, and twenty-five acres near the temple site in Independence, Missouri.

1904   March: President Smith became the first Church president to appear before the U. S. Senate when he was subpoenaed to testify at the Reed Smoot hearings.

Although he had apparently sanctioned and even performed plural marriages after the 1890 Manifesto, Joseph F. Smith accepted responsibility only for his personal violations of Church and legal decrees against polygamous cohabitation since 1890. He denied authorizing, performing, or even knowing about any plural marriages contracted after 1890.

April 6: President Smith issued an edict commonly called the "Second Manifesto," which defined the Wilford Woodruff Manifesto as having abolished plural marriage worldwide, not just in countries where it was illegal. Excommunication proceedings were initiated several years later, under the auspices of the Quorum of the Twelve, against Latter-day Saints who had entered polygamy after 1904, but Joseph F. Smith firmly resisted Reed Smoot's persistent urgings to prosecute those who had entered the system prior to 1904.

1911 April 11: Replying to Senator Reed Smoot's urgent appeal for an official statement on post-Manifesto polygamy, President Smith wired: "If the President inquire about new polygamy, tell him the truth, tell him that Prest. Cannon was the first to conceive the idea that the Church could consistently countenance polygamy beyond confines of the republic where there was no law against it, and consequently he authorized the solemnization of plural marriages in Mexico and Canada after manifesto of 1890, and the men occupying presiding positions who became polygamists since the manifesto married in good faith under those circumstances. This being the case could we consistently be expected to humiliate them by releasing them?"

Vision:

1918 October: Six weeks before his death, Joseph F. Smith experienced a "vision on salvation of the dead and visit of the Savior to the Spirit World," which was added to the Pearl of Great Price in 1976 and became section 138 of the Doctrine and Covenants in 1981.

Death:

1918   November 19: Died of pneumonia at 175 East South Temple in Salt Lake City. Due to the dangers of public gatherings during the national influenza epidemic, no public funeral was held. Buried in the Salt Lake City Cemetery.

Joseph Fielding Smith

(1876-1972)

Scriptorian
Historian
Tenth President of the Church

304 A Book of Mormons

Family Background:

1876   July 19: Born Joseph Fielding Smith, Jr., in Salt Lake City to Julina Lambson and future Church President Joseph F. Smith. He was the grandnephew of Joseph Smith, grandson of Church Patriarch Hyrum Smith, nephew of Church Patriarch John Smith, brother of Apostle Hyrum Mack Smith, and father-in-law of Apostle Bruce R. McConkie.

         Until his father's death Joseph Fielding signed his name, "Joseph F. Smith, Jr."; after Joseph F.'s death, he signed, "Joseph Fielding Smith."

         In 1898 he married Louie E. Shurtliff. Eight months after her death in 1908, he married Ethel G. Reynolds. Eight months after her death in 1938, he married Jessie Ella Evans. He was the father of eleven children.

Historian and Scriptorian:

1901   Following a two-year mission to Great Britain, he became a clerk in the Church historian's office. He was to work in various capacities in this office, including assistant Church historian (1906) and historian (1921), for the next sixty-nine years.

         In 1908 he became director and librarian of the Church Genealogical Society, and in 1934 was named president of the organization.

         "From the time I first could read," he recalled, "I have received more pleasure and greater satisfaction out of the study of the scriptures, and reading of the Lord Jesus Christ, and of the Prophet Joseph Smith, and the work that has been accomplished for the salvation of men, than from anything else in all the world."

         He wrote twenty-five books, including *Blood Atonement and Plural Marriage*, *Essentials in Church History*, *Teachings of the Prophet Joseph Smith*, *Doctrines of Salvation* (three volumes), *Answers to Gospel Questions* (five volumes), and *Man: His Origin and Destiny*.

Apostle:

1910   Called to the Quorum of the Twelve by his father, President Joseph F. Smith, after the death of John R.

Winder. The calling fulfilled an 1896 patriarchal blessing: "It is thy privilege to live to a good old age and the will of the Lord that you should become a mighty man in Israel .... It shall be thy duty to sit in counsel with thy brethren and to preside among the people."

In 1945 he was called as president of the Salt Lake Temple, and in 1951, at the age of seventy-four, became president of the Quorum. In 1965, at the age of eighty-nine, he was named a counselor to David O. McKay in the First Presidency.

Advocate of Righteousness:

President Smith often spoke and wrote fervently against the evils which Church members should avoid: "We should be on guard always to resist Satan's advances. He will appear to us in the person of a friend or a relative in whom we have confidence. He has power to place in our minds and whisper to us in unspoken impressions to entice us to satisfy our appetites or desires and in various other ways he plays upon our weaknesses and desires."

He was often viewed as a "stern and unbending judge of righteousness," as suggested by his views on capital punishment: "There is a growing notion in the world today that it is adding a crime to a crime to take the life of those who deliberately murder, . . . There are sins which cannot be forgiven, except by the guilty person paying a price by the shedding of his blood. Capital punishment was to benefit the guilty to obtain a better resurrection when the sin had been one unto death."

Father:

Despite a stern public manner, his family remember him as a loving husband and father. His wife Ethel, mother of nine of his eleven children, wrote, "I have often thought that when he is gone people will say, 'He is a very good man, sincere, orthodox, etc.' They will speak of him as the public knows him; but the man I know is a kind, loving husband and father whose greatest ambition in life is to make his family happy, entirely forgetful of self in his

Joseph Fielding Smith and wife Jessie.

efforts to do this. He is the man that lulls to sleep the fretful child, who tells bedtime stories to the little ones, who is never too tired or too busy to sit up late at night or to get up early in the morning to help the older children solve perplexing school problems. When illness comes, the man I know watches tenderly over the afflicted one and waits upon him. It is their father for whom they cry, feeling his presence a panacea that gives courage to the sufferer, his voice that remonstrates with them gently when they do err, until it becomes their happiness to do the thing that will make him happy."

Joseph Fielding Smith refused to waste time, and instilled the same discipline in his children. His son remembered, "Somehow it seemed immoral to lie in bed after six. Of course, I only tried it once. Father saw to that."

Physical punishment was not his method of discipline. His children remember him putting both hands on their shoulders, looking down into their eyes, and saying, "I wish my kiddies would be good."

President Smith's low-key humor delighted those who knew him well. Scolded by one of his sisters for never taking a day off, he quipped, "All my days are off." The sister advised, "Now I want you to go home and take a nap. George Albert Smith, Stephen L. Richards, and J. Reuben Clark always did, so you can too." "Yes," President Smith replied, "and where are they today? All dead!"

Relating a boyhood incident when his father had purchased a fine riding horse from George Q. Cannon, President Smith said,"She was so smart she learned how to unlock one kind of corral fastener after another that I contrived, until Father said to me, half humorously, that Juney seemed to be smarter than I was. So Father himself fastened her in with a strap and buckle. As he did so, the mare eyed him coolly; and, as soon as our backs were turned, she set to work with her teeth until she actually undid the buckle and followed us out, somewhat to my delight. I could not refrain from suggesting to Father that I was not the only one whose head compared unfavorably with the mare's."

Joseph Fielding Smith often took his sons to the Deseret Gymnasium, where, "with one hand—either hand, he gave us our choice—behind him he would beat the socks off us playing handball." He also enjoyed flying, a privilege of his position as honorary brigadier general of the Utah National Guard.

Tenth President of the Church:

1970 At the age of ninety-four Joseph Fielding Smith became the oldest man ever set apart as president of the Church. He succeeded David O. McKay and selected Harold B. Lee and N. Eldon Tanner as counselors. President Smith and his father, Joseph F. Smith, are the only father and son to become presidents of the Church.

During his administration the *Improvement Era, Relief Society Magazine,* and *Children's Friend,* all of which had been initiated during his father's administration, were replaced by the *Ensign,* the *Friend,* and the *New Era* (1970). He directed the Church's first area general conference (Manchester, England, 1971), reorganized the Church Educational System, and formed the Health Services Department. In 1972 he dedicated the Provo and Ogden temples.

During his life he delivered more than 125 general conference talks, and participated in over five thousand stake conferences. He loved music, often singing duets with his opera star wife, Jessie. He wrote the lyrics to several songs, including "The Best Is Not Too Good for Me," "Come, Come, My Brother, Wake!" "Does the Journey Seem Long?" and "We are Watchmen of the Tower of Zion."

Death:

1972   July 2: Died in Salt Lake City two weeks short of his ninety-sixth birthday; buried in the Salt Lake City Cemetery.

Lucy Mack Smith

(1776-1855)

Prophet's Mother
Prophet's Biographer

Family Background:

1776   July 8: Born in Gilsum, New Hampshire. In 1796 she married Joseph Smith; they had eleven children: Alvin (1798-1823), Hyrum (1800-1844), Sophronia (1803-?), Joseph (1805-1844), Samuel Harrison (1808-1844), Ephraim (1810-1810), William (1811-1894), Catherine (1812-1900), Don Carlos (1816-1841), and Lucy (1824-1882). Their first child, an unnamed daughter, died shortly after birth in 1797.

Lucy Smith was the matriarch of a Church patriarchy. Her son Joseph published the Book of Mormon and became the Church's founding Prophet in 1830. Her husband, Joseph, Sr., one of the Eight Witnesses, became Church patriarch in 1833 and assistant president in 1834. Hyrum, one of the Eight Witnesses, became assistant president in 1834, second counselor in 1837, Church patriarch in 1840, and associate president in 1841. Samuel H.—another of the Eight Witnesses—became a member of the Church's first high council in 1834, William became a member of the Quorum of the Twelve in 1835, and Don Carlos became president of the central high priests quorum of the Church in 1836.

Visionary:

Near death from consumption during adolescence, she promised to serve God if her life were spared, then heard a voice proclaim, "Let your heart be comforted; ye believe in God, believe also in me." Recovering rapidly, she sought out a "minister who was willing to baptize me, and leave me free in regard to joining any religious denomination, I stepped forward and yielded obedience to this ordinance; after which I continued to read the Bible as formerly."

Hard Times:

1803   Shortly after opening a store in Randolph, Vermont, the Smiths lost everything in a ginseng root venture. They drifted from Randolph to Royalton, to Sharon, to Tunbridge, and back to Royalton.

1811   The family moved to Lebanon, New Hampshire, where several of the children contracted typhus. Sophronia nearly died. Complications threatened young Joseph's leg; an operation— without anesthesia—left him with a permanent limp.

1816   Three consecutive crop failures forced the Smiths from Vermont. Joseph, Sr., went ahead to Palmyra, New York; Lucy and the eight children arrived later—with "barely two cents in cash." In Palmyra she earned money painting oilcloth coverings for tables and stands.

1823   November 19: Alvin, the eldest son, died of a physician's overdose of calomel. Shortly thereafter the family lost their farm.

Convert:

1830   April 6: Lucy was baptized the day the Church was organized. One year later she led a company of eighty Saints down the Erie Canal to Kirtland, Ohio. After nearly seven years in Kirtland, the Smiths moved to Caldwell County, Missouri, then to Nauvoo, Illinois.

Nauvoo:

In Nauvoo her house was often filled with needy Saints. "Many of the sick owed the preservation of their lives to her motherly care, attention and skill in nursing them, which she did without pecuniary consideration and the extent of which can only be appreciated by those who are personally acquainted with the dreadful scenes of sickness and distress, in consequence of the Missouri expulsion."

Widow:

1840   September 14: Shortly before he died, Joseph, Sr., said, "Mother, do you not know, that you are one of the most singular women in the world...? You have brought up all my children, and could always comfort them when I could not. We have often wished that we might both die at the same time, but you must not desire to die when I do, for you must stay to comfort the children when I am gone. Do not mourn, but try to be comforted. Your last days shall be your best days." Within four years Lucy Smith also lost four sons—Don Carlos, Joseph, Hyrum, and Samuel.

After her husband died, Lucy moved into the Mansion House with Joseph and Emma. To provide income, a small museum was established under her care in a lower room. Josiah Quincy, one-time mayor of Boston, wrote of an 1844 tour of the mansion with Joseph Smith, who introduced Mother Smith: "This is my mother, gentlemen. The curiosities we shall see belong to her. They were purchased with her own money at the cost of six thousand dollars." After disclosing four mummies, Joseph closed the cabinet with, "Gentlemen, those who see these curiosities generally pay my mother a quarter of a dollar."

Lucy Mack Smith received her endowment in 1843, and participated in the Holy Order prayer circle in 1843-44. After the deaths of Joseph, Hyrum, and Samuel in 1844, she briefly urged that her last surviving son, William, be named Church president. But in October, 1845, she publicly endorsed Brigham Young, and participated in the opening of the Nauvoo Temple two months later.

Mother Smith did not go west, choosing instead to remain in Nauvoo with her family. She felt wronged by Church trustees-in-trust Almon W. Babbitt, Joseph L. Heywood, and John S. Fullmer, who refused her Church financial assistance because of her allegiance to her ex-apostle son, William: "You restrict my conscience," she wrote them, "put limits to my affections, threaten me with poverty, if I do not drive my children from my doors because they resent insultance and abuse that has been heaped upon them without measure."

1845   Lucy wrote *Biographical Sketches of Joseph Smith the Prophet, and his Progenitors for Many Generations*, with the assistance of Howard and Martha Coray. It was published in England by Orson Pratt in 1853 and came under immediate attack from the First Presidency, who declared it "utterly unreliable as a history, as it contains many falsehoods." They recommended that "every one in the Church, male and female, if they have such a book . . . dispose of it so that it will never be read by any person again."

In retrospect, the errors in the book seem less glaring than the criticism suggests. Mother Smith did, however, treat her excommunicated son William favorably. "He is my son," she told Church agents, "and he has rights. As to the Twelve you say they have rights, but who shall decide between them. Are you the judge?"

Death:

Lucy Smith lived in Nauvoo with daughter Lucy Milliken until the last two years of her life, when she moved into the Nauvoo home of daughter-in-law Emma Smith Bidamon.

1856   May 5: Died in Nauvoo at age seventy-nine. She remained active to the end, reading the smallest print without glasses. Buried near her husband behind the Smith family homestead in Nauvoo.

Reed Smoot

(1862-1941)

Apostle
United States Senator

Family Background:

1862   January 10: Born in Salt Lake City to Anna Kristina Morrison and Mayor Abraham Owen Smoot. In 1872 the Smoots moved to Provo.

1876   At fourteen, he was one of the original twenty-nine students to enroll in the Brigham Young Academy. During summer vacations, he worked in the Church-owned Provo Woolen Mills, which were superintended by his father. After graduation Reed worked in the Provo Cooperative Institution, the first Church co-op organized by Brigham Young. The seventeen-year-old boy started on the bottom rung of the ladder, sacking fruit, sorting potatoes, and doing odd jobs. Eighteen months later he became superintendent.

1884   Called by President John Taylor to superintend the Provo Woolen Mills.
    September 17: Married Alpha M. Eldredge, daughter of Horace S. Eldredge, a member of the First Council of Seventy. She died in 1928, and he married Alice Taylor Sheets in 1930. He was the father of six children.

Missionary:

Smoot's 1880 mission call was rescinded because of his responsibilities with the Provo Co-op. His 1884 call was rescinded when he became superintendent of Provo Woolen Mills.

1890   After five years as second counselor in Provo's Utah Stake, he was called on a mission to Liverpool, England, where he worked in the mission office under President Brigham Young, Jr. He returned to Provo in 1891 to resume management of the woolen mills when his father was taken seriously ill.

Businessman:

Smoot eventually managed Provo Lumber Manufacturing and Building, served as president of Provo Commercial and Savings Bank and vice-president of Grant Central Mining, and was a director of Los Angeles and Salt Lake Railroad.

Apostle:

1900   April 8: Called to the Quorum of the Twelve by Lorenzo Snow after the death of Franklin D. Richards.

United States Senator:

Smoot's first political appointment was as director of the Utah Territorial Insane Asylum in Provo (1884). After 1890 the First Presidency encouraged only Republican general authorities to seek political office. Democrats Moses Thatcher and B. H. Roberts were censored in 1896 for not clearing their political plans with Church leaders.

1901   November 8: The First Presidency and Quorum of the Twelve considered Republican Smoot's desire to run for the U. S. Senate. According to Anthon H. Lund, "Bro [Lorenzo] Snow said he hoped to live to see us send an apostle there." But advised by President McKinley, Mark Hannah, and Archbishop Ireland that "it would not be wise to let a Mormon go to the senate this year," the Twelve and First Presidency decided to postpone Smoot's bid.

1902   With the approval of the First Presidency and Twelve, Smoot announced his candidacy for the Senate. Immediately the Salt Lake Ministerial Association objected that an apostle in Congress would violate the principle of separation of church and state.

1903   Smoot was the choice of an overwhelming majority of voters, but by the time he reached Washington a national campaign had formed against him. The Senate Committee on Privileges spent more than thirty months investigating charges that he belonged to a "self-perpetuating fifteen-member ruling body that controlled Utah's elections and economy . . . [which was] secretly continuing to preach and permit plural marriages" and that he had taken "a secret pledge of disloyalty to the American government."

After obtaining nearly four thousand pages of testimony from witnesses including President Joseph F. Smith and several apostles, the committee recommended Smoot's expulsion. But the full Senate, influenced by President Roosevelt, refused the recommendation: Smoot retained his seat.

During his thirty years in the Senate, Smoot came to be recognized as "the most influential figure in Utah's political history." A hard-working conservative, with "little political glamour," he was "no orator. He shunned the peccadilloes of his fellows; he staged no rebellions; he coined no phrases, he offered no intriguing new ideas. He merely worked without stint or respite and continued to win elections."

1908 Smoot won a seat on the powerful Senate Finance Committee—the "watchdog of the Treasury"—serving as its chairman during the Depression.

1909 Prohibition was the burning issue in Utah. Heber J. Grant, George Albert Smith, and David O. McKay urged Utah communities to eliminate liquor. Smoot, who supported the local option, helped defeat statewide prohibition. As the only apostle opposing prohibition, he was strongly criticized by constituents.

Smoot complained that Heber J. Grant had publicly referred to him as "his royal nibs." The Senator vehemently declared that no man "ever saw me take a drink of liquor in a saloon or anywhere else," and offered to resign his apostleship. President Joseph F. Smith soothed Smoot's feelings, assuring him "that his personal course was understood and approved, but would not be publicly supported." President Smith advised Smoot to "be patient and understanding with his more rabid brethren."

1919 Despite the support of the First Presidency and nearly all of the Twelve for the League of Nations, Smoot remained loyal to the Republican opposition.

An unabashed partisan, Smoot declared, "I am for the Republican ticket wherever put up, whether in Provo, Salt Lake, Montana or anywhere. Whenever my advice is asked

I always advise Republicans to stand by their entire ticket."

He attained national prominence in 1930 by co-sponsoring the Smoot-Hawley Tariff, imposing record high duties on imported raw materials, including sugar. The Church was the largest stockholder in the Utah-Idaho Sugar Company, and many Utah farmers depended on the sugar beet crop.

Republican President Taft declared Smoot "the most valuable man in the U. S. Senate." Republican President Hoover said that Reed Smoot "had acquired a knowledge of the working of the United States government unparalleled by any other man in the country."

Utah Democratic party chief James H. Moyle said, "I would not praise him for what he has done. I have followed up the praise and all the publicity regarding him and find that it comes from the selfish interests. Mr. Smoot has worked and is working, and has been and is for, the wealthy interests."

1932 A Democratic landslide swept Smoot from office by a plurality of 30,843 votes. Deeply hurt, he wrote, "Everywhere I go people ask me, 'What is the matter of Utah?' They can't understand the election results and nearly all remark that Utah will never again hold the position in our country that she does at the present time."

Secular Saint:

Before he joined the Quorum of the Twelve, Reed Smoot was widely considered to be a lackluster Saint, whose call to a stake presidency was due more to his administrative ability than to his religious devotion. He was loyal to his Mormon heritage and accepted his apostolic calling with resignation, but seemed embarrassed by much in Mormonism. Defending his dual role as Senator and apostle, he startled many Mormons by testifying that he had always been a semi-active Latter-day Saint, that he did not care much for the temple endowment, and that he ignored First Presidency instructions on political matters.

Even after the Senate certified his election, Smoot remained aloof from Church activity, aside from brief vacations in Utah. As the presiding authority in Washington, D.C., Apostle Smoot attended only evening sacrament meetings, working and relaxing during the day. It was not until his political defeat in 1932 that he devoted his full energies to his apostleship.

Death:

1941   February 9: The seventy-nine-year-old "apostle of economy" died in St. Petersburg, Florida, and was buried in the Provo City Cemetery.

Eliza R. Snow

(1804-1887)

"Zion's Poetess"
Wife of Prophets
Second President of the Relief Society
"Prophetess, Presidentess, Priestess"

Family Background:

1804   January 21: Born Eliza Roxcy Snow in Becket, Massachusetts. The family later moved to Ohio. She was the older sister of future apostle Lorenzo Snow and a distant cousin of Erastus Snow.

Convert:

1828   Eliza joined the Campbellites after studying with Sidney Rigdon and Walter Scott in Ohio.

1835   The night after her baptism as a Latter-day Saint, "as I was reflecting on the wonderful events transpiring around me, I felt an indescribable, tangible sensation . . . commencing at my head and enveloping my person and passing off at my feet, producing inexpressible happiness. Immediately following, I saw a beautiful candle with an unusual long, bright blaze directly over my feet. I sought to know the interpretation, and received the following, 'The lamp of intelligence shall be lighted over your path.'"

Eliza Snow taught Joseph Smith's children and boarded with the family in Kirtland and Nauvoo.

"Prophetess":

1838   When the Snow family moved to Adam-Ondi-Ahman, Missouri, the thirty-one-year-old teacher became friends with Zina Diantha Huntington (later Young). The two exercised the gift of tongues jointly throughout their lives—one would speak in tongues, the other interpret.

From Missouri through Nauvoo, the trek west, and well into the Utah period, Eliza R. Snow met often with other Mormon women to speak in tongues, bless each other, sing, and prophesy.

Many of Eliza's prophecies did not come to pass. People she promised would see the redemption of Jackson County did not. People she prophesied would see the Savior's face in the Independence Temple died. But Heber J. Grant related that when he was a young boy, she and Zina D. H. Young testified he would become an apostle. Mary Ann Chadwick Hull was promised by Eliza that her unborn child would reach womanhood: the girl lived to the age of twenty.

Nauvoo Ladies Society:

1842   March: Eliza R. Snow drew up the constitution for a benevolent society of women which met at Sarah Kimball's home in Nauvoo. When they presented the plan to Joseph Smith, he told them that the Lord had something better for them under the organization of the priesthood. The Relief Society was formed the next week, and Eliza Snow was elected secretary.

Plural Wife to Prophets:

1842   June 29: Eliza R. Snow became a plural wife of Joseph Smith, whom she described as "the choice of my heart, the crown of my life." "The Prophet Joseph had taught me the principle of plural, or celestial marriage, and I was married to him for time and eternity. In consequence of the ignorance of most of the Saints, as well as the people of the world, on this subject, it was not mentioned only privately between the few whose minds were enlightened on the subject."

1844   After the Prophet's death, she became a plural wife of Brigham Young. Their relationship appears to have been platonic, she serving as a counselor, he as a provider. She always referred to him with nineteenth-century formality as "President Young"; he called her "Sister Snow."

    Brigham Young did not always heed Eliza's counsel. On one occasion he gave his older daughters colorful sashes. When Phoebe Young laid her sash out on the bed while dressing for a dance, the ribbon disappeared. Confronted by President Young, Eliza replied, "I felt that you wouldn't approve of anything so frivolous for your girls so I put it away."

    "Sister Eliza," said her husband, "I gave the girls those ribbons, and I am judge of what is right and wrong for my girls to wear. Phoebe is to have her sash."

"Priestess":

1845   Called as Nauvoo Temple recorder by Brigham Young. In Salt Lake she directed the women's section of the Endowment House on Temple Square.

Eliza R. Snow and other Mormon women often administered to sick women and children. Elmina A. Shepard Taylor recorded in her journal: "Being quite debilitated and sick from the effect of my heart, Sisters Eliza, Horne, Margaret Young, and B. Smith laid their hands on my head and Sister Snow blessed me and rebuked the disease and I was much improved from that very time."

Their authority was confirmed by President Joseph F. Smith in 1914: "Women may indeed administer with consecrated oil, confirming rather than sealing the blessing, making no mention of authority. They may also continue the practice of washing and anointing women who are about to give birth."

Relief Society "Presidentess":

1867   Called as the second president of the Church Relief Society. For the next twenty years she was, in effect, a counselor to Brigham Young on matters pertaining to women, often being introduced as "Presidentess."

1869   Established the "Young Ladies' Retrenchment Association" under Brigham Young's supervision.

1872   Founded the *Woman's Exponent* on suggestion of her niece, Louisa Greene.

1878   Organized the Primary Association at the suggestion of Aurelia Rogers.

1881   President of the board of directors of the Deseret Hospital Association.

Unlike many Mormon women of her time, Eliza R. Snow was not a feminist. Though she supported women's right to vote, she did not play an active role in the suffrage movement. She believed that God's order required "submission on the part of women."

Board of Directors of the Deseret Hospital.
Standing, L-R: Dr. Ellis R. Shipp, Bathsheba W. Smith, Elizabeth Howard, Dr. Romania Pratt Penrose. Center Row: Phebe Woodruff, Mary Isabella Horne, Eliza R. Snow, Zina D. H. Young, Marinda Hyde. Front Row: Jane Richards, Emmeline B. Wells.

She argued, "The Lord has placed the means in our hands, in the Gospel, whereby we can regain our lost position. But how? Can it be done by rising, as women are doing in the world, to clamor for our rights? No. . . . It was through disobedience that woman came into her present position, and it is only by honoring God in all the institutions he has revealed to us, that we can come out from under that curse, regain the position originally occupied by Eve, and attain to a fulness of exaltation in the presence of God."

"Zion's Poetess":

Eliza R. Snow wrote from a very early age. She published ten books, including two volumes of poetry which many modern literary critics consider "superficial, maudlin, trite, and unimaginative." To nineteenth-century Mormons, however, she was "Zion's Poetess," "Utah's First Lady of Letters," the respected author of such beloved Mormon hymns as "How Great the Wisdom and the Love," "Truth Reflects Upon Our Senses," "Behold the Great Redeemer Die," and "O, My Father," which she wrote in Nauvoo after Joseph Smith's death.

Death:

1887   December 5: Died at the Lion House in Salt Lake City; buried in Brigham Young's private cemetery one block east of the Lion House.

Shortly before her death, she penned her epitaph:
In friendship's mem'ry let me live:
I know no selfish wish beside—
I ask no more; yet, O forgive
This impulse of instinctive pride.
The silent pulse of memory
That beats to the unuttered tone
Of tenderness, is more to me
Than the insignia of a stone.

Erastus Snow

(1818-1888)

Apostle
Colonizer
"The Late Erastus Snow"

Family Background:

1818   November 9: Born Erastus Fairbanks Snow in Saint Johnsbury, Vermont. He was a distant cousin to Lorenzo and Eliza R. Snow. He was father-in-law to Apostles Anthony W. Ivins and Moses Thatcher, and to President Spencer W. Kimball's maternal grandfather, Bishop Edwin D. Woolley.

He married Artimesia Beaman (or Beman), sister of Joseph Smith's first plural wife, in 1837, and later married Minerva White (1844), Elizabeth Rebecca Ashby (1847), and Julia Josephine Spencer (1856). He fathered thirty-five children.

Missionary:

1832   Converted by Orson Pratt and Lyman Johnson, Erastus was baptized by his brother William. Two years later, at sixteen, Erastus and his uncle James Snow served a brief mission in Ohio.

1835   Ordained a seventy during the Kirtland School of Prophets, and endowed in the Kirtland Temple with 360 others: "Then we all, like as did Israel when they surrounded Jericho, with one united voice gave shout of Hosannah, Hosannah, Hosannah to God and the Lamb; Amen, Amen, Amen. When this was done the Holy Ghost was shed forth upon us; some received visions of the Judgments that were to be poured out upon this generation; some spoke in tongues, some interpreted; others prophesied; others saw Zion in her glory, and the angels came and worshipped with us, and some saw them, yea, even twelve legions of them, the chariots of Israel and the horsemen thereof."

Snow served missions in Pennsylvania (1836)—"I left Kirtland on foot and alone with a small valise containing a few Church works and a pair of socks, with five cents in my pocket"; Ohio (1837); Pennsylvania-Maryland (1836)—a crowd "combined against me to abuse me and after disturbing the meeting considerably, lay in wait for me as I was going home with one of the brethren about a quarter of a mile, and besmeared me with rotten eggs"; Pennsylvania, New Jersey, and Massachusetts (1841); and Denmark (1849), where he opened Scandanavia to missionary work.

Pioneer:

1847 A member of the Council of Fifty, Snow went to Utah with the pioneer company. En route, Brigham Young chided him for failing to prevent company cattle from mixing with a buffalo herd: "It is a regular built dressing which I got from him this morning.... In attempting to exonerate myself from blame, I drew from him a severer chastisement; it is the first I have had since I have been in this Church, which is nearly fifteen years, and I hope it may last me fifteen years to come."

 July 21: Erastus Snow and Orson Pratt became the first Mormons to enter the Salt Lake Valley. "We involuntarily, both at the same instant, uttered a shout of joy at finding it to be the very place of our Destination and the Broad Bosom of the Salt Lake spreading itself before us."

Apostle:

1849 February 12: Snow's ordination filled the Quorum of the Twelve for the first time since Joseph Smith's death. Heber J. Grant, who served in the Quorum with him, declared, "My ideal of an apostle was Erastus Snow. When I was called to be an apostle, I prayed that the same spirit of self-sacrifice might inspire me."

Utah's Iron Works:

1852 Returning from a mission to Denmark, Snow stopped in England to organize and raise capital for Utah's Deseret Iron Company. Plagued by poor coal, low grade iron ore, and the lack of railroad transportation, the southern Utah industry soon failed.

Saint Louis:

1854 Called to preside over the Saints in Saint Louis and to establish a Church periodical. In its November 22 prospectus the *Luminary* promised "Science, Religion, General Intelligence and news of the day.... To those who delight in the filth and slander of the age, whose natural cravings are only satisfied with those upheavings and excitements of society which terminate in blood, to all such appetites the Luminary will furnish no provender."

Having endured his long absences without complaint, Snow's first wife, Artimesia, wrote in 1855, "I . . . hope all will be well with you while absent from us, but I can hardly reconcile myself to the thought of your staying two years and a half. The time looks long very long. But if even this would suffice for a few years that you might be permitted to stay at home and take a little rest and enjoy each others society I would reconcile myself to that. But I have about made up my mind that nothing will suffice but go go til you get so old that you cannot go any longer.... As it seems to be my lot to almost always live alone I will try to be content therewith." Artimesia died while he was on an exploring mission to Arizona in 1882.

Cotton Mission:

1861 When the Civil War cut off the North's supply of cotton, Brigham Young called Erastus Snow and Orson Pratt to preside over a "Cotton Mission" in the Rio Virgin and Santa Clara Valleys of southern Utah. The two apostles did not work well together.

According to Orson Pratt, Jr., "My father had not been down here long, when he found that there was a secret influence working against him.... The person would not come out like a man against him, but would keep himself in the dark and work against him like a snake in the grass .... He would even meet my wife in the dark and try to make her divide against me, by saying to her that 'Your husband is not in the right way, he is in the dark.' ... I will tell you who it was. The individual is Erastus Snow."

Snow presided over the Dixie Mission until his death twenty-seven years later.

Mexico:

1882   John Taylor called Snow to locate sites on both sides of the Mexican border where colonies could be established to conceal Mormon polygamists on the underground. Three years later he helped purchase Mexican land on which the Mormon colonies were built.

"The Late Erastus Snow":

Despite his busy schedule, Snow never pleaded the "excuse that he must hurry or he would be late for meeting; he listened patiently, then made his comments . . . . All this made him late for most of his meetings, whether business, civic, or church, and so earned the sobriquet, 'the late Erastus Snow,' which he carried all his life."

This habit caused difficulties between him and the punctual Brigham Young. When a carriage accident delayed Snow's arrival at a meeting in Cedar City, "Brigham Young was much annoyed, no doubt charging his tardiness to failure to start soon enough on the journey. 'Erastus,' he said crossly, 'get up and preach the people to sleep.' Apostle John Henry Smith, who was there, stated that Apostle Snow arose and 'without reference to President Young's unkind remark or his trouble with the buggy, delivered one of the most wonderful sermons he had ever heard in his life.'"

Elder Snow bore President Young's tongue-lashings without complaint. But his son Edward H. Snow recalled that once in Saint George, his father checked his "rising resentment by walking the floor all night long, repeating to himself the scripture, 'Whom the Lord loveth He chasteneth.'"

Snow's absentmindedness was so thorough that "he often removed meat or bread from the plate of the person seated on either side of him at the table, entirely unconscious . . . that he wasn't helping himself from the main platter."

Death:

1888 May 27: Died at sixty-nine of Bright's disease (uremic poisoning) at his 217 Canyon Road home in Salt Lake City. Despite his desire to be buried in the red soil of Saint George, he was interred in the Salt Lake City Cemetery.

Lorenzo Snow

(1814-1901)

Witness of Christ
Fifth President of the Church

Family Background:

1814   April 3: Born in Mantua, Ohio, a younger brother to Eliza R. Snow, and a distant cousin to future apostle Erastus Snow.

At age 30, married Harriet Amelia Squires and Charlotte Squires on the same day in October, 1844. He also simultaneously married Hannah and Mary Ann Goddard in 1845. Later wives were Sarah Ann Prichard (1845), Eleanor Houtz (1848), Caroline Horton (1853), Mary Elizabeth Houtz (1857), Phoebe Amelia Woodruff (1859), and Sarah Minnie Jenson (1871). His wife Hannah left him shortly after their marriage in 1845, though she did not divorce him until 1852. He had forty-two children.

As a youth Lorenzo was often "hid up with his book." He was so fascinated by military tactics that his sister Eliza made him a military uniform: "My brother took as much pride [in it], if not of military pride, of self-satisfaction, as ever Napoleon."

Convert:

1831   At seventeen, Lorenzo heard Joseph Smith preach in Hiram, Ohio, and concluded that he "could hardly be a false prophet." His mother and sister Leonora were baptized, but Lorenzo had no interest in Mormonism until after his first term at Oberlin College (Snow was the first Church president to attend college), when his recently-baptized sister Eliza urged him to come to Kirtland and study Hebrew under Joshua Seixas. Her real motive was to bring Lorenzo into contact with the Prophet. The strategy worked; Lorenzo was baptized in June, 1836.

Missionary:

1837   Sent alone on a local mission to Ohio, the first night he knocked on eight doors before finding lodging.

When Lorenzo spoke at a public meeting three days later, a man in the audience advised, "Now Elder Snow, I am a much older man than you. You are a young man, just starting out, I see, to be a minister. I want to give you a little counsel. If you continue to talk as loud as you talked tonight, in six months you will be taken to the cemetery." He "baptized a few, very few."

He later served missions to Kentucky, Illinois, and Missouri (1838); to England, where he presented a Book of Mormon to Queen Victoria (1840); and to Italy, where he translated the Book of Mormon into Italian and opened missionary work in Switzerland (1849). In 1864 he accompanied Joseph F. Smith and Ezra T. Benson to the Sandwich Isles (Hawaii), where he nearly drowned in a boating mishap.

While in England he felt inspired to compose the famous couplet, "As man now is, God once was; as God now is, man may become." When he presented the idea to Joseph Smith in Nauvoo, the Prophet confirmed it as true.

Reformed Hunter:

1838   In Adam-Ondi-Ahman, Missouri, "I took my gun with the intention of indulging in a little amusement in hunting turkeys. . . . It never occurred to my mind that it was wrong—that indulging in 'what was sport to me was death to them'; that in shooting turkeys, squirrels, etc., I was taking life that I could not give; therefore I indulged in the murderous sport without the least compunction of conscience. . . .

"While moving slowly forward in pursuit of something to kill, my mind was arrested with the reflection on the nature of my pursuit—that of amusing myself by giving pain and death to harmless, innocent creatures that perhaps had as much right to life and enjoyment as myself. I realized that such indulgence was without any justification, and feeling condemned, I laid my gun on my shoulder, returned home, and from that time to this have felt no inclination for that murderous amusement."

Apostle:

1849   February 12: Called to the Quorum of the Twelve by Brigham Young, Heber C. Kimball, and Willard Richards.

Founder of the Polysophical Society:

1852   Lorenzo Snow organized the Polysophical Society at his Salt Lake home on 3rd East and South Temple: "Brother Lorenzo Snow has a select party which meets at his Hall once a week, to continue through the winter; social improvement and to cultivate a taste for literature and refinement the object. The Presidency and Twelve are honorary members, and seem to take pleasure in meeting with us. The New Alphabet [Deseret Alphabet] is there introduced under the supervision of Brother Watt, and diagrams designed to call forth the ability of Professor [Orson] Pratt."

Patron Saint of Brigham City:

1853   Called to relocate with fifty families to Brigham City, Utah. There he organized the Brigham City Mercantile and Manufacturing Association—perhaps the most successful United Order in the Church. The cooperative operated a woolen mill, a blacksmith shop, sawmills, and a tannery, manufacturing shoes, hats, cheese, wagons, and tin products. 1875 production was valued at $260,000.

First Presidency:

1873   April 8: Sustained as a counselor to Brigham Young in the First Presidency.

Prisoner:

1885   November 20: Returning from a mission among Indian tribes in the Northwest, Snow was arrested for unlawful cohabitation. After a trial and unsuccessful appeals, the seventy-two-year-old leader was taken to the Utah Territorial Penitentiary on March 12, 1886.

Two Ogden physicians successfully petitioned that "in consideration of the advanced age of the bearer, Lorenzo Snow, and also of his unusually delicate condition, we the undersigned, take the liberty of stating that we fear his health would be seriously jeopardized by depriving him of his hair and beard, as he has worn the latter 16 years on this account." He was released on February 8, 1887, having served nine months.

"The Dead Shall Rise at Thy Bidding":

1891 An 1838 patriarchal blessing pronounced by Joseph Smith, Sr., had promised, " Thou shalt have . . . power to rend the [veil] and see Jesus Christ. . . . The dead shall rise and come forth at thy bidding. . . . Thou shalt have long life . . . yet not be old; age shall not come upon thee."

According to Brigham City's young Ella Jensen, "On Sunday the first of March, 1891, I was taken severely ill with the scarlet fever, and suffered very much for a week. . . . I then bade my dear ones good-bye, and my spirit left my body. . . . I heard Apostle Lorenzo Snow administer to me, telling me that I must come back, as I had some work to do on the earth yet. I was loath to leave the heavenly place, but told my friends that I must leave them. . . . But for a long time afterwards I had a great desire to go back to the place of heavenly rest, where I dwelt so short a time."

Witness of Christ:

1898 September 2: Lorenzo Snow, who had been president of the Quorum of the Twelve for nine years and president of the Salt Lake Temple for five, was informed of the death of President Wilford Woodruff. He immediately went to the Salt Lake Temple, donned his robes, and began a long session of prayer in the Holy of Holies.

A granddaughter later related his account: "It was right here that the Lord Jesus Christ appeared to me at the time of the death of President Woodruff. He instructed me to go right ahead and reorganize the First Presidency of the Church at once and not wait as had been done after the death of the previous presidents, and that I was to succeed President Woodruff. . . . He stood right here, about three feet above the floor. It looked as though he stood on a plate of solid gold. . . . I want you to remember that this is the testimony of your grandfather, that he told you with his own lips that he actually saw the Savior, here in the temple, and talked with him face to face."

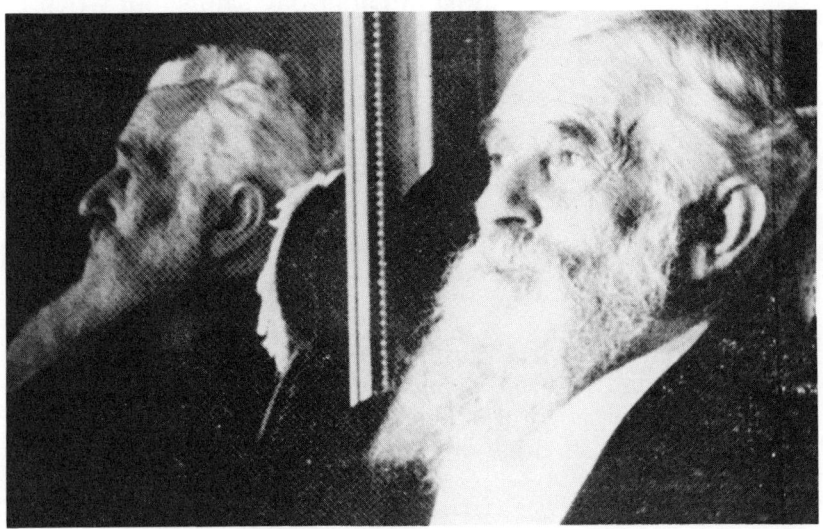

Fifth President of the Church:

1898 At the age of eighty four, Lorenzo Snow became the fifth president of the Church, with George Q. Cannon and Joseph F. Smith as counselors.

President Snow's administration broadened the work of the general authorities. He felt that the brethren were spending too much time on local matters, and advised them "by the appointment of the Almighty... to look after the interests of the world."

President Snow is perhaps best known for his success in relieving the Church's heavy indebtedness. His 1899 retrenchment stopped borrowing for investments, consolidated debts in a million-dollar bond issue, sold controlling interest in many operations, and launched a major reemphasis on tithing. Though he did not live to see the Church debt-free, he was responsible for the financial undertakings which ultimately restored Church solvency.

A South Carolina visitor, Reverend Prentis, described President Snow in 1898: "I had expected to find intellect, intellectuality, benevolence, dignity, composure and strength depicted upon the face of the President of the Church of Jesus Christ of Latter-day Saints; but when I was introduced to President Lorenzo Snow for a second I was startled to see the holiest face but one I had ever been privileged to look upon. His face was a poem of peace, his presence a benediction of peace. In the tranquil depths of his eyes were the 'home of silent prayer' and the abode of spiritual strength."

Death:

1901   October 10: Last Church president to know Joseph Smith personally, Lorenzo Snow died of pneumonia at age eighty-seven in the Beehive House in Salt Lake City. Buried in the Brigham City Cemetery.

Fanny Stenhouse

(1829-1904)

Expose' Writer

Family Background:

1829   Born Fanny Warn in Saint Heliers, Jersey—an island in the English Channel. In 1843 she joined the Baptist church, and became the governess of a British family in France. She taught English and embroidery in a Saint Brieux school until forced to resign because she refused to convert to Catholicism.

   She married T. B. H. Stenhouse February 6, 1850; they had ten children.

Convert:

1849   At nineteen, Fanny returned to England and found that her family had joined the Mormon church. Two weeks later she was converted by her future husband, T. B. H. Stenhouse.

1850   Soon after their marriage, Elder Stenhouse was called as the first English missionary to Italy, with Lorenzo Snow as his companion. Three years later, Fanny finally rejoined her husband in Switzerland. His request for a release from his mission was granted in 1854.

1855   Arriving in New York on New Year's Eve, T. B. H. Stenhouse found work in the offices of *The Mormon*; he later joined the staff of the *New York Herald*. The Stenhouses lived in New York for two years before emigrating to Salt Lake by handcart.

1860   In Salt Lake City Fanny Stenhouse acted in occasional theater productions and established herself as "Milliner, Dress and Cloak Maker, First House West of the Tabernacle."

Opponent of Plural Marriage:

1862   T. B. H. asked, "Are you not satisfied that it is right for me to take another wife?" Fanny replied, "I have never yet really doubted that the revelation was from God for I cannot believe that any man would be so blasphemous and wicked as to set forth such a revelation in God's name, unless he received it as he said he did. If it is from God, of course you are right to obey it; but if I were to consult my own feelings I would never consent to live in Polygamy. I would rather risk salvation."

T. B. H. married Belinda Pratt, daughter of Parley P. Pratt, and was sealed the same day to Fanny's deceased friend, Carrie Grant, daughter of Salt Lake City Mayor Jedediah M. Grant and sister of Heber J. Grant.

"Had I been able to consider the whole affair as an outrage upon humanity in general, and an insult to my sex in particular, I should have replied with scorn and defiance," Fanny later wrote. "Had I implicitly believed in the divinity of the Revelation, I should have bowed my head in meek submission. But I did neither of these. The feelings of my heart naturally led me to hate with a most perfect hatred the very mention of the word Polygamy, while at the same time I still believed, or tried to make myself believe, that the Revelation was from God, and must therefore be obeyed."

Fanny never felt the same about the Church again: "To doubt one doctrine was to doubt all, and I soon felt that my religion was rapidly crumbling away before my eyes, and that I was losing confidence in everything and everybody. I was like a ship at sea without a compass, not knowing where to go or what to do."

"Heretic":

1868 T. B. H. Stenhouse, considered the "founder of Utah journalism," moved his *Salt Lake Telegraph* to Ogden on advice of Brigham Young. When the paper failed, so did Stenhouse's faith: "I gave evidence of my obedience, and it brought ruin, as I expected. Henceforth I will follow the best experience of my life."

A year later, he was disfellowshipped for "failure to attend the School of Prophets." Commenting on Brigham Young's role in the proceeding, T. B. H. mused, "What will he not do next? To submit would be to acknowledge him absolute, and myself a slave. There is but one alternative now—slavery or freedom. Cost me what it may, I will be free."

Stenhouse wrote his bishop that he had "no faith in Brigham's claim to an Infallible Priesthood, and that he considered that he ought to be cut off from the Church." Fanny added a postscript: "I wish to share my husband's fate." T. B. H. was excommunicated shortly after divorcing his plural wife Belinda November 25, 1869. Church action against Fanny was not taken until October 5, 1874, two years after she wrote her first expose' of Mormonism.

The Stenhouses, resolving to "walk into the jaws of death," joined William S. Godbe's "New Movement." She wrote, "Little did I imagine at that period... that I should ever have the boldness, either with tongue or pen, to plead the cause of the Women of Utah. But, impelled by those unseen influences which shape our destinies, I took my stand with the 'heretics'; and, as it happened, my own was the first woman's name enrolled in their cause."

Expose' Writer:

1872   Fanny Stenhouse published *A Lady's Life Among the Mormons—A Record of Personal Experience as One of the Wives of a Mormon Elder*. She followed this up in 1874 with *"Tell It All": The Story of a Life's Experience in Mormonism*. The first expose' was popular, but never matched the popularity of *"Tell It All,"* which included an introductory preface by Harriet Beecher Stowe.

Death:

Assaulted one evening in Salt Lake City by a group of unknown men, the Stenhouses moved to San Francisco, where T. B. H. served as West Coast correspondent for the *New York Herald*. He died of jaundice in 1882 at the age of fifty-eight, and was buried in San Francisco.

Fanny Stenhouse eventually moved near her children in Los Angeles. She was blinded in an accident ten years before her death in 1904. Buried in Los Angeles.

James E. Talmage

(1862-1933)

University President
Scientist
Apostle

Family Background:

1862   September 22: Born James Edward Talmage in Hungerford, England. Talmage was baptized in England in 1873 and emigrated with his family to Provo, Utah, in 1876.

Scholar:

An Oxford Diocesan Scholar at the age of twelve, Talmage entered Brigham Young Academy in 1876 as a student of Karl G. Maeser. In 1879 he completed high school and became a teacher of elementary science and English at the academy. In the 1880s he attended LeHigh University and Johns Hopkins University. An avid scientific researcher, he conducted personal experiments to supplement theoretical investigation; in 1884 he even used hashish for two weeks to study the effects of narcotics.

1884   Named professor of geology and chemistry at Brigham Young Academy and later elected to the board of trustees. During four years in Provo, Talmage became a U. S. citizen, Provo city councilman, alderman, and justice of the peace.

1888   Married Merry May Booth in Salt Lake City. He called her "Maia," after the Roman goddess of the spring. They had eight children.

University President:

1888   Called at twenty-six to be president of Latter-day Saints College in Salt Lake City. In 1894 he was named president of the University of Utah and joined the faculty as a professor of geology.

1896   Awarded a Ph.D. by Illinois Wesleyan University for nonresident work.
        March 12: Working feverishly on the *Articles of Faith*, in addition to his duties as university president, Talmage

undermined his health. The First Presidency "learned that my health has been jeopardized," he wrote in his journal, "and, as they said, my sanity, and life threatened by insomnia and other evidences of nervous disorders.... Pres. Woodruff, Pres. Geo. Q. Cannon, and Pres. Jos. F. Smith gave me combined counsel to try the effect of moderate smoking: indeed said Pres. Cannon, 'We give you this rather as an instruction than as counsel. . . .'"

Despite his lack of experience with tobacco and his successful determination to prevent therapy from becoming habit, Talmage found that "a good cigar produced a marvelous quieting of my over-wrought nerves."

1897 Resigned as president of the University of Utah, though continuing as professor of geology. Ten years later he resigned as chairman of the geology department to be a full-time mining consultant.

Talmage was a Fellow of the Royal Microscopical Society, and a member of the Royal Scottish Geographical Society, Geological Society, Geological Society of America, Royal Society of Edinburgh, and American Association for Advancement of Science.

Apostle:

1911 December 8: Ordained an apostle after the death of Charles Penrose.

1924 Called as president of the European Mission for four years.

Author:

During the 1920s and early 1930s organic evolution was widely publicized in the United States. The Church took no specific stand on the theory, except to reaffirm that "man was created by God, that Adam was the parent of the human race, and that the destiny of man would be worked out according to the plan of God, which included the reality of the atonement of the Savior." Talmage went a step further in a 1930 radio address, "The Earth and Man," reconciling propositions of science and religion.

A prolific writer, Talmage produced such scientific works as *First Book of Nature* (1888), *Domestic Science* (1891), and *The Great Salt Lake, Present and Past* (1900). His theological works include *The Articles of Faith* (1899), *The Great Apostasy* (1909), *The House of the Lord* (1912), and *Jesus the Christ* (1915).

Workaholic:

Talmage was thoroughly converted to the Mormon work ethic. "In his later years he had no interests in the conventional sense, no sports or games or hobbies that were not closely associated with his work. His work was *his* recreation."

Family, friends, and associates were concerned about his long working hours. President Grant, an avid golfer, urged Talmage to take up the sport, and after much persuasion, reached a compromise: Talmage would give the game an honest trial. His lessons would continue until he was able to hit a shot which President Grant rated as satisfactory, "a real golf shot." Then President Grant would allow him to make his own decision about further play.

After a brief lesson on addressing the ball, Talmage teed up. Instead of missing or slicing the ball into the rough, he hit a clean, two-hundred-yard drive. When President Grant congratulated him on a "real golf shot," Talmage responded, "If I have carried out my part of the agreement, then I shall call on you to live up to yours.... I should like to get back to the office, where I have a great deal of work waiting."

Death:

1933 July 27: Died at seventy-one of a throat infection complicated by overwork into acute myocarditis. He had stayed in his office at 47 East South Temple overnight July 23, suffering from a slightly irritated throat which was not relieved by his favorite drink, root beer. He remained in his office on the 24th, but on the 25th was so ill he required help getting home.

His gravestone at the Salt Lake City Cemetery is an unusual geological phenomenon, a "xenolith" (rock within a rock)—dark limestone engulfed in granite.

His epitaph expresses the breadth of his scholarly and religious perspective: "Within the Gospel of Jesus Christ There Is Room and Place for Every Truth Thus Far Learned by Man or Yet to be Made Known."

Annie Clark Tanner

(1864-1942)

Plural Wife
"Mormon Mother"
Author

Family Background:

1864   September 24: Born in Farmington, Utah. Baptized in 1873, Annie Clark was rebaptized a year later during a reformation movement. She remembered, "We raised our right hand and promised not to trade with outsiders. Also, as children, we promised never to touch tea, coffee, or tobacco. To take the Lord's name in vain was a great offense. The punishment for disregard of high moral standards among young people was severe indeed. The young people who transgressed were required to make an acknowledgement of their sin in a public meeting and ask the forgiveness of the Saints."

Plural Wife:

1880   At sixteen, Annie attended the University of Utah and served as a counselor to Farmington Primary President Aurelia Rogers. From 1882 to 1883 she attended the Brigham Young Academy, where Karl G. Maeser acclaimed her as the most brillant student in her class.

    Professor Joseph M. Tanner made a strong impression on Annie's classmate, Alice Louise Reynolds: "Had I not seen a guide in Rome in 1906," she said, "I should be tempted to say he was the most handsome man I have ever seen."

    On his first visit to Annie Clark's home, the circumspect Tanner brought along his first wife, Jennie. After returning from a buggy ride in the country the next day, "Mrs. Tanner, having observed that I had been comparatively indifferent to her husband, brought up the subject of polygamy. I told her that without her approval, our affair was at an end.

    "'Why,' she answered, 'don't you love him?' 'Independent of that,' I replied, 'without your approval, our interest in each other will go no farther.' She then related her father and mother's miserable experience in the principle, and excused herself for the aversion she felt for it, but concluded, 'I have no children although I have been married five years. I can't deprive Marion of a family, and of all the girls I know, you are my choice.'" Annie became his plural wife in 1883. He became president of Utah State University and superintendent of Church schools.

Anti-polygamy pressures demanded that Annie's marriage be kept secret. Her wedding night was spent in her parents' home: "As I sat down to a glass of bread and milk the thought came to me, 'Well, this is my wedding supper.' In those few minutes I recalled the elaborate marriage festivals which had taken place in our own family, of the banquets I had helped to prepare and the many lovely brides among my friends. I even began to compare their wedding gowns."

Six months later, Tanner married a third wife. "I had not seen the third wife, but I did wonder wherein I lacked that so soon he should take another wife. Then I remembered the doctrine of the Trinity as taught by the Church—that if one wanted to attain the very pinnacle of glory in the next world there must be, at least, three wives."

When Tanner was called on a mission to Europe, "Annie Clark" supported him and herself as a school teacher. In 1888, pregnant with the first of her ten children, she went underground until the baby was born.

Throughout her marriage, Annie Clark Tanner, like many plural wives, was essentially a hard-working widow: "I had the attitude of many Mormon women in polygamy. I felt the responsibility of my family, and I developed an independence that women in monogamy never know. A woman in polygamy is compelled by her lone position to make a confidant of her children. How much more is this true when that woman is left entirely alone."

Modernist:

1910 Annie Clark Tanner rented out her Farmington home and moved to Provo so her children could obtain better educations. She took a Bible class from BYA professor Joseph Peterson, a popular instructor later dismissed for teaching evolution and "higher criticism." "I had been a teacher of the Bible in several of the organizations of the Church and now for the first time in my life I was learning some truths which made reasonable explanation of Bible difficulties," she wrote. "I fully believed that the men who had done research on the old Hebrew records were just as honest as any scientist. Why should we turn down their findings?"

Her son Obert observed that in Provo "the basis of her authority for truth gradually shifted from the authority of sacred scriptures to the authority of scholars and universities. She continued to love the scriptures, but on a selective basis. One scripture story or doctrine, one after another, became of doubtful value to her, if not simply incredible. She ultimately cast her lot, not mainly with scriptures, but gradually and more finally with scholars and their books . . . from the warm and trusting security of a religious foundation, she gleaned whatever solace she could find in the scientific approach of the less certain, the less positive, the more tentative."

Ex-wife:

Returning to Farmington, she continued to rent out part of her home to make ends meet. Though Wilford Woodruff had announced discontinuance of plural marriage on her twenty-sixth birthday, Marion and Annie Tanner continued to live together after the Manifesto. She bore eight children after 1890, and he entered into three plural marriages.

On a Sunday morning in 1913, J. M. Tanner made one of his infrequent trips home, a visit Annie never forgot. He informed her "that he would not come to Farmington to see us any more. There had been no previous differences between us except the children's education to which no reference had recently been made, so the statement was a great shock to me at the time.

"Inwardly, I felt impelled to persuade him otherwise, and I was sure he had expected me to. I nevertheless controlled myself and made no response to his far-reaching decision. My silence at the moment was not an easy thing. Yet, I am aware now that the years of preceding struggle to live polygamy had all helped to steel me for whatever may come. I thought in those few moments before he departed: 'I'll be equal to whatever must come.'" Thus ended the thirty-year marriage. Annie was forced to find work as a practical nurse in Salt Lake City.

After thirty years as a plural wife, Annie Clark Tanner concluded the "companionship between husband and wife in polygamy could not be so close as in monogamy. There was more independence on both sides in polygamy. . . . It is needless to observe that monogamous marriages are by far the more successful. They give security and confidence, and these are the requirements for happiness."

Author:

Annie Clark Tanner wrote *A Biography of Ezra T. Clark*, her father, in 1934, and in 1941, the last year of her life, her autobiography, *A Mormon Mother*.

Death:

1942   Died at the age of seventy-eight in Farmington, Utah, the hometown she always hated to leave. Her gravestone in the Farmington Cemetery has no epitaph, but words from her autobiography are appropriate: "It is but a small part that the average person contributes to improve mankind. My life has been simple, full of love, devotion, and service for my family. I might have thought mine a hard row to hoe had not the plants I cultivated responded so magnificently to the culture I gave them."

John Taylor

(1808-1887)

Father of Utah Sugar Industry
Third President of the Church
"King, Priest, and Ruler Over Israel on Earth"

Family Background:

1808   November 1: Born in Milnthorpe, England, he married Leonora Cannon in 1833. When Joseph Smith explained plural marriage to him in 1843, Taylor wrote, "I had always entertained strict ideas of virtue. . . . Nothing but a knowledge of God, and the revelations of God, and the truth of them, could have induced me to embrace such a principle as this."

He embraced the principle thoroughly, marrying fifteen plural wives—Elizabeth Kaighin (1843), Jane Ballantyne (1844), Mary Ann Oakley (1846), Mary Amanda Utley (1846), Ann Hughlings Pitchforth (1846), Ann Ballantyne (1846), Mary Ramsbottom (1846), Lydia Dibble Smith (1846), Sarah Thorton Coleman (1846), Mercy Thompson Smith (1846), Sophia Whittaker (1847), Harriet Whittaker (1847), Caroline Hooper Saunders Gillian (1847), Margaret Young (1847), and Josephine Elizabeth Rouche (1886). Three of his wives later divorced him: Mercy R. Thompson Smith (1847), Sarah Thornton Coleman (1852), and Ann Ballantyne (1854).

He was the father of thirty-five children, including John W. Taylor and an adopted son (his wife's nephew), George Q. Cannon, who became apostles. Another son, William W., became a president of the Council of the Seventy, and President Joseph F. Smith was the nephew of his wife Mercy Thompson Smith.

Convert:

Two years after the Taylors immigrated to Canada from England, John became active in the Methodist church. Convinced that no denomination they knew followed the New Testament pattern, the Taylors and their friends prayed for someone to bring them the true church.

1836   Converted and baptized by Parley P. Pratt.

Taylor once said, "If it were not for the religion I profess, which gives me to know something about the matter, by revelation for myself, I would not have anything to do with religion at all. . . . I never would submit to be gulled with the nonsense that exists in the world, under the name of religion."

After serving as the Church's presiding officer in Canada for a year, Taylor moved to Kirtland, Ohio, then to Far West, Missouri.

Apostle:

1838   December 19: Ordained an apostle at Far West by Brigham Young and Heber C. Kimball, following the excommunication of John F. Boynton. Joseph Smith was in Liberty Jail.

1839   Taylor went with other members of the Twelve to Great Britain, where he opened Ireland and the Isle of Man to missionary work. He later served missions to Great Britain (1846-1847) and France (1850-1852). In France he wrote several pamphlets, including *Government of God.*

Editor:

In Nauvoo, Taylor received his second anointings, became a member of the Council of Fifty (1844), served on the city council (1841-1844) and the board of regents for the university, and was judge advocate of the Nauvoo legion.

He edited the last three volumes of the *Times and Seasons* and published the *Nauvoo Neighbor.* In recognition of his polished editorials, W. W. Phelps, Nauvoo's toastmaster supreme, dubbed Taylor "Champion of Right."

Taylor established the first Church periodicals in France and Germany (1851) and published the *Mormon,* a New York City newspaper (1852).

Martyrdom Witness:

1844   June 27: Jailed with Joseph Smith, Hyrum Smith, and Willard Richards in Carthage, Illinois. To cheer up the group, Taylor sang "A Poor Wayfaring Man of Grief." He suggested escape to the Prophet: "If you permit it, and say the word, I will have you out of this prison in five hours, if the jail has to come down to do it." The offer was refused.

Asked to sing the song again, Taylor said he did not feel like singing. Hyrum entreated, "Oh, never mind; commence singing and you will get the spirit of it." Shortly after Taylor completed the song again, an armed mob overwhelmed the guard and rushed up the stairs to the prisoner's room while gunmen outside fired into the building:

"After parrying the guns for some time, which now protruded thicker and farther into the room, and seeing no hope of escape or protection there, as we were now unarmed, it occurred to me that we might have some friends outside, and that there might be some chance of escape in that direction but here there seemed to be none. As I expected them every moment to rush into the room—nothing but extreme cowardice having thus far kept them out—as the tumult and pressure increased, without any other hope, I made a spring for the window, which was right in front of the jail door where the mob was standing, and also exposed to the fire of the Carthage Greys. . . .

"I was struck by a ball from the door about midway of my thigh, which struck the bone, and flattened out almost the size of a quarter of a dollar, and then passed on through the fleshy part to within about half an inch of the outside. I think some prominent nerve must have been severed or injured for as soon as the ball struck me, I fell like a bird when shot, or an ox when struck by a butcher, and lost entirely and instantaneously all power of action or locomotion. I fell upon the window-sill, and cried out, 'I am shot!'

"Not possessing any power to move, I felt myself falling outside of the window, but immediately I fell inside, from some, at that time, unknown cause. When I struck the floor my animation seemed restored, as I have seen it sometimes in squirrels and birds after being shot. As soon as I felt the power of motion I crawled under the bed, which was in a corner of the room, not far from the window where I received my wound.

"While on my way and under the bed I was wounded in three other places; one ball entered a little below the left knee, and never was extracted; another entered the forepart of my left arm, a little above the wrist, and, passing down by the joint, lodged in the fleshy part of my hand, about midway, a little above the upper joint of my little finger; and another struck me on the fleshy part of my left hip, and tore away the flesh as large as my hand, dashing the mangled fragments of flesh and blood against the wall."

When he reached Nauvoo, Taylor and his family were "not a little startled to find that my watch had been struck with a ball. I sent for my vest, and, upon examination, it was found that there was a cut as if with a knife, in the vest pocket which had contained my watch. In the pocket the fragments of the glass were found literally ground to powder. It then occurred to me that a ball had struck me at the time I felt myself falling out of the window, and that it was this force that threw me inside."

Father of Utah Sugar Industry:

1847   Mechanically gifted, Taylor built one of the first sawmills in Utah.

1849   On a mission to examine French methods of producing sugar from sugar beets, he purchased a French sugar factory for the Church and brought it across the plains in forty-four wagons. The factory was set up at the present site of Sugarhouse Park in Salt Lake Valley without any written instructions for assembling the complicated mechanism.

    The venture proved a failure. Instead of sugar, the process produced a thick brown syrup which even cattle would not eat. The Church lost more than $50,000 on the experiment. Brigham Young blamed Taylor for mismanagement and refused to compensate his personal losses. When Taylor became president thirty years later, he was compensated by the Quorum of the Twelve.

Civil Servant:

Taylor served as associate judge in the provisional State of Deseret (1849-50), territorial legislator (1853-54, 1857-79),

Third President of the Church:

1875   Brigham Young made John Taylor president of the Quorum of the Twelve by rearranging seniority.

1877   On Brigham Young's death, Taylor led the Church as president of the Quorum of the Twelve.

1878   Organized the Primary Association.

1880   October 10: Sustained as president of the Church, with George Q. Cannon and Joseph F. Smith as counselors.

1882   Wrote *Mediation and Atonement of Our Lord and Savior Jesus Christ*.

"King, Priest, and Ruler Over Israel on Earth":

During the Taylor administration, Congress passed a series of laws intended to disfranchise, fine, and imprison Mormon polygamists. Despite the Supreme Court's 1879 decision upholding anti-polygamy laws, President Taylor received a revelation in 1882 indicating "all officers in the Priesthood must enter into plural marriage." In 1884 he reported another revelation urging "monogamists to resign ecclesiastical offices in the church."

During an 1885 visit to California he received word that federal officials had ordered his arrest, but returned to Salt Lake City January 27, 1885. February 1 he preached his last public sermon, explaining that he would submit to arrest "if the law would only be a little more dignified." That night he disappeared from public view and went into hiding on the "Mormon underground."

1885   February 4: In a secret meeting of two members of the First Presidency, seven apostles, and two clerks at the Salt Lake City Endowment House, "President Taylor . . . directed Br Nuttall to read a Revelation which he said he received more than a year ago requiring him to be anointed & set apart as King Priest and Ruler over Israel on the Earth—over Zion & the Kingdom of Christ our King of Kings." Notices of the ceremony appeared in the *Salt Lake Tribune* three months later. But the coronation had little practical effect on Utah politics—the Council of Fifty had ceased to meet, and within six years Mormons would be encouraged to divide along national party lines.

The federal anti-polygamy crusade severely disrupted Church activities. First Presidency guidance at general conferences came in the form of letters signed by President Taylor and his first counselor, George Q. Cannon. Joseph F. Smith, second counselor, had escaped into exile in Hawaii.

President Taylor moved constantly to avoid arrest. According to his son, Apostle John W. Taylor, President

Taylor received an 1886 revelation which declared "the Law of Plural Marriage was Eternal." By 1887 nearly every settlement in Utah had been raided by federal marshals, hundreds of Saints had escaped to Mexico or Canada, and almost all of the Church leaders were in hiding.

Shortly before President Taylor's death in July, the First Presidency, hoping that plural marriage could survive under state-enforced laws, agreed to a compromise whereby Utah would adopt an anti-polygamy constitution in return for statehood. But the plan failed when the Scott Amendment was defeated in Congress.

Death:

1887 July 25: Died of congestive heart failure in Kaysville, Utah, while on the underground to preserve his religious principles. "I do not believe in a religion that cannot have all my affections, but in a religion for which I can both live and die," he had said. Buried in the Salt Lake City Cemetery.

John W. Taylor

(1858-1916)

Apostle
"Prophet of the Quorum"
Champion of Plural Marriage

Family Background:

1858   May 15: Born John Whittaker Taylor in Provo, Utah, to John Taylor and Sophia Whittaker, whom his father married on a carriage ride in Salt Lake City's Liberty Park.

1883   Married May Leona Rich. He later married plural wives Nellie Eva Todd (known to the family as his "Canadian wife"), and—after the Wilford Woodruff Manifesto—Janetta Maria Woolley (1890), Eliza Roxey Welling (1901), and Rhoda Welling (1901)—(his "Mexican wives"), and Ellen Georgena Sandburg (1909). He was the father of thirty-five children.

Vision:

Abraham Cannon reported that Taylor, as a young man working in a Summit County sawmill, saw a bright light which "continued to increase in intensity and with the increase he seemed to be pushed further away from its source. Finally he clasped his arms around the stump of a tree for the purpose of keeping himself in position. He saw the Son of God appear in the brilliancy of the light and then his hold upon the stump began to slip and he knew that should he release his grasp he would be thrust back with such violence that he would be dashed to pieces.

"His father told him that the interpretation of the dream was that the bright light was the truth which would banish all truthhaters from before it, and the tree stump to which he was holding was a similar representation to that of the rod of iron in the Book of Mormon."

"Prophet of the Quorum":

1884   Called to the Quorum of the Twelve by his father, John Taylor. John W. so frequently pronounced public and private prophecies that during the next two decades he was referred to as "the prophet of the Quorum."

Business Speculator:

1894　After "laboring for nearly six months almost entirely in his own interests," Taylor was charged by President Lorenzo Snow to attend "more faithfully to his ecclesiastical duties, and less to his personal affairs." John W.'s business speculations brought financial ruin to several friends, including J. Golden Kimball. By 1902 Taylor's business prospects were so abysmal that the Twelve appointed Reed Smoot to persuade creditors to settle $140,000 of Taylor's debts at ten cents on the dollar. A decade later, Taylor's Mormon friends in Canada endured similar losses as his speculative schemes again collapsed.

Champion of Plural Marriage:

1892　Two years after the Church sustained the Wilford Woodruff Manifesto, Taylor said, "I do not know that that thing was right though I voted to sustain it, and will assist to maintain it; but among my father's papers I found a revelation given him of the Lord, and which is now in my possession, in which the Lord told him that the principle of plural marriage would never be overcome. President Taylor desired to have it suspended, but the Lord would not permit it."

1905　John W. Taylor and Matthias Cowley, with tacit approval of members of the First Presidency, had entered plural marriages after the Manifesto and had performed such marriages in the United States, Canada, and Mexico.
　　Apostle Reed Smoot, committed by his election to the U. S. Senate to vote against known offenders of the Manifesto, withheld his sustaining vote for the Quorum of the Twelve Apostles in the 1905 October Conference. Taylor, asked about the possibility of resigning his apostleship, replied, "I told you brethren that while I didn't support you in the policy of deposing the apostles to make a showing in Congress and said I would not approve of the policy of the Church in this regard, I would not oppose it." Both Taylor and Cowley resigned their apostleships, but their resignations were not announced for several months.

Excommunication:

1911   Charged with entering into plural marriages after the 1904 "Second Manifesto," and of aiding others to do likewise, Taylor told the Twelve, "I have never married any one without the endorsement and authority of the President of the Church, and if you desire I will give the names of those I have married, but I think this would be unwise."

"I have no aspirations in an ecclesiastical way," he added. "I have a large family of children, my wives to take care of and my business needs my attention. I don't say these things out of disrespect, but I would like you to do as you think best, not because of lack of testimony, but feel free in regard to my case. . . .

"I am a different man to what I have been. I am not a man of spiritual temperament as I was at one time. . . . In my parting with you, I desire to go with a spirit of kindness and with the best purposes. I feel freerer [sic] today than I have felt for the past four or five weeks."

1911   March 28: Excommunicated by the Quorum of the Twelve for "insubordination."

Death:

1916   October 10: Died of cancer at the age of fifty-eight in Salt Lake City.

Prior to his death, he had told his wives, "No tears . . . I will be waiting for you over there. I must go now to prepare a place. And when I leave I want no mourning, I want no flowers, no public display. No funeral. I am a nomad. Let the ashes of this wandering body blow with the winds from some mountain peak."

Speculation as to whether the ex-apostle would be buried in his temple clothes caused curious onlookers to attempt to view the body. Family security prevented this. His wife Nettie related that on the night of Taylor's death, President Joseph F. Smith, regretting his role in Taylor and Cowley's dismissal, called privately at her home and gave her a package containing temple robes. He was buried in the Salt Lake City Cemetery.

Blessings Restored:

1965   May 21: Reinstated as a Church member in full standing by authorization of President David O. McKay.

Moses Thatcher

(1842-1909)

Businessman
Apostle
Political Dissident

Family Background:

1842   February 2: Born in Sangamon County, Illinois. His family migrated to the Salt Lake Valley in 1847. Two years later, touched with the gold fever, they moved to Sacramento, California, where his father operated an "eating house."

Moses earned his keep by watering miners' horses for as much as five dollars a drink. He also mined, extracting moss and gold from the crevices of rocks on the banks of the American River with a butcher knife and a milk pan.

Missionaries frequently visited the Thatcher home, and fourteen-year-old Moses was baptized in the Rio Puta in 1856. Three months later he was ordained an elder. In 1858 Moses and his brothers moved to Salt Lake City, where he joined the police force. In 1860 the Thatcher family moved to Cache Valley, Utah, where Moses married Lettie Farr in 1861. He later married Lydia Ann Clayton (1868) and Georgie Snow, daughter of Erastus Snow (1885).

Businessman:

1870   Appointed superintendent of Cache Valley schools, as well as director and secretary of the Utah Northern Railroad, a company which he eventually managed. As his wealth increased, Thatcher became a vice-president and director of ZCMI and Deseret National Bank, and president of Thatcher Brothers' Banking Company. He was well respected in Cache and Rich counties, serving as territorial legislator for ten years.

Apostle:

1879   April 9: After two years as a stake president in Logan, Utah, Thatcher was ordained an apostle and, six months later, called on a mission to Mexico.

1880   February: He returned to Salt Lake City with a proposal to colonize Utah Saints in Mexico, but the Twelve decided against the measure and Thatcher returned to Mexico City in December.

1881   April: Dedicated Mexico for the preaching of the gospel. The first Mormon mission to Mexico was in 1874.

1883   Prosecution of federal anti-polygamy laws made the prospect of Mexican colonies more attractive. Thatcher and his future father-in-law, Erastus Snow, were dispatched to find suitable sites. Thatcher knew key Mexican officials, and his business acumen qualified him to negotiate complicated agreements.

Dedicating Colonia Juarez on a 75,000-acre tract in Corrales Basin in 1887, Thatcher promised, "As long as saloons are banned, and profanity kept off the streets, this spot will remain a place of refuge for all who need it." Mormon polygamists found refuge in Juarez and seven other Mexican colonies until 1910, when they were abondoned during the Mexican Revolution.

Political Dissident:

> Abraham H. Cannon alleged that Thatcher "constantly opposed the increase of power in the hands of the President of the Church."

1885   February 4: According to Cannon, "The Council of Fifty met in the old City Hall, and Moses opposed the proposition to anoint John Taylor as Prophet, Priest and King." In 1889 Thatcher objected to the selection of Wilford Woodruff as president of the Church on grounds that the eighty-two-year-old apostle could not cope with increasing Church difficulties over polygamy.

1892   Moses Thatcher, B. H. Roberts, and Charles W. Penrose, campaigning for the Democratic Party, were censured by their Republican brethren, who felt it unwise for them to "take to the political stump at that time."

1896   Thatcher, a Democratic Senatorial candidate, and B. H. Roberts, Democratic candidate for Congress, suffered disciplinary action for accepting nomination without approval from Church leaders. Wilford Woodruff explained: "When a man was appointed to the apostleship, or presidency, or in any office, as a teacher of the people, it placed on him a very grave responsibility; and no man was counted at liberty, from the organization of the church, to engage in any branch of business, politics, or anything else to take him entirely away from his calling, business, duty or responsibility for a length of time, without first counseling with the presidency of the church, or with his quorum, on its propriety, and getting permission to do so."

After both Thatcher and Roberts were defeated, the First Presidency prepared a "political manifesto" which stipulated that "before accepting any position, political or otherwise, which would interfere with the proper and complete discharge of his ecclesiastical duties, and before accepting a nomination or entering into engagements to perform new duties, [every leading] official should apply to the proper authorities and learn from them whether he can, consistently with the obligations already entered into with the church upon assuming his office, take upon himself the added duties and labors and responsibilities of the new position."

Although B. H. Roberts eventually endorsed the document, Thatcher steadfastly refused. He was convinced that the manifesto would be used selectively to stifle Democratic candidates: "I could not consent to the adoption of a rule that would effect the political liberty of so many people, and give so great power to the church authorities."

The entire matter was complicated by Thatcher's prolonged ill health and morphine addiction. Heber J. Grant recorded during this time that he called on Moses one evening "and found him very low indeed. . . . He told me that he felt impressed with the idea that he had a cancer in his stomach. He is a wonderfully sick man and it looks to me that he can not live long unless there is a change for the better." He did not die for fifteen years. His refusal to sign the manifesto resulted in his name not being presented for endorsement in April conference.

Deposed Apostle:

1896   November 19: Dropped from the Quorum of the Twelve

and deprived of the right to use his priesthood. One year later, to avoid excommunication, he signed a prepared statement: "That in taking the position that the authorities of the Church, by issuing the declaration of principles on April 6, 1896, acted in violation of pledges previously given and contrary to what they had published in the *Deseret News* and given to the *Salt Lake Times*, he was in error and in the dark. . . . That he was mistaken in conveying the idea that the church authorities desired and intended to unite church and state to exercise undue influence in political affairs."

Death:

1909   August 21: Having returned to his business interests and family in Logan, Moses Thatcher died there at the age of sixty-seven. Buried in the Logan Cemetery.

Chief Walker

(1801-1855)

"Hawk of the Mountains"
Mormon Elder
Friend of Brigham Young

Family Background:

1808 Wakara was born on the banks of Pequirarynoquint ("Stinking River"—the Spanish Fork) near the present Spanish Fork, Utah, to Timpanogos Ute parents. His name, which means "yellow," was anglicized to "Walker." Wakara's father, a member of the band that had welcomed Spanish explorers Escalante and Dominquez to Utah Valley in 1776, was killed early in Wakara's life during a tribal feud.

Walker tried to kill his own aged mother when she became a burden, but "she was a quick, wiry, plucky little creature and though well advanced in years, after receiving several severe cuts, and bruises at his hands, any one of which would have ended a common mortal's career, made good her escape, and remained hidden among the bullrushes of Sanpitch swamps."

"Hawk of the Mountains":

Wakara earned the name "Hawk of the Mountains" and his position as chief through his skills as a horse thief. His legendary raiding parties into California and Mexico also won him the nickname "Napoleon of the Desert."

He looked the part, "attired in a suit of the finest broadcloth, cut in the latest fashion," and complemented by "a cambric shirt and a beaver hat."

White settlers viewed Wakara as "a fine figure of a man . . . a crack shot, a rough rider, and a great judge of horse flesh. He is very clever, in our sense of the word. He is a peculiarly eloquent master of the graceful alphabet of pantomime, which stranger tribes employ to communicate with one another. He has picked up some English, and is familiar with Spanish and several Indian tongues."

Friend of Brigham Young:

1847 When Brigham Young declared Salt Lake Valley "the right place" for Mormon pioneers, Wakara's band was camped seventy miles southeast in Spanish Fork Canyon. Ute tradition holds that Wakara attempted to incite a band of young firebrands to oppose white settlement; his elder brother, the wise Sowiette, needed a horsewhip to drive home the finer points of his argument opposing violence.

Mormon tradition has it, however, that Wakara had envisioned the coming of white people: "He died and his spirit went to heaven. He saw the Lord sitting upon a throne dressed in white. The Lord told him he could not stay, he had to return to earth, that there would come to him a race of white people that would be his friends, and he must treat them kindly."

Mormon Elder:

1849   When Wakara and Brigham Young met, the Ute chief invited the Mormons to move south to settle on his lands. One year later, Wakara was baptized by Manti settler Isaac Morley. In 1851 Wakara and other chiefs were brought to Salt Lake, ordained elders, and told they now had "power and authority from the Great Spirit."

Slaver:

1851   Wakara was given a "talking paper" by George A. Smith, certifying "that Captain Walker and Peteetneet of the Eutah Indians and their band have resided here about 3 weeks and as they have showed themselves friends and gentlemen and are now leaving to visit your settlements it is my desire that they should be treated as friends, and as they wish to Trade horses, Buckskins and Piede children, we hope them success and prosperity and good bargains."

The endorsement of child slavery did not last long. The Ute band had been preying on weaker tribes, stealing their children or buying them with horses, which were prized as food. On the Mexico-California market, young boys were worth $100; girls brought as much as $200. Shortly before the territorial legislature passed an anti-slavery bill, Brigham Young declared in the *Deseret News*, January 10, 1852, "Human flesh to be dealt in as property is not consistent or compatible with the principles of government."

"Captain Walker":

1853   Wakara's disaffection over the slavery issue festered into open rebellion during a ten-month war. The "Walker War" resulted in the massacre of twenty white men, including Captain John W. Gunnison and seven members of his U. S. government survey team near Fillmore. After the fledgling territorial government expended some $200,000 in an attempt to quell the outbreak, Governor Young sent a letter proposing peace to "Capt. Walker":

"I send you some tobacco for you to smoke in the mountains when you get lonesome. You are a fool for fighting your best friends, for we are the best friends, and the only friends that you have in the world. Everybody else would kill you if they could get a chance.... When you get good natured again I would like to see you. Don't you think you should be ashamed? You know that I have always been your best friend."

Wakara replied, "Tell Brother Brigham, we have smoked the tobacco he sent us in the pipe of peace; I want to be at peace, and be a brother to him."

"That is all right," Brother Brigham responded. "But it is truly characteristic of the cunning Indian, when he finds he cannot get advantage over his enemy, to curl down at once, and say, I love you."

Peace was arranged in May, 1854. At the war's conclusion, Wakara denied ever personally killing a white man. President Young officially exonerated "Indian Walker" of responsibility for "the foundation of the difficulties," stating in general conference that he personally could vouch that at the "very commencement of the fuss, he [Wakara] was not in favour of killing whites."

"Mrs. Walker":

George A. Smith claimed that before the Walker war "Walker himself... teased me for a white wife; and if any of the sisters will volunteer to marry him, I believe I can close the war forthwith.... If any lady wishes to be Mrs. Walker, if she will report herself to me, I will agree to negotiate the match."

The "Potato Saint" had no takers. At the conclusion of

the war Wakara approached Brigham Young, who advised, "If you can find one that will give her consent you may marry her." Rejected by two Manti women, the sulking chief retreated to his winter campground, lamenting that "Brigham did not know how to use a chief like him for when he came down [to Salt Lake City] Brigham would not allow him a squaw to sleep with like the Moquintches and Navajos."

Death:

1855   Wakara wintered on Meadow Creek near Fillmore, Utah. During a heated tribal gambling session, the chief ruptured a blood vessel in his neck. This led to a general weakening and ultimately the development of "lung fever"—probably pneumonia.

Brigham Young, on hearing of the illness, sent David Lewis to deliver a letter to the Ute camp. Wakara was so sick he had to be supported on his horse to receive the emissary. Lewis promised to return the next day to read President Young's letter. But during the night the forty-four-year-old chief died.

Horrified settlers discovered the next day that his death had triggered ritual slaying of Piede slaves. At least two women and two children, plus twelve or fifteen of Wakara's best Spanish horses, were killed to accompany him to the spirit world.

Wakara was entombed with blankets, rifles, robes, buckskin clothing, cooking utensils, and bows and arrows, high on a mountainside above his winter camp. The unread letter from Brigham Young was placed on his body.

Most accounts of the burial agree that a slave boy was sealed alive in the tomb of aspen logs and boulders, with instructions to "watch Wakara." Three days later a group of Wakara's braves, inspecting the area, ignored pleas of the thirst-crazed boy, who complained that Wakara was "beginning to stink."

The authors rediscovered the gravesite on Walker Mountain above Meadow, Utah, in 1979. It had previously been found by Charles Kelly in 1946, whose Indian guide related the grave had been robbed in 1909 of every "single bead."

Daniel H. Wells

(1814-1891)

Member of the First Presidency
"Brigham Young's Statesman"

Family Background:

1814   October 27: Born Daniel Hanmer Wells in Trenton, New Jersey. He married Eliza Rebecca Robinson in 1837, and plural wives Louisa Free Lee (1849), Martha Harris (1849), Hanna Free Hotchkiss (1851), Lydia O. Alley (1851), Susan H. Alley (1852), Emmeline B. Woodward Harris Whitney (1852), Clara Gorder (1863), Sarah Gomber (1869), Sarah C. Nielson (1870), Elizabeth Harper (1871), Jane Smith (1871), Charlotte Foreman (1871), Caroline C. Raleigh (1879), and Eliza Foscue Lee (1889). Two of his wives were sisters of wives of Brigham Young and John D. Lee. He often reminded his thirty-seven children that they "should be very grateful to me for providing them with such good mothers."

    Son-in-law Orson F. Whitney described the Wells families in a parody of Edgar Allan Poe's "The Bells":

Ho the gathering of the Wells,—
Heaps of Wells,—
What a world of census-takers
This family foretells. . . .
A lot of little Wells,
Babbling Wells,
Blabbing Wells,
Youngsters counted by the score
Knee-deep on the parlor floor.

"Squire Wells":

1834   He moved with his widowed mother to Commerce (later Nauvoo), Illinois, where he was elected town constable and subsequently justice of the peace.

1839   When Mormon refugees began to arrive in Commerce, Wells sold them his land cheaply. It was on his property that the Nauvoo Temple was eventually built.

1841   A non-Mormon, Wells was elected commissary general of the Nauvoo Legion and made a trustee of the University of Nauvoo.

Convert:

1846   August 9: Baptized by Almon W. Babbitt in the Mississippi River. His wife Eliza would not join the Church.

When the Saints vacated Nauvoo in the spring of 1846, Wells remained. During the "Battle of Nauvoo" in September he urged surrender: "There is no use of the small handful of volunteers trying to defend Nauvoo against such an overwhelming force. What interests have the Saints to expect from its defense? Our interests are not identified with it, but in getting away from it. Who could urge the propriety of exposing life to defend a place for the purpose of vacating it?"

September 17: Wells crossed the Mississippi with the remaining Saints. In a "one-horse buggy" he dashed a message to Brigham Young in Winter Quarters apprising him of the situation in Nauvoo. The Wells family spent the winter of 1846-1847 in Burlington, Iowa, then moved to Galesburg, Illinois, until the spring of 1848. Unable to convince his wife to join the main body of Saints in Winter Quarters, he wrote to Brigham Young, "I see no prospect short of a complete sacrifice of everything I hold dear on earth." Wells left his wife and young son in Nauvoo and headed west, never to see them again.

Superintendent of Church Public Works:

1848   Named to the Council of Fifty in Salt Lake Valley. In 1849 he was appointed attorney general of the "Provisional State of Deseret." As superintendent of public works, Wells supervised construction of the Council House (1850), the Old Tabernacle (1852), the Church Office Building (1852), the Beehive House (1852), the Social Hall (1853), the Endowment House (1855), the Lion House (1856), Salt Lake Theatre (1862), Salt Lake Tabernacle (1867), and Salt Lake Temple (1893).

One of the most well-read men in Utah, Wells served on the University of Deseret's first board of regents, and as chancellor of the school for nine years.

Commander of the Nauvoo Legion:

1849   Made commander of the Nauvoo Legion—the territorial

militia. He was responsible for protecting settlers against Indian depredations, and commanded the Echo Canyon Expedition against the Utah Expeditionary Force (1857).

His daughter Emmeline recalled, "Father had the finest uniform that could be made here. His long sash was of heavy yellow silk and his wonderful steel sword was engraved half-way down the blade; he had a large black hat with a beautiful black feather dropping over the rim."

Member of the First Presidency:

1857   Ordained an apostle and named Brigham Young's second counselor after the death of Jedediah M. Grant.

Brigham Young's Statesman:

A self-trained lawyer, Wells served as chief justice of Utah, administering the oath of office to Governor Brigham Young. He labored for statehood throughout his life, serving in four constitutional conventions and for many years in the territorial legislature. Brigham Young called Wells "my statesman."

1864   Served for a year as president of the European Mission. He presided over the same mission from 1885 to 1887.

Salt Lake City Mayor:

1866   February 12: Elected mayor of Salt Lake City, serving ten turbulent years of increasing anti-Mormon hostility.

1871   October 28: Charged with Hosea Stout and William H. Kimball for the 1857 murder of Richard Yates. The three were confined at Camp Douglas, east of the city. William Hickman apparently killed the man, but no one ever came to trial.

1874   When U. S. marshals attempted to interfere with a municipal election, an unruly mob gathered at the polling place. Mayor Wells "commanded the crowd to disperse and leave the entrance clear.... Some of the leaders, now more or less intoxicated, when the order was given to disperse, instead of obeying, made an attack on the mayor.... Mayor Wells resisted this move. Several others now caught hold of him, tearing his clothes."

Counselor to the Twelve:

1877 Daniel H. Wells was never a member of the Quorum of the Twelve, but on the death of Brigham Young, John Taylor called Wells to be a counselor to the Quorum.

Hero:

1879 Presiding over the Endowment House, Wells married John H. Miles to Caroline Owen. The new Mrs. Miles alleged that on the same day, just prior to her marriage, Wells had married her husband to Emily Spencer. Following a quarrel between the two wives, Caroline swore out a complaint of polygamy against her husband.

When asked to testify about the endowment ceremony in court, Wells refused to answer. "I consider any person who reveals the sacred ceremonies of the Endowment House a falsifier and a perjurer; and it has been and is a principle of my life never to betray a friend, my religion, my country or my God. It seems to me that this is sufficient reason why I should not be held in contempt." Wells was sentenced to two days in the penitentiary.

On his release, a large, well-planned parade escorted him home. The anti-Mormon *Salt Lake Tribune* reported the event on May 7: "Never has such a crowd thronged the streets, nor such a cavalcade of human beings and brutes in point of numbers, promiscuous and motley confusion, been witnessed before, as that presented on our public streets on the occasion of the triumphal entry into town from the Penitentiary of Daniel H. Wells, First Counsellor in the Mormon Church.... Hundreds of poor dupes were forwarded by all the trains centering in this city, to participate in a celebration, which in spirit and substance, was designed as a public defiance of the national judicial authorities."

Temple President:

1888　Appointed president of the Manti Temple.

Death:

1891　March 24: Died of pleuro-pneumonia in Salt Lake City at age seventy-seven. His epitaph in the Salt Lake City Cemetery reads:
> It is inter-woven into my character
> Never to betray a friend or brother,
> My country, my religion, or my God.

Emmeline B. Wells

(1828-1921)

Women's Advocate
Fifth President of the Relief Society

Family Background:

1828   February 29: Born Emmeline Blanche Woodward in Petersham, Massachusetts. While she was attending boarding school in New Salem, her mother joined the Church; Emmeline was baptized on a visit home in 1842.

A fifteen-year-old school teacher, Emmeline married James Harvey Harris and moved to Nauvoo, where she gave birth to a son. He died within the month. Shortly after, her husband left her, seeking fame in New Orleans.

The desertion was devastating: "Last night there came a steam boat up the river. O how my youthful heart fluttered with hope.... Not all that has yet been said can shake my confidence in the only man I ever loved.... I saw a person approaching. My heart beat with fond anticipation. It walked like James. It came nearer and just as I was about to speak his name, he spoke and I found I was deceived by the darkness."

Plural Wife:

1845   James never returned. Two years later, she became Bishop Newel K. Whitney's second wife. He was fifty, she sixteen; they had two children before he died in 1850.

1852   Some time after Whitney died in 1850, she wrote his friend Daniel H. Wells, asking him to "consider the lonely state" of his friend's widow. She asked him to "declare his feelings" for her, for she had often seen herself "united with a being noble as thyself."

Wells married her as his sixth plural wife. They had three children, but it was a disappointing, unhappy union for Emmeline. "O, if my husband could only love me even a little and not seem to be perfectly indifferent to any sensation of that kind," she wrote in her 1874 diary. "He cannot know the craving of my nature; he is surrounded with love on every side, and I am cast out.... O my poor aching heart when shall it rest its burden only on the Lord.... Every other avenue seems closed against me."

1874   On their twenty-second anniversary she wrote, "Anniversary of my marriage with Pres. Wells. O how happy I was then how much pleasure I anticipated and how changed alas are all things since that time, how few thoughts I had then have ever been realized, and how much sorrow I have known in place of the joy I looked forward to."

         Daniel H. Wells was a busy man, and Emmeline did not blend well with his other wives. She was not an efficient homemaker, preferring to spend her time reading and in pleasant conversation. She also dressed differently than most women, preferring pastels to the usual dark colors. The other wives are said to have made fun of Emmeline's love poems to Daniel.

Women's Advocate:

1877   Emmeline B. Wells edited and published the *Woman's Exponent* for thirty-eight years. Her editorials covered a broad range of women's issues—equal pay for equal work, women's voting rights, even equality in athletic programs.

         Upset at women who allowed themselves to be placed on pedestals, she complained, "See the manner in which ladies—a term for which I have little reverence or respect—are treated in all public places! . . . She must be preserved from the slightest blast of trouble, petted, caressed, dressed to attract attention, taught accomplishments that minister to man's gratification; in other words, she must be treated as a glittering and fragile toy, a thing without brains or soul, placed on a tinselled and unsubstantial pedestal by man, as her worshipper."

1879   Church leaders encouraged Emmeline B. Wells and Zina Young Williams to attend a meeting of the National Women's Suffrage Association. There they petitioned Congress to recognize the rights of the children of plural marriages.

1882   Wells and her close friend Zina D. H. Young traveled to a National Women's Suffrage Association convention, where Emmeline delivered a paper on Mormon life in Utah. In 1899 she attended the Women's International Council and Congress in England and was received by Queen Victoria.

Fifth President of the Relief Society:

1910   Set apart as president of the Church Relief Society by Joseph F. Smith. Since 1888 she had been a member of the general board; she also assisted in the organization of the YLMIA and the Primary Association.

In 1895, as general Relief Society Secretary, she wrote a history of the organization, defining its main objectives: "The care of the needy, the sick, the helpless and the unfortunate, to visit the widow and the fatherless, to administer comfort and consolation as well as temporal relief of physical wants, to see that none are left to suffer... also to care for the dying and the dead, to be at the bedside of the lonely ones when death is near, to robe the body neatly and properly for burial when all is over, and to perform those kindly deeds with tenderness and grace."

Death:

1921   April 25: Died at the age of eighty-four in her home at 1354 South 900 East in Salt Lake City; buried in the Salt Lake City Cemetery near her husband Daniel.

David Whitmer

(1805-1888)

Book of Mormon Witness
Joseph Smith's Nominated Successor
Dissident

Family Background:

1805   January 7: Born in Harrisburg, Pennsylvania, David was the brother of fellow Book of Mormon witnesses Peter, Jacob, John, and Christian Whitmer. His sister Catherine married Hiram Page, and another sister, Elizabeth, married Oliver Cowdery.

Of "Pennsylvania Deutsch" heritage, Whitmer still spoke with a "German twang" in his eightieth year. His family moved to a farm near Seneca Lake, New York, when he was a boy. He was elected sergeant in the local militia, the "Seneca Grenadiers," at age twenty. In 1830 Whitmer married Julia A. Jolley; they had two children.

Book of Mormon Benefactor:

1829   June: Whitmer first heard of Joseph Smith and the "gold plates" from his friend Oliver Cowdery in 1828. After receiving a sample of the Book of Mormon translation and several letters from Cowdery, Whitmer made a two-hundred-mile wagon trip to bring Joseph and Oliver from Harmony, Pennsylvania, to his home in Fayette, New York.

The Whitmer family was close to the translation process as the Book of Mormon manuscript increased day by day. Whitmer even served briefly as a scribe in June. His 1887 account relates:

"I will now give you a description of the manner in which the Book of Mormon was translated. Joseph Smith would put the seer stone into a hat, and put his face in the hat, drawing it closely around his face to exclude the light; and in the darkness the spiritual light would shine. A piece of something resembling parchment would appear, and on that appeared the writing. One character at a time would appear, and under it was the interpretation in English. Brother Joseph would read off the English to Oliver Cowdery, who was his principal scribe, and when it was written down and repeated to Brother Joseph to see if it was correct, then it would disappear, and another character with the interpretation would appear. Thus the Book of Mormon was translated by the gift and power of God, and not by any power of man."

Book of Mormon Witness:

1829 June: Whitmer, Oliver Cowdery and Martin Harris reported a visitation from the angel Moroni. In 1878 Orson Pratt and Joseph F. Smith recorded an interview with Whitmer in which he said that Moroni had shown the Three Witnesses the "plates of the Book of Mormon, also the sword of Laban, the Directors—i.e., the ball which Lehi had—and the Interpreters... I heard the voice of the Lord, as distinctly as I ever heard anything in my life, declaring that the records... were translated by the gift and power of God."

For many years Whitmer maintained possession of the "printer's copy" of the Book of Mormon manuscript (in Oliver Cowdery's handwriting). This document is now in the possession of the Reorganized Church of Jesus Christ of Latter Day Saints.

Whitmer was baptized, confirmed, and ordained an elder by Joseph Smith in June, 1829. In April of the following year he became one of the six original members of the Church.

Joseph Smith's Nominated Successor:

1834 July 3: Whitmer was sustained as president of the high council in Missouri. Later in the year he was ordained as Joseph Smith's successor "on condition that he [Joseph Smith] did not live to God himself."

1838 Whitmer was sustained as "President of the Church" in Far West, Missouri—the modern equivalent of stake president.

Dissident:

1838 According to a March, 1829, revelation, Joseph Smith was given "a gift to translate the [Book of Mormon], and I have commanded him that he shall pretend to no other gift, for I will grant him no other" (Book of Commandments 4:2). Whitmer opposed Joseph Smith as president of the Church, feeling that the Prophet's only gift was to translate the Book of Mormon. The revelation was revised in the 1835 edition of the Doctrine and Covenants to read, "I have commanded that you should pretend to no other gift until my purpose is fulfilled in this; for I will grant unto you no other gift until it is finished."

Whitmer also objected to high priest ordinations, though he himself had been so ordained by Oliver Cowdery at the age of twenty-six. "This error was introduced at the instigation of Sidney Rigdon. The office of high priests was never spoken of, and never thought of being established in the church until Rigdon came in. . . . Rigdon . . . would persuade Brother Joseph to inquire of the Lord about this doctrine and that doctrine, and of course a revelation would always come just as they desired it."

Jealous of Rigdon's popularity, Whitmer wrote, "Rigdon was a thorough Bible scholar, a man of fine education, and a powerful orator. He soon worked himself deep into Brother Joseph's affections, and had more influence over him than any other man living. . . . Brother Joseph rejoiced, believing that the Lord had sent to him this great and mighty man Sidney Rigdon, to help him in the work. Poor Brother Joseph! He was mistaken."

February 5: A Far West meeting of the "whole Church in Zion" voted to remove David Whitmer, John Whitmer, and W. W. Phelps from their positions as "Presidents of the Church" in Missouri. David Whitmer was accused of persisting "in the use of tea, coffee, and tobacco." All three men allegedly encouraged the sale of Jackson County lands, a transgression which Joseph Smith had earlier declared "a denial of our faith, as that is the place where the Zion of God shall stand, according to our faith and belief in the revelations of God."

April 13: Found guilty of "possessing the same spirit with the dissenters," David Whitmer was excommunicated for failure to observe the Word of Wisdom, neglecting meetings, writing unfavorable letters about Joseph Smith, and signing his name to official Far West documents after being removed from the presidency there.

Fifty years after the fact, Whitmer said, "If you believe my testimony to the Book of Mormon; if you believe that God spake to us three witnesses by his own voice, then I tell you that in June, 1838, God spake to me again by his own voice from the heavens, and told me to separate myself from among the Latter-day Saints for as they sought to do unto me, so should it be done unto them."

Whitmer left Far West after his excommunication and settled in Richmond, Missouri, where he operated a "Livery and Feed Stable," advertising that "customers may rely on promptness, good turnouts, safe horses, and moderate charges." The Whitmer business, as described by a great-granddaughter, "filled hauling contracts, rented out carriages and buggies, and met two trains a day at Lexington Junction with a beautifully decorated yellow bus."

1839 Spring: When the Mormons were expelled from Far West in the spring of 1839, Whitmer recalled, the local militia "pressed me and my team into service, and I was forced to go and drive a wagon load of baggage to Far West. I told them if I had to go I would take no gun. They said 'all right'; and I took no gun." During the confusion of the evacuation of the city, "he was handed a musket by the soldiery and ordered to shoot Joseph Smith, but threw the musket down, declaring he 'would not harm the Lord's anointed.'"

Whitmer became involved in the leadership of several "reorganizations." In 1848 he gave approval to organize a church in Kirtland around his name and former ordinations, but the collapse of that effort embarrassed him. Thirty years later, he ordained his nephew to organize a new "Church of Christ," claiming an identical organization to the 1829-1830 Church. After his death adherents of this group continued to publish materials supporting his claims.

Union Loyalist:

1860 During a Richmond political meeting at which non-secessionists were urged to leave Missouri, Whitmer walked to the platform and delivered a short speech declaring that "no resolutions or threats would cause him to run away.... He was a citizen of the United States, and should remain such. He proposed to live or die under the old flag. If anyone desired to shoot him, then was a good time." He walked away a respected man.

Most-Interviewed Witness:

During the last years of his life, constantly interviewed about his experiences with the Book of Mormon, Whitmer never denied his testimony. When the Book of Mormon manuscript was examined in 1884 by a committee from the Reorganized Church, Joseph Smith, III, said that a skeptical Richmond military officer suggested to Whitmer that he possibly "had been mistaken and had simply been moved upon by some mental disturbance or hallucination, which had deceived him into *thinking* he saw" the angel, plates, and Urim and Thummim:

"Elder Whitmer arose and drew himself up to his full height—a little over six feet—and said, in solemn and impressive tones: 'No sir! I was not under any hallucination, nor was I deceived! I saw with these eyes, and I heard with these ears! *I know whereof I speak!*' "

Death:

1888   January 25: Died at the age of eighty-three in Richmond, Missouri, the last surviving witness to the Book of Mormon. Buried in the "new" Richmond Cemetery.

John A. Widtsoe

(1872-1952)

Scientist
University President
Apostle

Family Background:

1872   January 31: Born John Andreas Widtsoe in Froen, Norway. In 1879 his widowed mother took a pair of his shoes to a Mormon cobbler, who stuffed the toes with Mormon pamphlets when he returned them. Anna Widtsoe read the pamphlets, then attended a Mormon meeting. Two years later the family was baptized, and in 1883 emigrated to Logan, Utah.

In 1898 John married Leah Eudora Dunford, daughter of Susa Young Gates. Susa, who had met Widtsoe in Boston, was so impressed by him she "wooed" him for her daughter. The Widtsoes had seven children.

Scholar:

Widtsoe graduated from Brigham Young College in 1891 and from Harvard, with high honors, in 1894. Returning to Utah, he became the first Mormon faculty member at Utah Agricultural College (Logan), where he taught chemistry.

Awarded the Parker Traveling Scholarship shortly after his wedding, he took his new bride to Europe. In 1899 he was awarded a Ph.D. with high honors from the University of Goettingen, Germany.

Back at Logan, Widtsoe became director of the Utah Agricultural Experiment Station, which did research work in crop, soil, and irrigation techniques. In 1905 he went to Brigham Young University.

University President:

His phenomenal success at BYU prompted the Utah Agricultural College to offer him its presidency. He accepted in 1907. Ten years later he became president of the University of Utah. His administration brought the school to full university status.

Apostle:

1921   Called to the Quorum of the Twelve and appointed

commissioner of education, president of the Utah Historical Society, and director of the Genealogical Society. In addition he was elected to the Victoria Institute in England, an honor received by only one other Mormon scholar—James E. Talmage.

Widtsoe's sermons stressed the search for truth: "The doctrine of the Church cannot be fully understood unless it is tested by mind and feelings, by intellect and emotions, by every power of the investigator. Every Church member is expected to understand the doctrine of the Church intelligently. There is no place in the Church for blind adherence."

"The essential thought must ever be that a man does not, except in his spiritual infancy, accept a statement merely because the Church or someone in authority declares it correct, but because, under mature examination, it is found to be true and right and worthwhile. Conversion must come from within."

Author:

1935   After six years as president of the European Mission, Widtsoe served for several years as editor of the *Improvement Era.*

He wrote more than thirty books. His Church works include *Joseph Smith as Scientist, Discourses of Brigham Young, Priesthood and Church Government, Evidences and Reconciliations,* and his autobiography, *In a Sunlit Land.* Among his professional publications are *Dry Farming, Principles of Irrigation Practices, Arid Farming in Utah,* and *How the Desert Was Farmed.*

His interest was "to help the common man": "Hence have come teaching young people, taking the problems of the toiler, notably the farmer, and lifting all into a spiritual realm, hence my devotion to the spread of Gospel knowledge."

Death:

1952   November 29: Died in Salt Lake City at age eighty; buried in the Salt Lake City Cemetery.

Wilford Woodruff

(1807-1898)

Fourth President of the Church

Family Background:

1807 March 1: Born in Farmington, Connecticut. He married Phoebe W. Carter in 1837, and later wed Mary Ann Jackson (1846), Mary Caroline Barton (1846), Mary Meek Giles (1852), Clarissa Hardy (1852), Sarah E. Brown (1853), Emma Smith (1853), and Sarah Delight Stocking (1857). Two of his plural wives divorced him: Mary Jackson (1848) and Clarissa Hardy (1853).

He was the father of sixteen daughters and seventeen sons, including Apostle Abraham Owen Woodruff. He was a father-in-law of President Lorenzo Snow.

Accident Prone:

Wilford Woodruff recorded that he was involved in twenty-seven serious accidents during his lifetime, breaking every bone in his body except his spine and neck. He fell into a cauldron of scalding water, fell on his face from a barn beam, was gored by a bull, kicked in the stomach by an ox, nearly drowned in a river, split his instep with an ax, nearly froze to death, and was bitten by a mad dog.

Convert:

1833 December 29: Wilford Woodruff attended a meeting in Richland, New York, where Zera Pulsipher proclaimed the restoration. "I thought it was what I had long been looking for. I could not feel it my duty to leeve the house without bearing witness to the truth before the people. I opened my eyes to see, my ears to hear, my heart to understand, and my doors to entertain him who had administered to us. Brother Pulsipher continued labouring with us for several days and on the 31th of December I with my Brother—Azmon Woodruff with two yong females which had been healed by the laying on of hands went forward in baptism."

A Freewill Baptist minister and several of his congregation followed the next day, and on January 2, 1834, Elder Pulsipher established a branch, ordaining

Azmon Woodruff and the former minister elders, and Wilford Woodruff a teacher. "I truly felt that I could exclaim with the servant of God that it was better to be a door keeper in the house of God than to dwell in the tents of wickedness."

1834   April 1: Parley P. Pratt arrived in Richland to recruit members for Zion's Camp. Ten days later Wilford Woodruff sold his sawmill and gristmill and moved to Kirtland, Ohio, where he and the rest of the camp began the two-thousand-mile march May 1.

December 31: Wilford Woodruff consecrated "myself together with all my properties and affects unto the Lord." The inventory consisted of "One Due Bill payable in one year, One trunk and its contents principly books, Hat Boots and clothing, One Valiece, One english watch, One rifle and equpments, One sword, One pistol, Also Sundry articles, And Notes which are doubtful and uncertain"—total value $240.00.

Missionary:

1835   January 13: A priest, Woodruff began a two-year mission to Arkansas and Tennessee, where he was ordained an elder by Warren Parrish. During 1835 he "traveled 3,248 miles, baptized forty-three people, held one hundred seventy meetings, and organized three branches."

1836   Ordained a seventy, he served a mission to the Eastern States and the Fox Islands (now Vinalhaven, off the coast of Maine.)

1840   As a member of the Quorum of the Twelve, Wilford Woodruff served on the mission to Great Britain. During an eight-month period in Herefordshire, Worcestershire, and Gloucestershire, he converted 1800 people, including a 600-member United Brethren congregation.

He later presided over the European (1844-1845) and Eastern States (1848-1850) missions.

"Wilford the Faithful":

1838 Ordained an apostle in Missouri by Brigham Young while Joseph Smith was in Liberty Jail.

1842 As business manager for the Nauvoo *Times and Seasons*, he was dubbed "Wilford the Faithful" by the Prophet.

1847 July 24: A member of the pioneer company, Wilford Woodruff viewed the Salt Lake Valley for the first time and wrote, "We gazed with wonder and admiration upon the vast rich fertile valley."

1856 Appointed Church historian. Throughout his life Wilford Woodruff kept a detailed journal which has provided extensive records of the early history of the Church.
 A Woodruff eulogizer, J. M. Tanner, said, "He loved to work.... To sweat, was a divine command, as much so as to pray." Whenever he could escape his responsibilities, however, he went fishing in the Jordan River.
 In 1895 President Woodruff recorded that since he had joined the Church he had traveled 172,369 miles, attended 7,655 meetings, including 75 semi-annual conferences and 344 quarterly conferences, given 3,526 discourses, confirmed 8,952 people, received 18,977 letters and written 11,519.

Temple Worker:

1877 Called to be the first president of the newly completed Saint George Temple, where it was revealed to him that work for the dead could be performed by persons not related. August 21, "I, Wilford Woodruff, went to the temple of the Lord this morning and was baptized for 100 persons who were dead," including the signers of the Declaration of Independence, Napoleon Bonaparte, Christopher Columbus, Johann Wolfgang Goethe, and William Wordsworth. The only U.S. presidents excluded were Ulysses S. Grant (who was still alive), Martin Van Buren (who declined to intervene on behalf of Mormon losses in Missouri), and James Buchanan (who sent federal troops to Utah in 1857).

As president of the Church, Woodruff presided over the dedication of the Salt Lake Temple on April 6, 1893.

President Woodruff changed the policy of "adoption," whereby many individuals had sealed themselves to prominent Church leaders, in 1894. "When a man receives the endowments, adopt him to his father; not to Wilford Woodruff, nor to any other man outside the lineage of his fathers."

Woodruff himself, according to the March 28, 1894 journal of Abraham H. Cannon, had previously had four hundred unmarried female ancestors sealed to him in a single day.

Fourth President of the Church:

1889   April 7: Sustained as fourth president of the Church, with George Q. Cannon and Joseph F. Smith as counselors. Wilford Woodruff had served as president of the Quorum of the Twelve since 1880.

1890   September 25: "I have arrived at a point in the history of my life as the President of the Church of Jesus Christ of Latter-day Saints," he wrote, "where I am under the necessity of acting for the temporal salvation of the Church. The United States government has taken a stand and passed laws to destroy the Latter-day Saints on the subject of polygamy, or patriarchal order of marriage; and after praying to the Lord and feeling inspired, I have issued the ... proclamation [Wilford Woodruff Manifesto] which is sustained by my counselors and the twelve apostles."

The Church had been disincorporated and all its property in excess of $50,000 confiscated by the federal government; more than a thousand men had been sentenced to prison for unlawful cohabitation. In February the Supreme Court had upheld the Idaho law which disfranchised anyone unwilling to take an oath denouncing plural marriage.

1891   October 19: Church leaders hoped that the Manifesto would unlock the door to statehood for Utah and provide relief from federal legislation. But testifying before the

Master in Chancery for the return of escheated Church property, President Woodruff extended the Manifesto beyond its original intent. When asked if the Manifesto prohibited "living or associating in plural marriage by those already in the status," he replied, "I intended the proclamation to cover the whole ground—to obey the laws of the land entirely."

He had been "placed in such a position on the witness stand," he told the Twelve, "that he could not answer other than he did." But according to Abraham H. Cannon, it had previously been agreed that "any man who deserts and neglects his wives or children because of the manifesto, should be handled on his fellowship.... Men must be careful to avoid exposing themselves to arrest or conviction for violations of the law, and yet they must not break their covenants with their wives."

A few days later, President Woodruff reasoned with the Saints in northern Utah: "Which is the wisest course for the Latter-day Saints to pursue—to continue to attempt to practice plural marriage with the laws of the nation against it and the opposition of sixty millions of people, and at the cost of the confiscation and loss of all the Temples, and the stopping of all the ordinances therein, both for the living and the dead, and the imprisonment of the First Presidency and Twelve and the head of families in the Church, and the confiscation of personal property of the people . . . or after doing and suffering what we have through our adherence to this principle to cease the practice and submit to the law. . . ?

"The Lord showed me by vision and revelation exactly what would take place if we did not stop this practice. If we had not stopped it... all ordinances would be stopped throughout the land of Zion. Confusion would reign throughout Israel, and many men would be made prisoners. This trouble would have come upon the whole Church, and we should have been compelled to stop the practice."

For thirteen years the Manifesto was frequently interpreted as an inspired expedient. Though some, like Lorenzo Snow, ceased living with their plural wives, most continued to violate the unlawful cohabitation statute, and, until 1904, hundreds of new plural marriages were authorized in Mexico, Canada, and the United States.

1896 Political differences among leading Church officials induced President Woodruff and his counselors to issue a "political manifesto" which stipulated that "men called to spend all their time in the ministry shall not run into politics to the neglect of their spiritual calling without being properly released for that purpose."

During the final two years of his administration Wilford Woodruff changed Fast Day from Thursdays to Sundays, ordained his son Abraham Owen Woodruff to the Quorum of the Twelve, became the first president of the Church to make a voice recording, and officiated at the Pioneer Jubilee celebration, dedicating the Brigham Young Monument on South Temple Street [Brigham Street] in Salt Lake City.

Death:

1898 Wilford Woodruff suffered from severe insomnia in his later years because of asthma. Occasionally he traveled to the Pacific Coast, where he could sleep better. He died in San Francisco from asthmatic complications at the age of ninety-one on September 2. Buried in the Salt Lake City Cemetery.

Brigham Young

(1801-1877)

"Lion of the Lord"
Colonizer
Second President of the Church

Family Background:

1801   June 1: Born in Whitingham, Vermont, Brigham Young was cousin to Apostles Franklin D. Richards and Willard Richards. He was son-in-law of Albert Rockwood (First Council of Seventy), and brother-in-law to Lorenzo Snow, Amasa Lyman, Heber C. Kimball, and Church architect Truman Angell. He was Heber C. Kimball's uncle by marriage.

Early Years:

Soon after Brigham's birth, his family moved to Sherburne, New York. "When I was young," Brigham recalled, "I was kept within very strict bounds and was not allowed to walk more than half-an-hour on Sunday for exercise. . . . I had not a chance to dance when I was young, and never heard the enchanting tones of the violin until I was eleven years of age; and then I thought I was on the highway to hell, if I suffered myself to linger and listen to it."

At age sixteen, Brigham learned carpentry, joining, painting, and glazing. The family was poor. His sisters made him "Jo Johnson" caps to ease the New York winter. He had to work year round, ill clad, with "insufficient food until my stomach would ache."

Throughout his life Brigham Young was conscious of the fact that he had little formal education—only eleven days. "When I meet ladies and gentlemen of high rank, they must not expect from me the same formal ceremony and etiquette that are observed among the great in the courts of kings. In my youthful days, instead of going to school, I had to chop logs, to sow and plant, to plow in the midst of roots barefooted, and if I had on a pair of pants that would cover me I did pretty well."

Despite his lack of formal education, he was the leading spirit in endowing three institutions of higher learning in Utah—Brigham Young College (Logan, Utah), the University of Deseret (now University of Utah in Salt Lake City), and Brigham Young Academy (now Brigham Young University in Provo). His educational philosophy was summed up in a prize-winning definition submitted posthumously for him to the San Francisco World's

Fair: "Education is the power to think clearly, to act well in the world's work, and to appreciate life."

Marriages:

He married Miriam Works in 1824. She died in 1832, and he married Mary Ann Angel in 1834.

Brigham Young described himself as a "great lover of women. In what particular? I love to see them happy, to see them well fed and well clothed, and I love to see them cheerful. I love to see their faces and talk with them, when they talk in righteousness; but as for anything more, I do not care. There are probably but few men in the world who care about the private society of women less than I do."

He married at least fifty-five plural wives, including Zina D. Huntington, Eliza R. Snow, Amelia Folsom, Ann Eliza Webb, and seven widows of Joseph Smith. Several wives left him and six obtained formal divorces.

He fathered thirty-one daughters and twenty-five sons, including sons who married daughters of apostles Jedediah M. Grant, Parley P. Pratt, Erastus Snow, and Lorenzo Snow. Susa Young Gates was perhaps his most prominent daughter.

President Young ordained three of his sons apostles when the youngest was only eleven years old. Appointing them his counselors, he became the only president of the Church to have sons serving with him in the First Presidency. Brigham Jr. was the only son to become a member of the Quorum of the Twelve. John W. was publicly sustained as a member of the First Presidency in 1876, but Joseph A. remained apostle without portfolio.

Convert:

1830   A Methodist since 1822, Brigham Young read the Book of Mormon left in Mendon, New York, by Joseph Smith's brother Samuel. Two years later, on April 14, 1832, he was baptized, confirmed, and ordained an elder by Eleazer Miller.

1832   Served a mission to Canada with his brother Joseph.

1834   Marched in Zion's Camp.

Apostle:

1835   February 14: Called to the original Quorum of the Twelve by the Three Witnesses.

1838 October: When David Patten was killed, Young became the senior member of the Quorum and led the Saints from Missouri to Illinois while Joseph Smith was in Liberty Jail.

1839 September 14: Brigham Young left Nauvoo on a mission to England "without purse or scrip." His wife was ill, with no means of support, caring for a day-old baby. In England he founded the *Millennial Star* and established the European Emigration Bureau, which sent the first company of forty European Saints to Nauvoo.

1841 Called to be president of the Quorum of the Twelve (D&C 124:127), Young returned to Nauvoo in July.

"President of the Whole Church":

1844 July: Young was on a Council of Fifty assignment promoting Joseph Smith's U. S. presidential candidacy when he learned of the martyrdom. Despite attempts by Sidney Rigdon to assume control of the Church after Joseph's death, the Church membership sustained the Quorum of the Twelve with Young as its president. As early as December 5, Brigham Young was signing Church documents as "President of the Church."

1845 April 7: Sustained as "President of the Quorum of the Twelve Apostles to this Church and nation, and all nations, and also as President of the whole Church of Latter-day Saints."

1847 December 5: Sustained as President of the Church by the Quorum of the Twelve "with authority to nominate his two counselors," Heber C. Kimball and Willard Richards.
December 24: The First Presidency was formally sustained by a general conference in Kanesville, Iowa.

Colonizer:

1847 President Brigham Young led the pioneer vanguard to the Salt Lake Valley and directed colonizing efforts in more than two hundred settlements. He was appointed governor of the Provisional State of Deseret (1849) by the provisional legislature, organized the "Perpetual Emigration Fund" (1849), established the *Deseret News*, with Willard Richards as editor (1850), and was appointed governor of Utah Territory by President Millard Fillmore (1850).

A charter member of the Council of Fifty, Brigham Young noted in a meeting of the Salt Lake School of the Prophets that "some of the brethren think that the Priesthood should not govern us in political affairs but the Priesthood is supreme; even in financial affairs. . . . Some would say as with the Democrats [in the] east, each party wanting their man but we must quit that: I hope we may never hear of an opposition in this city or country again. . . . We will learn that the Priesthood must dictate."

1857 Reports that the Mormon "theodemocracy" was getting out of hand provoked President James Buchanan to send federal troops to install a new governor and other officials. Governor Young, who had not been contacted by the president, declared martial law and forbade the army to enter the Salt Lake Valley. In the spring of 1858, as the Utah Expeditionary Force approached, Young evacuated northern Utah. Thomas L. Kane worked out a settlement whereby the army passed through the deserted Salt Lake City to Cedar Valley, thirty miles southwest, and the new territorial officials were accepted without further incident.

1861 October 18: At the outbreak of the Civil War Brigham Young wired the first telegraph message east on the new Overland Telegraph line: "Utah has not seceded, but is firm for the Constitution and laws of our once happy country."

"Lion of the Lord":

The "Lion of the Lord"—so named by toastmaster W. W. Phelps in 1845—was imposing in every dimension. He stood 5'10" tall, weighed 188-200 pounds, and boasted a 44-inch chest.

He also wore false teeth. "One morning he was cleaning his artificial dentures at the family wash bench just outside a back door [of the Erastus Snow home in Saint George, Utah] when little Flora caught sight of him at this very private chore. Quickly he plopped his teeth into his mouth when he beheld her staring at him in open-mouthed, wide-eyed fascination. She bounced up and down with excitement, shrilly crying 'Oh, Brother Brigham, show me your teeth; show me your teeth, Brother Brigham!' The Lion of the Lord, touched by childhood's whims, kindly obliged."

He was not always the confident preacher moderns tend to envision. Even in his later years, he approached the public forum with uneasiness. "Although I have been a public speaker for thirty-seven years," he once said, "it is seldom that I rise before a congregation without feeling a child-like timidity; if I live to the age of Methusaleh I do not know that I shall outgrow it."

Visitors to Salt Lake City often commented on his language: "He says 'leetle', 'beyene' and 'disremember.' An irrepressible conflict between his nominatives and verbs now and then crops out in expressions like 'they was.'"

"When he speaks," reported one contemporary, "the words seem to be calmly weighed by the brain, clipped by the teeth, and finally squeezed through the left half of the almost locked up lips."

His sermons were usually practical—filled with hints on stock raising, fence building, tales of sufferings of Saints, advice to the lovelorn. He admonished the breathing of fresh mountain air, the use of homemade cloth, the eating of thick-crusted bread.

Man of Contradictions:

Brigham Young was not averse to contradicting himself. He condemned novel reading as profitless, but allowed the practice in his own home. He consistently denounced the purchase of manufactured "states goods" as a breach of self-sufficiency, but admitted buying more of them than any man in the territory. He demanded strict obedience from members of the Church, yet counseled:

"I am more afraid that this people have so much confidence in their leaders that they will not inquire for themselves of God whether they are led by Him. I am fearful they settle down in a state of blind self-security, trusting their eternal destiny in the hands of their leaders with a reckless confidence that in itself would thwart the purposes of God in their salvation, and weaken that influence they could give to their leaders, did they know for themselves, by the revelations of Jesus, that they are led in the right way. Let every man and woman know, by the whispering of the Spirit of God to themselves, whether their leaders are walking in the path the Lord dictates, or not."

A journalist described Brigham Young as "a self-reliant and strong-willed man . . . one born to be master of himself and many others." But his children remember him as an "easy touch." He himself declared, "I do not rule my family with an iron hand, as many do, but in kindness and with pleasant words; and if soft words would teach them, they would know as much as any family on this earth."

Temple Builder:

Brigham Young worked as a carpenter on the Kirtland and Nauvoo temples. He laid the cornerstone for the Salt Lake Temple (1853) and dedicated sites for the Logan and Manti temples (1877). At the Manti dedication he told Warren Snow: "Here is the spot where the Prophet Moroni stood and dedicated this piece of land for a temple site, and that is the reason why the location is made here, and we can't move it from this spot."

Businessman:

Heber J. Grant recalled Brigham Young's saying, "Daniel Wells is my statesman, Heber Kimball is my prophet, and I am a business man looking after the best interests of the people."

"Before I had been one year in this place [Salt Lake City]," Brigham Young said, "the wealthiest man who came from the mines, Father Rhodes, with seventeen thousand dollars could not buy the possessions I had made in one year." During the years 1862-1872 President Young's annual personal income averaged $32,000.

His wealth came from a "dairy in Hampton, Utah, which produced over 150 tons of cheese per year, a 10,000-acre ranch between Mendon and Logan on which grazed 600 head of cattle and hundreds of sheep, a carding factory and grist mill on City Creek, a large wagon and repair shop in Salt Lake City, a cotton and woolen factory at the mouth of Parley's Canyon, a leather tannery in St. George, a saddle-manufacturing shop, and a shoe factory which employed a dozen men."

His farming and ranching operations were blue-ribbon quality. He won many prizes at the annual Deseret fairs—"second best apples," "second best pecks of silver and red onions," "best drumhead cabbage," "best bunches of grapes," "best pigs," "best brood mare," "best yearling colt," "best Devon Bull."

At his death, he was the wealthiest man in Utah, with an estate of approximately $2.5 million, which was embroiled in legal battles between his family and the Church for years afterwards.

Death:

1877   August 29: Died of complications related to appendicitis.

Brigham Young was typically practical in arranging his own burial details, requesting a coffin "made of plump 1-1/4 inch (redwood) boards, not scrimped in length . . . my body dressed in my temple clothing . . . the coffin to have the appearance that if I wanted to turn a little to the right or the left, I should have plenty of room to do so." Buried in the family burial plot one block east of the Lion House in Salt Lake City.

During World War II a United States Navy liberty ship was named in his honor, and in 1950 a twelve-foot marble statue of Brigham Young, created by his grandson Mahonri M. Young, was placed in the Capitol Building in Washington, D. C.

Brigham Young, Jr.

(1836-1903)

President of the Quorum of the Twelve

Family Background:

1836   December 18: Born in Kirtland, Ohio, to Brigham Young and Mary Ann Angell. His twin sister, Mary, died at the age of seven.

He married Catherine Curtis Spencer in 1885, and later Jane Carrington (1857), Elizabeth Fenton (1868), Rhoda Elizabeth Perkins (1886), Abbie Stevens (1888), and Helen Armstrong (1890). He was the father of thirty-one children.

"Young Brigy":

1855   Two army officers lodged a complaint with Salt Lake City Mayor Jedediah Grant that "young Brigy" and three others rode "violently by them & bowing, while they were riding the streets with some Ladies."

A year earlier, Young was injured in a Christmas Day street fight between a group of Salt Lake City citizens and drunken soldiers from Ft. Douglas.

Nineteen-year-old Apostle:

1855   November 22: Secretly ordained an apostle by his father. Wilford Woodruff related, "President Young said, 'I am going to tell you something that I have never before mentioned to any other person. I have ordained my sons, Joseph A., Brigham & John W., Apostles and My Counsellors. Have you any objections?' J. Taylor and G. A. Smith said they had not, that it was his own affair & they considered it under his own direction. He further stated, 'In ordaining my sons I have done no more than I am perfectly willing that you should do with yours. And I am determined to put my sons into active service in the Spiritual Affairs of the Kingdom and keep them there just as long as possible. You have the same privilege.'"

Missionary:

1862   Called on a mission to England. President Young wrote his son before his return, "In all probability you will be able to entirely omit the use of tobacco on your mission, if you have not already done so.... Permit us to welcome you home with your mouth and breath free from the use and smell of tobacco. It is now going on two years and a half since I have used a particle of tobacco, and I guess a little resolution and faith on your part will also enable you to dispense with its use."

Brigham Young, Jr., returned to Liverpool to preside over the European Mission in 1865, 1867, and 1890.

Brigham Young Agent:

1868   Appointed with his brother John W. to serve as their father's agent for Union Pacific Railroad grading contracts.

1869   Called to preside over the Saints in Cache County, Utah.

1878   Served with George Q. Cannon and Albert Carrington as an executor of the Brigham Young estate.

        A small group of heirs brought suit against the Church and executors. When a $50,000 contempt of court bond was required for each executor in addition to the $300,000 already posted, President Cannon declared the extra bonding excessive and decided it was better to go to jail than further obligate themselves and their friends financially. The three spent three weeks in the penitentiary before the Utah Supreme Court set aside the decision of the lower court.

1885   Young was instrumental in securing Mexican permission to establish Mormon colonies south of the border in 1885 as havens for those harried by anti-polygamy regulations in the United States.

President of the Quorum of the Twelve:

Young Brigham, though appointed special counselor to his father in 1864, was not admitted to the Quorum of the Twelve until 1868, after the death of George A. Smith. In 1873 Brigham was called as one of five assistant counselors to his father. At the time of his father's death in 1877, there was much speculation, both within and without the Church, that Brigham Jr. would succeed his father as president.

1890   Sustained as president of the Quorum of the Twelve.

1898   Though the Spanish-American War was popular with the American public and Church officials, Young opposed it. He counseled against enlistment and even preached publicly against the call for volunteers. The First Presidency asked him to stop his personal efforts against the war. When he did, the First Presidency issued a statement supporting the war effort.

1900   Seniority in the Twelve was changed to reflect date of entry into the Quorum rather than date of ordination. Thus Joseph F. Smith became senior apostle and hence Church president in 1901 instead of Young.

Death:

1903   April 11: Died of bronchitis of the liver in Salt Lake City at the age of sixty-nine. He was buried in the Salt Lake City Cemetery.

Zina D. H. Young

(1821-1901)

Plural Wife of Prophets
Third President of the Relief Society
Women's Rights Advocate

Family Background:

1821   January 21: Born Zina Diantha Huntington in Watertown, New York. She married Henry B. Jacobs in March, 1841, and was sealed to Joseph Smith seven months later, seven months pregnant with Jacobs's child.

        T. B. H. Stenhouse reported that some time after Joseph Smith's death, "within the hearing of many Saints ... [Brigham Young] ordered those walking in other men's shoes to step out of them. 'Brother Jacobs,' Young declared, 'the woman you claim for a wife does not belong to you. She is the spiritual wife of brother Joseph sealed up to him. I am his proxy, and she is, in this behalf, with her children, my property. You can go where you please, and get another, but be sure to get one of your own kindred spirit.'"

        In 1846 Jacobs "stood approving as [Zina's] earlier sealing to Joseph Smith was confirmed by proxy in the Nauvoo Temple," and "witnessed her sealing 'for time' to Brigham Young."

        Zina and Brigham had only one child, but she also reared four of his children by Clara Ross after the death of their mother.

Convert:

1835   After baptism by Hyrum Smith, Zina's entire family moved to Kirtland, Ohio, where she exercised the "gift of tongues and interpretation thereof." Eliza R. Snow and Zina often worked as a revelatory team, one speaking in tongues while the other interpreted.

Pioneer Midwife and Teacher:

        Zina D. H. Young took a medical course in the early 1850s and became a midwife and nurse. She also taught school. She frequently administered "washings and anointings" to women prior to childbirth.

        As president of the Church Silk Association, she traveled the territory promoting the cultivation of mulberry trees and silkworms. She was the manager of Brigham Young's cocoonery.

Plural Marriage Advocate:

1876   At a women's mass meeting in Salt Lake City she proclaimed, "The principle of plural marriage is honorable. It is a principle of the Gods, it is heaven born. God revealed it to us as a saving principle; we have accepted it as such, and we know it is of him for the fruits of it are holy. Even the Savior, himself, traces his lineage back to polygamic parents. We are proud of the principle, because we know its true worth, and we want our children to practice it, that through us a race of men and women may grow up possessing sound minds in sound bodies, who shall live to the age of a tree."

She advised, "I think that much of the unhappiness found in polygamous families is due to the women themselves. They expect too much attention from the husband, and because they do not get it, or see a little attention bestowed upon one of the other wives, they become sullen and morose, and permit their ill-temper to finally find vent."

A successful polygamous wife "must regard her husband with indifference, and with no other feeling than that of reverence, for love we regard as a false sentiment; a feeling which should have no existence in polygamy. The marriages which we read of in the Old Testament were not love matches, as of instance, the marriage of Isaac to Rebekah, of Jacob to Leah; and we believe in the good old custom by which marriages should be arranged by the parents of the young people."

Third President of the Relief Society:

1888   A charter member of the Nauvoo Relief Society, Zina D. H. Young was selected second counselor to President Eliza R. Snow in 1879. In 1888 Wilford Woodruff called her to be the third president of the Relief Society.

Death:

1901   August 28: Died of old age—sexton's records list "senility"—at her home at 146 Fourth Street in Salt Lake

City at the age of eighty. Buried in the Salt Lake City Cemetery family plot of her first husband, Henry B. Jacobs, who had died of Bright's disease in 1886. Her epitaph is the motto of the Relief Society: "Charity never faileth."

Bibliography

Elijah Abel
Bringhurst, Newell G. "Elijah Abel and the Changing Status of Blacks Within Mormonism." *Dialogue: A Journal of Mormon Thought* 12 (1979):22-36.
Bush, Lester E. "Mormonism's Negro Doctrine: An Historical Overview." *Dialogue: A Journal of Mormon Thought* 8 (1973):11-68.
Carter, Kate B. *The Negro Pioneer.* Salt Lake City: Daughters of the Utah Pioneers, 1965.
History of the Church 4:365.
Jenson, Andrew. *LDS Biographical Encyclopedia.* 4 vols. Salt Lake City: Andrew Jenson Historical Company, 1901-1936.
Journal History, 20 December 1836, 2 January 1837, 1 June 1839.
Messenger and Advocate 2:335.
Provo, Utah. Brigham Young University. Harold B. Lee Library. Adam S. Bennion Papers. "Council of Twelve Meeting Minutes," 4 June 1879, 26 August 1908.
———. John Nuttal, diary of August 1878-June 1879.
Salt Lake City. LDS Church Archives. A Record of All the Quorums of Seventy in the Church of Jesus Christ of Latter-day Saints 1859-1863.
———. First Quorum of Seventies Minute Book, 6 June 1877.
———. Book B. General Record of Seventies 1844-1847.
———. Book B75:2955. Index to Missionary Records: 1830-1970, 1883.
———. Minutes of a Conference of the Church of Jesus Christ of Latter-day Saints held in Cincinnati, 25 June 1843.
———. Minutes of First Council of Seventy: 1859-1863, 5 March 1879.
———. 6175, Part 1. Missionary Records: 1860-1906. 1883, p. 75.

Almon W. Babbitt
Barrett, Gwynn W. "John M. Bernhisel—Mormon Elder in Congress." Ph.D. dissertation, Brigham Young University, 1968.
Crescent City Oracle, 22 May 1857.
Frontier Guardian, 21 February 1849, 29 April 1852.
History of the Church 2:252; 3:346; 4:164-166, 187, 424, 276.
Millennial Star 19:443; 17:307.
Nauvoo Neighbor, 20 January 1845.
Ridd, Jay D. "Almon Whiting Babbitt." Master's thesis, University of Utah, 1953.
Roberts, B. H. *Comprehensive History* 2:524
Salt Lake City, Utah. LDS Church Archives. Brigham Young Papers. John M. Bernhisel to Brigham Young, 19 July 1851.
———. Thomas L. Kane to Brigham Young, 24 September 1850.
———. Brigham Young to Orson Hyde, 19 July 1849.

John C. Bennett
Bennett, John C. *The History of the Saints: Or an Expose' of Joe Smith and Mormonism.* Boston: Leland & Whiting, 1842.
Hill, Donna. *Joseph Smith: The First Mormon.* Garden City, New York: Doubleday & Co., 1977.
History of the Church 4:341.

Hogan, Mervin B. "The Confrontation of G. M. Abraham Jonas and John Cook Bennett at Nauvoo." Mimeographed. Salt Lake City. LDS Church History Library.

McKiernan, F. Mark. *The Voice of One Crying in the Wilderness: Sidney Rigdon, Religious Reformer.* Lawrence, Kansas: Coronado Press, 1971.

New Haven, Connecticut. Yale University. Beinecke Rare Book and Manuscript Library. John C. Bennett Letters in James D. Strang Papers.

Salt Lake City, Utah. LDS Church Archives. *Proceedings of the Grand Lodge of Illinois A. F. and M. for 1952.*

The History of the Reorganized Church of Jesus Christ of Latter Day Saints. 3 vols. Independence, Missouri: Herald House, 1967.

Times and Seasons 2:404.

Tyler, Dr. James J. *John Cook Bennett: Colorful Freemason of the Early Nineteenth Century.* Grand Masonic Lodge of Ohio, 1947.

John M. Bernhisel

Barrett, Gwynn W. "John M. Bernhisel: Mormon Elder in Congress." Ph.D. dissertation, Brigham Young University, 1968.

Blanche, Rose. "Early Utah Medical Practice." *Utah Historical Quarterly* 10 (1942):18-19

Salt Lake City, Utah. LDS Genealogical Society Library. Endowment House Record Books E and F.

Salt Lake City, Utah. LDS Church Archives. John M. Bernhisel Papers. John M Bernhisel to Thomas L. Kane, 4 December 1849; to Brigham Young, 8 November 1852, 14 December 1854.

———. Manuscript History of Brigham Young, 26 November 1849.

Sam Brannan

Archuleta, Kay. *The Brannan Saga.* San Jose, California: Smith McKay Printing Co., 1977.

Bailey, Paul. *Sam Brannan and the California Mormons.* Salt Lake City: Westernlore Press, 1959.

Provo, Utah. Brigham Young University. Harold B. Lee Library. Sam Brannan Letters.

Salt Lake City, Utah. LDS Church Archives. Brigham Young Papers. Wilford Woodruff to Brigham Young, 3 December 1844.

———. Brigham Young to Sam Brannan, 6 June 1847, 5 April 1849.

Stellman, Louis J. *Sam Brannan, Builder of San Francisco: A Biography.* New York: Exposition Press, 1954.

Tyler, Daniel. *A Concise History of the Mormon Battalion in the Mexican War.* Salt Lake City, 1881.

George H. Brimhall

Pardoe, T. Earl. *The Sons of Brigham.* Provo, Utah: Brigham Young University Alumni, 1969.

Provo, Utah. Brigham Young University. Harold B. Lee Library. George H. Brimhall Journal.

———. Benjamin Cluff, Jr., Presidential Papers.

———. "Pedagogical History of the Brigham Young Academy Class of '93."

Provo Daily Herald, 17 March 1911, 31 July 1932.

Salt Lake Telegram, 30 July 1932, p. 2

Sherlock, Richard. "Campus in Crisis: BYU, 1911." *Sunstone* 4 (January-February 1979):10-16

Smith, Joseph F. "Philosophy and the Church Schools." *Juvenile Instructor*, April 1911, pp. 208-209.
Wilkinson, Ernest L. *Brigham Young University: The First One Hundred Years*. 4 vols. Provo, Utah: Brigham Young University Press, 1975.

Fawn M. Brodie

American Literature 46 (January 1975):581.
Brodie, Fawn M. "Can We Manipulate the Past?" Paper read at First Annual American West Lecture. Salt Lake City, 1970.
Los Angeles Times, 20 February 1877, 12 January 1981.
Provo, Utah. Barbara Mckay Smith Letter Collection.
———. Fawn Brodie Memorial Services.
Salt Lake City, Utah. University of Utah. J. Willard Marriott Library. Fawn M. Brodie Interview at California State University at Fullerton, 30 November 1975.
———. Fawn M. Brodie Letter Collection.

Hugh B. Brown

Brown, Hugh B. "Be Aware—Beware," baccalaureate address, Brigham Young University, 24 May 1962.
———. *Continuing the Quest*. Salt Lake City: Bookcraft, 1961.
———. *The Abundant Life*. Salt Lake City: Bookcraft, 1965.
Campbell, Eugene E., and Poll, Richard D. *Hugh B. Brown: His Life and Thought*. Salt Lake City: Bookcraft, 1975.
Deseret News, 3 December 1975.
Improvement Era 56:914.

Abraham H. Cannon

Cannon, Frank J., and Higgins, Harvey J. *Under the Prophet in Utah*. Boston: C. M. Clark Publishing Co., 1911.
Deseret News, 20 July 1896.
Jenson, Andrew. *Latter-day Saint Biographical Encyclopedia*. 4 vols Salt Lake City: Andrew Jenson Historical Company, 1901-1936.
Salt Lake City, Utah. LDS Church Archives. Abraham H. Cannon Journal.

Frank J. Cannon

Cannon, Frank J., and Higgins, Harvey J. *Under the Prophet in Utah*. Boston: G. M. Clark Publishing Co., 1911.
Salt Lake City, Utah. LDS Church Archives. Abraham H. Cannon Journal.
———. George F. Gibbs Papers.
———. Joseph F. Smith Letters.
Salt Lake Tribune, 7 March 1905, 26 July 1933.
Snow, Reuben Joseph. "The American Party in Utah: A Study of Political Party Struggles During the Early Years of Statehood." Master's thesis, University of Utah, 1964.
Whitney, Orson F. *History of Utah*. 4 vols. Salt Lake City: George Q. Cannon & Sons, 1890-1904.

George Q. Cannon

Cannon, Frank J., and Higgins, Harvey J. *Under the Prophet in Utah*. Boston: G. M. Clark Publishing Co., 1911.
Cannon, Mark W. "The Mormon Issue in Congress, 1872-1882: Drawing on the Experience of Territorial Delegate George Q. Cannon." Ph.D. thesis, Harvard University, 1960.

Cannon, M. Hamlin. "Prison Diary of a Mormon Apostle." *Pacific Historical Review* 16 (November 1947):395-409.
Evans, Beatrice Cannon, and Cannon, Janath Russell, eds. *Cannon Family Historical Treasury.* Salt Lake City: G. Q. Cannon Family Association, 1967.
Jenson, Andrew. *Latter-day Saint Biographical Encyclopedia.* 4 vols. Salt Lake City: Andrew Jenson Historical Company, 1901-1936.
Journal of Discourses 12:290-291, 297.
Quinn, D. Michael. "The Council of Fifty and Its Members: 1844-1945." *Brigham Young University Studies* 20 (Winter 1980):163-197.
Roberts, B. H. *Comprehensive History* 6:381-382.
Salt Lake City, Utah. LDS Church Archives. Abraham H. Cannon Journal.

Martha Hughes Cannon

Salt Lake City, Utah. LDS Church Archives. Angus M. Cannon Papers.
Salt Lake City, Utah. Utah State Historical Society. Elizabeth Cannon McCrimmon, "Martha Hughes Cannon."
San Francisco Examiner, 8 November 1896.
White, Jean Bickmore, "Martha H. Cannon." *Sister Saints.* Edited by Vicky-Burgess-Olson. Provo, Utah: Brigham Young University Press, 1978.

Butch Cassidy

Betenson, Lula, as told to Dora Flack. *Butch Cassidy, My Brother.* Provo, Utah: Brigham Young University Press, 1975.
Kelly, Charles. *The Outlaw Trail: A History of Butch Cassidy and His Wild Bunch.* New York: Bonanza Books, 1959.
Luke, Theron. "Butch Cassidy: Man or Legend?" *Provo Daily Herald,* 7 September 1969.
Pointer, Larry. *In Search of Butch Cassidy.* Norman, Oklahoma: University of Oklahoma Press, 1977.
Wyoming State Tribune, 16 June 1939.

J. Reuben Clark

Clark, J. Reuben, Jr. "Address of J. Reuben Clark, Jr." *American Bar Association Journal* 26 (1940):901-902.
Clark, J. Reuben, Jr. *Stand Fast by Our Constitution.* Salt Lake City: Deseret News Press, 1959.
Conference Reports, April 1940.
Congressional Record, 11 June 1940.
Deseret News, 13 August 1938, 6 October 1961.
Flake, Lawrence. *Mighty Men of Zion.* Salt Lake City: Karl D. Butler, 1974.
Fox, Frank W. *J. Reuben Clark: The Public Years.* Provo, Utah: BYU Press/Deseret Book Company, 1980.

Oliver Cowdery

Anderson, Richard Lloyd. *Investigating the Book of Mormon Witnesses.* Salt Lake City: Deseret Book Company, 1981.
Gunn, Stanley R. *Oliver Cowdery: Second Elder and Scribe.* Salt Lake City: Bookcraft, 1962.
History of the Church 2:379-383, 3:16.
Lang, W. *History of Seneca County from the Close of the Revolutionary War to July 1880.* Tiffin, Ohio: Transcript Printing Co., 1880.
Larson, A. Karl, and Larson, Katharine Miles. *The Diary of Charles Lowell Walker.* 2 vols. Logan, Utah: Utah State University Press, 1980.

Quinn, D. Michael. "Echoes and Foreshadowings: The Distinctiveness of the Mormon Community." *Sunstone* 3 (March-April 1978):12-17.

———. "The Mormon Succession Crisis of 1844." *Brigham Young University Studies* 16 (Winter 1976):187-233.

Salt Lake City, Utah. LDS Church Archives. Pottawattamie High Council Minutes, 4-5 November 1848.

Matthew Cowley

Cowley, Matthew. *Matthew Cowley Speaks*. Salt Lake City: Deseret News Press, 1954.

Salt Lake City, Utah. LDS Church Archives. Abbie Hyde Cowley Journal, 28 July 1895.

Smith, Henry A. *Matthew Cowley: Man of Faith*. Salt Lake City: Bookcraft, 1968.

Richard L. Evans

Deseret News, 1 November 1971.

Evans, Richard L. *Thoughts for One Hundred Days*. Salt Lake City: Publishers Press, 1966.

Evans, Richard L. *Richard L. Evans: The Man and the Message*. Salt Lake City: Bookcraft, 1973.

Flake, Lawrence. *Mighty Men of Zion*. Salt Lake City: Karl D. Butler, 1974.

Woolsey, Heber G. *Memorial Services for Richard L. Evans*. Provo: Brigham Young University Press, 1971.

Green Flake

Brooks, Juanita, ed. *On the Mormon Frontier: The Diary of Hosea Stout*. 2 vols. Salt Lake City: University of Utah Press/Utah State Historical Society, 1964.

Brown, John Zimmerman. *Autobiography of Pioneer John Brown: 1820-1896*. Salt Lake City, 1941.

Carter, Kate B. *Our Pioneer Heritage*. Salt Lake City: Daughters of Utah Pioneers, 1959.

Flake, Osmer D. *Life of William Jordan Flake*. Salt Lake City: Church News, 1948.

Lythgoe, Dennis L. "Negro Slavery in Utah." *Utah Historical Quarterly* 39 (1971):40-54.

Madsen, Steven K. Interview, 21 October 1979.

Salt Lake City, Utah. LDS Church Archives. William J. Flake to Church Historian's Office, 14 February 1894.

Salt Lake City, Utah. LDS Genealogical Society Library. Jordan Flake Will. North Carolina Wills, Anson County, 1751-1942.

Susa Young Gates

Cornwall, Rebecca Foster. "Susa Young Gates: The Thirteenth Apostle." *Sister Saints*. Edited by Vicky Burgess-Olson. Provo, Utah: Brigham Young University Press, 1978.

Cracroft, R. Paul. "Susa Young Gates: Her Life and Her Work." Master's thesis, University of Utah, 1959.

Gates, Susa Young, "The Editor Presumes to Talk About Herself." *Young Woman's Journal* 7(1896):200-203.

———."Woman's Power." *Young Woman's Journal* 1 (1890):442.

Jakeman, James T. *Album Daughters of the Utah Pioneers and Their Mothers*. Salt Lake City: Western Publishing Co. Inc., 1916.

Person, Carolyn W. D. "Susa Young Gates." *Mormon Sisters*. Edited by Claudia Bushman. Cambridge, Massachusetts: Emmeline Press, 1976.

William Godbe

Arrington, Leonard J. *Great Basin Kingdom.* Cambridge, Massachusetts: Harvard University Press, 1958.

———. "Taxable Income in Utah." *Utah Historical Quarterly* 24 (January 1956):21-47.

Deseret News, 2 August 1902.

Godbe, Hampton. Family Records.

Journal History, 19 September 1868, 3 October 1868.

Phrenological Journal, July 1871.

Tullidge's Quarterly Magazine, October 1880.

Tullidge, Edward. *Life of Brigham Young or Utah and Her Founders.* New York, 1877.

Utah Magazine, 27 November 1869.

Walker, Ronald W. "The Commencement of the Godbeite Protest: Another View." *Utah Historical Quarterly* 42 (Summer 1974):216-244.

———. "The Godbeite Protest in the Making of Modern Utah." Ph.D. dissertation, University of Utah, 1977.

Heber J. Grant

Allen, James B., and Leonard, Glen M. *The Story of the Latter-day Saints.* Salt Lake City: Deseret Book Company, 1976.

Conference Reports, April 1900, October 1941.

Durham, G. Homer. *Gospel Standards: Selections from the Writings of Heber J. Grant.* Salt Lake City: *Improvement Era,* 1941.

Gibbons, Francis M. *Heber J. Grant: Man of Steel, Prophet of God.* Salt Lake City: Deseret Book Company, 1979.

Jorgensen, Victor W., and Hardy, B. Carmon. "The Taylor-Cowley Affair and the Watershed of Mormon History." *Utah Historical Quarterly* 48 (Winter 1980):4-36.

Quinn, D. Michael. "The Council of Fifty and Its Members, 1844 to 1945." *Brigham Young University Studies* 20 (Winter 1980):163-197.

———. "Organizational Development and Social Origins of the Mormon Hierarchy, 1832-1932: A Prosopographical Study." Master's thesis, University of Utah, 1973.

Salt Lake City, Utah. LDS Church Archives. Abraham H. Cannon Journal, 8 April 1894.

———. Heber J. Grant Correspondence and Journals.

Walker, Ronald W. Crisis In Zion: Heber J. Grant and the Panic of 1893." *Sunstone* 5 (January-February 1980):26-34.

Jedediah M. Grant

Brooks, Juanita, ed. *On the Mormon Frontier: The Diary of Hosea Stout.* 2 vols. Salt Lake City: University of Utah Press/Utah Historical Society, 1964.

Journal of Discourses 3:60-61, 4:85-87.

Judd, Mary G. *Jedediah M. Grant.* Salt Lake City: Deseret News Press, 1969.

Salt Lake City, Utah. LDS Church Archives. Wilford Woodruff Journal, 6 August 1847.

Walker, Ronald. "Jedediah and Heber Grant." *Ensign,* July 1979, pp. 48-50.

Jacob Hamblin
Arnold, Frank R. "Utah Piety on the North Rim of the Grand Canyon." *Improvement Era*, June 1926, p. 765.
Christensen, C. L. "Personal Experiences of an Indian Interpreter of the Navajo Tribe." *Contributor* 16 (1895):555.
Corbett, Pearson H. *Jacob Hamblin: the Peacemaker.* Salt Lake City: *Deseret News* Press, 1952.
Little, James A. *Jacob Hamblin.* Salt Lake City: *Deseret News* Press, 1909.
Peterson, Charles S. "Lamanites and the Indian Mission." *Journal of Mormon History* 2 (1975):21-34.
Salt Lake City, Utah. LDS Church Archives. James G. Bleak, "Annals of the Southern Utah Mission."

Martin Harris
Anderson, Richard Lloyd. *Investigating the Book of Mormon Witnesses.* Salt Lake City: Deseret Book Company, 1981.
Contributor 5 (1884):406.
Deseret News, 24 September 1856.
History of the Church 1:21, 2:95, 2:510, 2:575, 4:424.
Jenson, Andrew. *LDS Biographical Encyclopedia.* 4 vols. Salt Lake City: Andrew Jenson Historical Company, 1901-1936.
Journal of Discourses 18:160.
Millennial Star, 31 October 1846.
Nibley, Preston, ed. *History of Joseph Smith By His Mother.* Salt Lake City: Deseret Book Company, 1973.
Salt Lake City, Utah. LDS Church Archives. William Pilkington, Jr. "The Dying Testimony of Martin Harris as given to William Pilkington, Jr., by Martin Harris Himself in Clarkston, Cache Co., Utah."
———. William Pilkington, Jr. "Autobiography."

Bill Hickman
Arrington, Leonard J., and Hilton, Hope A. "William A. Hickman: Setting the Record Straight." Mimeographed. Task Papers in LDS History #28. Salt Lake City: LDS Church Historical Department, 1979.
Deseret News, 24 August 1883, 23 August 1885.
Hickman, William A. *Brigham's Destroying Angel: Being the Life and Confessions of the Notorious Bill Hickman, Danite Chief of Utah.* Edited by J. H. Beadle. Salt Lake City: Shepherd Publishing Company, 1904.
Hickman, William A., Family Organization. *Profiles of William Adams Hickman.* Salt Lake City: William A. Hickman Family Organization, 1980.
Hilton, Hope A. *Some Progenitors and Descendents of Edwin and Eleanor Webber Hickman.* Salt Lake City: Hope A. Hilton, 1978.
Hunter, Milton R. *Brigham Young, the Colonizer.* Salt Lake City: Deseret News Company, 1940.
Jenson, Andrew. *Historical Record* 6:343.
New York Times, 29 September 1859.
Salt Lake City, Utah. LDS Church Archives. Brigham Young Office Journal and Papers.

Orson Hyde
Barron, Howard H. *Orson Hyde: Missionary-Apostle-Colonizer.* Salt Lake City: Horizon Publishers, 1977.
Deseret News, 3 October 1877.

Hill, Marvin. "Orson Hyde." Master's thesis, Brigham Young University, 1955.
History of the Church 1:415, 3:167-168, 4:106, 4:446-459, 6:98, 6:345.
Hyde, Orson. "History of Orson Hyde." *Millennial Star* 26 (1864):742-792.
Journal of Discourses 2:81.
Page, Albert R. *Orson Hyde and the Carson Valley Mission, 1855-1857*. Provo, Utah: Brigham Young University Press, 1970.
Roberts, B. H. *Comprehensive History* 1:473, 2:45.

Anthony W. Ivins
Deseret News, 24 September 1934.
Dryden, David. "Task Papers in LDS History." Mimeographed. Salt Lake City: LDS Church Historian's Office, 1976.
Durham, G. Homer. *Gospel Standards: Selections from the Writings of Heber J. Grant*. Salt Lake City: Improvement Era, 1941.
Hatch, Nelle Spilsbury. *Colonia Juarez: An Intimate Account of A Mormon Village*. Salt Lake City: Deseret Book Company, 1954.
Jorgensen, Victor W., and Hardy, B. Carmon. "The Taylor-Cowley Affair and the Watershed of Mormon History." *Utah Historical Quarterly* 48 (Winter 1980):4-36.
Romney, Thomas Cottah. *The Mormon Colonies in Mexico*. Salt Lake City: Deseret Book Company, 1938.
Salt Lake City, Utah. Utah State Historical Society Library. Anthony W. Ivins Collection.

Heber C. Kimball
Conference Reports, October 1910.
Deseret News, 31 March 1858.
Journal of Discourses 1:161; 4:138; 5:28, 154; 10:240.
Kimball, Stanley B. *Heber C. Kimball: Mormon Patriarch and Pioneer*. Urbana, Illinois: University of Illinois Press, 1981.
McIntyre, Myron, and Barton, Noel R. *Christopher Layton*. Salt Lake City: Christopher Layton Family Organization, 1966.
Salt Lake City, Utah. LDS Church Archives. Heber C. Kimball Journal and Private Memorandum Book.
———. Solomon F. Kimball, "Sacred History."
Watson, Elden Jay, ed. *Manuscript History of Brigham Young: 1801-1844*. Salt Lake City: By the Author, 1968.
Whitney, Orson F. *Life of Heber C. Kimball, An Apostle: The Father and Founder of the British Mission*. Salt Lake City: The Kimball Family, 1888.
Woman's Exponent, January 1884, p. 127.

J. Golden Kimball
Cheney, Thomas E. *The Golden Legacy: A Folk History of J. Golden Kimball*. Salt Lake City/Santa Barbara, California: Peregrine Smith Inc., 1974.
Deseret News, 3 September 1938.
Fife, Austin, and Fife, Alta. *Saints of Sage & Saddle*. Bloomington, Indiana: University of Indiana Press, 1956.
Richards, Claude J. *J. Golden Kimball: The Story of a Unique Personality*. Salt Lake City: Deseret News Press, 1934.
Salt Lake City, Utah. LDS Church Archives. J. Golden Kimball Journals.

Jesse Knight
Allen, James B., and Leonard, Glen M. *The Story of the Latter-day Saints*. Salt Lake City: Deseret Book Company, 1976.

Butterworth, Edwin, Jr. *1,000 Views of 100 Years*. Provo: Brigham Young University Press, 1975.

Knight, Jesse William. *The Jesse Knight Family*. Salt Lake City: Deseret News Press, 1940.

Harold B. Lee

Deseret News, 27 December 1973.

Conference Reports, October 1961, October 1973.

Improvement Era, July 1953.

Lee, Harold B. *From the Valley of Despair to the Mountain Peaks of Hope*. Salt Lake City: Deseret Book Company, 1971.

My Kingdom Shall Roll Forth. Salt Lake City: Corporation of the President of the Church of Jesus Christ of Latter-day Saints, 1980.

John D. Lee

Brooks, Juanita. *John D. Lee*. Glendale, California: Arthur H. Clark Company, 1972.

Cleland, Robert Grass, and Brooks, Juanita, eds. *A Mormon Chronicle: The Diaries of John D. Lee 1848-1876*. 2 vols. San Marino, California: Huntington Library, 1955.

Deseret News, 21 April 1894.

Lee, John D. *Mormonism Unveiled*. St. Louis: Bryan, Brand, & Co., 1877.

Salt Lake City, Utah. LDS Church Archives. John D. Lee Journals.

Amasa Lyman

History of the Church 3:209, 5:255.

Jenson, Andrew. *LDS Biographical Encyclopedia*. 4 vols. Salt Lake City: Andrew Jenson Historical Company, 1901-1936.

Journal of Discourses 3:170, 7:299.

Lyman, Albert R. *Amasa Mason Lyman*. Fillmore, Utah: Melvin A. Lyman, 1957.

Lyman, Albert R. *Francis Marion Lyman: Apostle*. Delta, Utah: Melvin A. Lyman, 1958.

Millennial Star 24:231, 27:473.

Salt Lake City, Utah. LDS Church Archives. Abraham H. Cannon Journal.

———. Amasa M. Lyman Journal.

Times and Seasons 6:664.

Walker, Ronald, "The Godbeite Protest in the Making of Modern Utah." Ph.D. dissertation, University of Utah, 1977.

Amy Brown Lyman

Deseret News, 13 November 1943.

Hefner, Loretta L. "Amy B. Lyman." *Sister Saints*. Edited by Vicky Burgess-Olson. Provo, Utah: Brigham Young University Press, 1978.

Lyman, Amy Brown. *In Retrospect*. Salt Lake City: General Board of the Relief Society, 1945.

Provo, Utah. Brigham Young University. Harold B. Lee Library. Amy Brown Lyman Papers. Transcript of KSL Radio interview with Amy Brown Lyman.

Francis M. Lyman

Lyman, Albert R. *Amasa Mason Lyman*. Fillmore, Utah: Melvin A. Lyman, 1957.

Lyman, Albert R. *Francis Marion Lyman: Apostle*. Delta, Utah: Melvin A. Lyman, 1958.

Salt Lake City, Utah. University of Utah. J. Willard Marriott Library. Samuel W. Taylor Papers.

Karl G. Maeser
Gates, Susa Young. "Dr. Karl G. Maeser." *Young Woman's Journal* 3 (August, 1892):481-486.

Maeser, Reinhard. *Karl G. Maeser.* Provo: Brigham Young University, 1928.

Pardoe, T. Earl. *The Sons of Brigham.* Provo: Brigham Young University Alumni, 1969.

Wilkinson, Ernest L. *Brigham Young University: The First One Hundred Years.* 4 vols. Provo: Brigham Young University Press, 1975.

Thomas B. Marsh
Journal of Discourses 5:116, 206-210.

History of the Church 3:167.

Roberts, B. H. *Comprehensive History* 1:429.

Salt Lake City, Utah. LDS Church Archives. Wandle Mace Journal: 1809-1890.

———. Brigham Young Letter Collection.

Smith, Hyrum M., and Sjodahl, James M. *Doctrine and Covenants Commentary.* Salt Lake City: Deseret Book Company, 1951.

Van Wagoner, Richard, and Walker, Steven C. "The Return of Thomas B. Marsh." *Sunstone*, 6 (July 1981):28-30.

David O. McKay
Conference Reports, April 1964.

Hinckley, Bryant S. "David O. McKay." *Improvement Era*, May 1932, pp. 391-443.

McKay, David O. *Home Memories of President David O. McKay.* Salt Lake City: Deseret Book Company, 1956.

Nibley, Preston. *The Presidents of the Church.* Salt Lake City: Deseret Book Company, 1971.

West, Emerson R. *Profiles of the Presidents.* Salt Lake City: Deseret Book Company, 1973.

Edward Partridge
Collette, D. Brent. "In Search of Zion: A Description of Early Mormon Millennial Utopianism as Revealed Through the Life of Edward Partridge." Master's thesis, Brigham Young University, 1977.

History of the Church 1:390-391.

Jenson, Andrew. *LDS Biographical Encyclopedia.* 4 vols. Salt Lake City: Andrew Jenson Historical Company, 1901-1936.

Quinn, D. Michael. "Evolution of the Presiding Quorums of the LDS Church." *Journal of Mormon History* 1 (1974)21-38.

David Patten
Berlin. Elliott. "Abraham Owen Smoot, Pioneer Mormon Leader." Master's thesis, Brigham Young University, 1955.

Jenson, Andrew. *LDS Biographical Encyclopedia.* 4 vols. Salt Lake City: Andrew Jenson Historical Company, 1901-1936.

Lee, John D. *Mormonism Unveiled.* Saint Louis: Bryan, Brand, & Co., 1877.

Millennial Star 16:408.

Report of Sashiel Woods and Joseph Dickson to Governor Boggs. *Documents, Correspondence, Orders, etc., in Relation to the Disturbances with the Mormons.* Published by order of the Missouri Legislature, 1841.

Salt Lake City, Utah. LDS Church Archives. Abraham H. Cannon Journal.

———. Wilford Woodruff Journal, 25 June 1857.

Wilson, Lycurgus Arnold. *the Life of David Patten: The First Apostolic Martyr.* Salt Lake City, 1900.

Romania Pratt Penrose

Salt Lake City, Utah. LDS Church Archives. Romania B. Pratt. "Memoir of Romania B. Pratt, M.D." Uncatalogued manuscript.

Waters, Christine Croft. "Romania P. Penrose." *Sister Saints.* Edited by Vicky Burgess-Olson. Provo: Brigham Young University Press, 1978.

Woman's Exponent 7:217.

Young Woman's Journal 2:534.

W. W. Phelps

Bowen, Walter Dean. "The Versatile W. W. Phelps: Mormon Writer, Educator, and Pioneer." Master's thesis, Brigham Young University, 1958.

Brooks, Juanita, ed. *On the Mormon Frontier: The Diary of Hosea Stout.* 2 vols. Salt Lake City: University of Utah Press/Utah Historical Society, 1964.

Esshom, Frank. *Pioneers and Prominent Men of Utah.* Salt Lake City: Utah Pioneers Book Publishing Company, 1915.

History of the Church 1:390-391, 4:164, 5:390, 6:477, 7:268.

Jennings, Warren A. "Factors in the Destruction of the Mormon Press in Missouri: 1833." *Utah Historical Quarterly* 35 (Winter 1967):57-76.

Jenson, Andrew. *Church Chronology.* Salt Lake City: *Deseret News*, 1899.

———. *LDS Biographical Encyclopedia.* 4 vols. Salt Lake City: Andrew Jenson Historical Company, 1901-1936.

Salt Lake City, Utah. LDS Church Archives. W. W. Phelps Papers.

———. Brigham Young Papers.

Times and Seasons 5:765.

Orson Pratt

Bergera, Gary James. "The Orson Pratt-Brigham Young Controversies: Conflict Within the Quorums, 1853-1868." *Dialogue* 13 (Summer 1980):7-49.

Cannon, Joseph J. "George Q. Cannon: Relations with Brigham Young." *The Instructor*, June 1945, p. 259.

Durham, Reed C., and Heath, Stephen H. *Successsion in the Church.* Salt Lake City: Bookcraft, 1970.

History of the Church 5:60-61, 139.

Journal of Discourses 4:297.

Larson, A. Karl, and Larson, Katharine. *Diary of Charles Lowell Walker.* 2 vols. Logan, Utah: Utah State University Press, 1980.

Lundwall, N. B. *Masterful Discourses and Writings of Orson Pratt.* Salt Lake City: Bookcraft, 1962.

Lyon, T. Edgar. "Orson Pratt: Early Mormon Leader." Master's thesis, University of Chicago, 1932.

Lyon, T. Edgar. "Orson Pratt: Pioneer and Proselyter." *Utah Historical Quarterly* 24 (July 1956):261.

Millennial Star 41:788.

Salt Lake City, Utah. LDS Church Archives. Mrs. Orson Pratt, "The Workings of Mormonism."

Utah Genealogical and Historical Magazine 27:113-115.

Watson, Elden J., ed. *Orson Pratt Journals.* Salt Lake City: By the Author, 1975.

Parley P. Pratt

Journal of Discourses 6:15.

New York Herald, 23 November 1869.

Pratt, Parley P. *Autobiography of Parley P. Pratt*. Salt Lake City: Deseret Book Company, 1966.

Pratt, Steven. "Eleanor McLean and the Murder of Parley P. Pratt." *Brigham Young University Studies* 15 (Winter 1975):225-256.

Smith, Joseph Fielding. *Essentials in Church History*. 26th ed. Salt Lake City: Deseret Book Company, 1973.

Stanley, Reva. *Biography of Parley P. Pratt: The Archer of Paradise*. Caldwell: Caxton Printers Ltd., 1937.

Alice Louise Reynolds

Keele, Reba L. "Alice L. Reynolds." *Sister Saints*. Edited by Vicky Burgess-Olson. Provo, Utah: Brigham Young University Press, 1978.

Lyman, Amy Brown. *A Lighter of Lamps: The Life Story of Alice Louise Reynolds*. Provo: The Alice Louise Reynolds Club, 1947.

Provo, Utah. Brigham Young University. Harold B. Lee Library. "Autobiography of Alice Louise Reynolds."

———. Alice Louise Reynolds, "History of George Reynolds."

Reynolds, Alice Louise. "Music That Pays Dividends." *National Education Association Journal of Proceedings and Addresses*. Chicago: University of Chicago Press, 1913.

Willard Richards

Barrett, Gwynn W. "John M. Bernhisel: Mormon Elder in Congress." *Utah Historical Quarterly* 36 (Spring 1968):143-167.

Deseret News, 16 March 1854.

Jenson, Andrew. *LDS Biographical Encyclopedia*. 4 vols. Salt Lake City: Andrew Jenson Historical Company, 1901-1936.

Times and Seasons 5:76.

Sidney Rigdon

Chase, Daryl. "Sidney Rigdon: Early Mormon." Master's thesis, University of Chicago, 1931.

Gregory, Thomas J. "Sidney Rigdon: Post Nauvoo." *Brigham Young University Studies* 21 (Winter 1981):51-67.

History of the Church 4:341; 5:8, 46, 532, 553-556; 6:47-49.

Hunt, James. *Mormonism*. Saint Louis: Ustick and Davies, 1844.

Keller, Karl, ed. "'I Never Knew A Time When I Did Not Know Joseph Smith': A Son's Record of the Life and Testimony of Sidney Rigdon." *Dialogue* 1 (Winter 1966):15-42.

Latter Day Saints Messenger and Advocate 1 (January 1845).

McKiernan, F. Mark. *The Voice of One Crying in the Wilderness: Sidney Rigdon, Religious Reformer (1793-1876)*. Lawrence, Kansas: Coronado Press, 1971.

Quinn, D. Michael. "Latter-day Saint Prayer Circles." *Brigham Young University Studies* 19 (Fall 1978):79-105.

———. "The Mormon Succession Crisis of 1844." *Brigham Young University Studies* 16 (Winter 1976):187-233.

Rollmann, Hans. "The Early Baptist Career of Sidney Rigdon in Warren, Ohio." *Brigham Young University Studies* 21 (Winter 1981):37-50.

Salt Lake City, Utah. LDS Church Archives. Reynolds Cahoon Diary.

———. Stephen Post Papers.

———. Sidney Rigdon Papers.

———. Salt Lake City School of the Prophets Minutes.

———. Brigham Young Papers.
Times and Seasons 5:660-666.

B. H. Roberts
Bitton, R. Davis. "The B. H. Roberts Case of 1899-1900." *Utah Historical Quarterly* 25 (Spring 1957):27-46.
Improvement Era, December 1933, p. 839.
Jenson, Andrew. *LDS Biographical Encyclopedia.* 4 vols. Salt Lake City: Andrew Jenson Historical Company, 1901-1936.
Madsen, Truman G. *B. H. Roberts: Defender of the Faith.* Salt Lake City: Bookcraft, 1981.
Malan, Robert H. *B. H. Roberts.* Salt Lake City: Deseret Book Company, 1966.
Provo, Utah. Brigham Young University. Harold B. Lee Library. Reed Smoot Diary.
Salt Lake City, Utah. LDS Church Archives. Alma Eldredge Journal.
———. Heber J. Grant Journal.
———. J. Golden Kimball Journal.
———. Journal History, 11 July 1907, 31 October 1908, 23 December 1933.
———. Seymour B. Young Journals and Notebooks.
Salt Lake Tribune, 15 September 1898, 7 November 1910.
Whitney, Orson F. *History of Utah.* 4 vols. Salt Lake City: George Q. Cannon and Sons Co., 1892-1894.

Porter Rockwell
Bennett, John C. *The History of the Saints: Or an Expose' of Joe Smith and Mormonism.* Boston: Leland & Whiting, 1842.
Clayton Family Association. *Journal of William Clayton.* Salt Lake City: Deseret News Press, 1921.
Deseret News, 10 October 1855, 31 August 1935.
History of the Church 5:305, 6:152.
Ludlow, Fitz Hugh. "Among the Mormons." *The Atlantic Monthly*, April 1864, p. 492.
Salt Lake Tribune, 30 September 1877, 11 June 1878, 13 June 1878, 24 February 1924.
Schindler, Harold. *Orrin Porter Rockwell: Man of God, Son of Thunder.* Salt Lake City: University of Utah Press, 1966.
Wyl, Wilhelm W. *Mormon Portraits: Joseph Smith the Prophet, His Family and His Friends.* Salt Lake City, 1886.

Aurelia Rogers
Madsen, Carol Cornwall, and Oman, Susan Staker. *Sisters and Little Saints.* Salt Lake City: Deseret Book Company, 1979.
Rogers, Aurelia S. *Life Sketches of Orson Spencer and Others, and History of Primary Work.* Salt Lake City: George Q. Cannon and Sons Co., 1898.
Ritchie, Elizabeth Kohler. "Aurelia S.Rogers." *Sister Saints.* Edited by Vicky Burgess-Olson. Provo, Utah: Brigham Young University Press, 1978.

Ellis Shipp
Casterline, Gail Farr. "Ellis R. Shipp." *Sister Saints.* Edited by Vicky Burgess-Olson. Provo, Utah: Brigham Young University Press, 1978.
Salt Lake City, Utah. LDS Church Archives. Journal History, 13 August 1878.
Musser, Ellis Shipp. *The Early Autobiography and Diary of Ellis R. Shipp, M.D.* Salt Lake City: Deseret News Press, 1962.

Emma Smith

Avery, Valeen Tippetts, and Newell, Linda King. "The Elect Lady: Emma Hale Smith." *Ensign*, September 1979, pp. 65-67.

———. "Lewis Bidamon: Stepchild of Mormonism." *BYU Studies* 19 (Spring 1979):375-88.

———. "The Lion and the Lady: Brigham Young and Emma Smith." *Utah Historical Quarterly* 48 (Winter 1980):81-97.

Bailey, Raymond T. "Emma Hale: Wife of the Prophet Joseph Smith." Master's thesis, Brigham Young University, 1952.

History of the Church 5:107, 6:249-250.

History of the Reorganized Church. 3 vols. Independence, Missouri: Herald House, 1967.

Independence, Missouri. RLDS Church Archives. Emma Smith Bidamon Letter Collection.

Provo, Utah. Brigham Young University. Harold B. Lee Library. Charles Bidamon Letter.

Saints' Herald, 1 October 1879.

Salt Lake City, Utah. LDS Archives. Journal History, 22 January 1848.

———. Brigham Young Papers.

Smith, Lucy Mack. *History of Joseph Smith.* Edited by Preston Nibley. Salt Lake City: Bookcraft, 1958.

Smith, Mary Audentia, ed., condensed by Vertha Audentia Anderson Hulmes. *Joseph Smith III and the Restoration.* Independence, Missouri: Herald House, 1952.

Snow, Eliza R. *Poems, Religious, Historical, Political.* Liverpool: F. D. Richards, 1856.

Times and Seasons, 10 June 1841.

George A. Smith

Church News, 30 May 1951.

Gleave, Ray Haun. "The Effect of the Speaking of George A. Smith on the People of the Iron Mission of Southern Utah." Master's thesis, Brigham Young University, 1957.

Jenson, Andrew. *LDS Biographical Encyclopedia.* 4 vols. Salt Lake City: Andrew Jenson Historical Company, 1901-1936.

Journal of Discourses 1:95-97, 2:360, 3:24-25, 15:97.

Ludlow, Fitz Hugh. *The Heart of the Continent: A Record of Travel Across the Plains and in Oregon, with an Examination of the Mormon Principle.* New York: Hurd and Houghton, 1870.

McCarthy, Justin. *Reminiscences.* New York and London, 1889.

Palmer, William. "Pioneers of Southern Utah." *Instructor* 79 (January 1944):21-24.

Pusey, Merlo J. *Builders of the Kingdom: George A. Smith, John Henry Smith, George Albert Smith.* Provo, Utah: Brigham Young University Press, 1981.

Quinn, D. Michael. "Organizational Development and Social Origins of the Mormon Hierarchy, 1832-1932: A Prosopographical Study." Master's thesis, University of Utah, 1973.

Salt Lake City, Utah. LDS Church Archives. Journal History, 29 July 1847, 12 June 1858.

———. Bathsheba Smith Autobiography.

———. George A. Smith Journal and Letter Collection.

Whitney, Orson F. *History of Utah.* 4 vols. Salt Lake City: George Q. Cannon and Sons Co., 1892.

George Albert Smith

Ballard, Melvin R. *Melvin J. Ballard: Crusader for Righteousness.* Salt Lake City: Bookcraft, 1966.

Conference Reports, October 1947.

My Kingdom Shall Roll Forth: Readings in Church History. Salt Lake City: The Church of Jesus Christ of Latter-day Saints, 1980.

Nibley, Preston. *The Presidents of the Church.* Salt Lake City: Deseret Book Company, 1971.

Pardoe, T. Earl. *The Sons of Brigham.* Provo: Brigham Young University Alumni, 1969.

Provo, Utah. Brigham Young University. Harold B. Lee Library. Reed Smoot Diary.

Pusey, Merlo J. *Builders of the Kingdom: George A. Smith, John Henry Smith, George Albert Smith.* Provo, Utah: Brigham Young University Press, 1981.

Salt Lake City, Utah. University of Utah. J. Willard Marriott Library. George Albert Smith Diary.

———. John Henry Smith Diary.

Stubbs, Glen R. "A Biography of George Albert Smith: 1870 to 1951." Ph.D. dissertation, Brigham Young University, 1974.

Hyrum Smith

Corbett, Pearson H. *Hyrum Smith: Patriarch.* Salt Lake City: Deseret Book Company, 1963.

History of the Church 1:466; 2:294-297, 335-343; 3:419-428; 5:107.

Independence, Missouri. RLDS Church Archives. Minutes of First Presidency and Quorum of the Twelve Apostles.

Quinn, D. Michael. "Organizational Development and Social Origins of the Mormon Hierarchy, 1832-1932: A Prosopographical Study." Master's thesis, University of Utah, 1973.

Roberts, B. H. *Comprehensive History* 2:162, 6:527-530.

Salt Lake City, Utah, LDS Church Archives. Brigham Young Papers.

Smith, Hyrum M., and Sjodahl, Janne M. *Doctrine and Covenants Commentary* Salt Lake City: Deseret Book Company, 1951.

Smith, Joseph Fielding. *Essentials in Church History.* 26th ed. Salt Lake City: Deseret Book Company, 1973.

Smith, Lucy. *Biographical Sketches of Joseph Smith the Prophet and His Progenitors for Many Generations.* Liverpool/London: Published for Orson Pratt by S. W. Richards, 1853.

Times and Seasons 3:799.

Joseph Smith

Brodie, Fawn M. *No Man Knows My History: The Life of Joseph Smith, the Mormon Prophet.* 2nd ed. New York: Alfred A. Knopf, 1971.

Conkling, Christopher. *A Joseph Smith Chronology.* Salt Lake City: Deseret Book Company, 1979.

Hill, Donna. *Joseph Smith: The First Mormon.* Garden City: Doubleday & Co., Inc., 1977.

History of the Church 2:170; 6:116, 244, 366, 605; 7:107.

Journal of Discourses 2:213.

Matthews, Robert J. *Joseph Smith's Translation of the Bible.* Provo, Utah: Brigham Young University Press, 1975.

Millennial Star 26:834.

Pratt, Parley P., Jr., ed. *Autobiography of Parley Parker Pratt.* Salt Lake City: Deseret Book Company, 1966.
Quinn, D. Michael. "The Council of Fifty and Its Members: 1844 to 1945." *Brigham Young University Studies* 20 (Winter 1980):163-197.
———. "Joseph Smith III's 1844 Blessing and the Mormons of Utah." *John Whitmer Historical Association Journal* 1 (1981):12-27
———. "Latter-day Saint Prayer Circles." *Brigham Young University Studies* 19 (Fall 1978):79-105.
Saints' Herald 26:289.
Salt Lake City, Utah. LDS Church Archives. Aroet L. Hale Journal.
———. Joseph Smith, Jr., Papers.

Joseph F. Smith

Allen, James B., and Leonard, Glen M. *The Story of the Latter-day Saints.* Salt Lake City: Deseret Book Company, 1976.
Arrington, Leonard J., and Bitton, Davis. *The Mormon Experience: A History of the Latter-day Saints.* New York: Alfred A. Knopf, 1979.
Arrington, Leonard J.; Esplin, Ron; and Rigby, Christine. "Joseph F. Smith: From Impulsive Young Man to Patriarchal Prophet." Address presented at the Joseph Smith Family Reunion, 1975.
Campbell, Eugene E., and Poll, Richard D. *Hugh B. Brown: His Life and Thought.* Salt Lake City: Bookcraft, 1975.
Conference Reports, April 1906, April 1930.
Clark, James R., ed. *Messages of the First Presidency of the Church.* 6 vols. Salt Lake City: Bookcraft, 1965-1975.
Jorgensen, Victor W., and Hardy, B. Carmon. "The Taylor-Cowley Affair and the Watershed of Mormon History." *Utah Historical Quarterly* 48 (Winter 1980):4-36.
Nibley, Preston. *The Presidents of the Church.* Salt Lake City: Deseret Book Company, 1971.
Quinn, D. Michael. "Organizational Development and Social Origins of the Mormon Hierarchy, 1832-1932: A Prosopographical Study." Master's thesis, University of Utah, 1973.
Salt Lake City, Utah. LDS Church Archives. Hyrum Smith Papers.
———. Joseph F. Smith Papers.
Salt Lake City, Utah. University of Utah. J. Willard Marriott Library. Joseph Fielding Smith Family Papers.
San Francisco, California. Fourth District Court, Case 14685, Levira A. Smith vs. Joseph F. Smith.
Smith, Joseph F. "Christmas and New Year." *Improvement Era,* January 1919, pp. 266-267.
Smith, Joseph Fielding. *Life of Joseph F. Smith.* Salt Lake City: Deseret News Press, 1938.

Joseph Fielding Smith

Conference Reports, April 1930.
Heslop, J. M., and Van Orden, Dell R. *Joseph Fielding Smith: A Prophet Among the People.* Salt Lake City: Deseret Book Company, 1971.
Hinckley, Bryant S. "Joseph Fielding Smith." *Improvement Era,* June 1932.
McConkie, Joseph F. *True and Faithful.* Salt Lake City: Bookcraft, 1971.
Nibley, Preston. *The Presidents of the Church.* Salt Lake City: Deseret Book Company, 1971.

Smith, Joseph Fielding, Jr., and Stewart, John J. *The Life of Joseph Fielding Smith.* Salt Lake City: Deseret Book Company, 1972.

West, Emerson R. *Profiles of the Presidents.* Salt Lake City: Deseret Book Company, 1973.

Lucy Mack Smith

Barrett, Ivan J. *Heroines of the Church.* Provo, Utah: Extension Publications Division of Continuing Education, Brigham Young University, 1966.

Bergera, Gary James. "The Orson Pratt-Brigham Young Controversy: Conflict Within the Quorums, 1853 to 1868." *Dialogue* 13 (Summer 1980):7-49.

Clark, James R., ed. *Messages of the First Presidency of the Church.* 6 vols. Salt Lake City: Bookcraft, 1956-1975.

History of the Church 7:471, 519.

Quinn, D. Michael. "Latter-day Saint Prayer Circles." *Brigham Young University Studies* 19 (Fall 1978):79-105.

———. "The Mormon Succession Crisis of 1844." *Brigham Young University Studies* 16 (Winter 1976):187-233.

Salt Lake City, Utah. LDS Church Archives. Brigham Young Papers.

Smith, Lucy Mack. *Biographical Sketches of Joseph Smith the Prophet, and His Progenitors for Many Generations.* Liverpool/London: Published for Orson Pratt by S.W. Richards, 1853.

Reed Smoot

Allen, James B. "The Great Protectionist, Sen. Reed Smoot of Utah." *Utah Historical Quarterly* 45 (Fall 1977):325-345.

———. "Personal Faith and Public Policy: Some Timely Observations on the League of Nations Controversy in Utah." *Brigham Young University Studies* 14 (Autumn 1973):77-98.

Jenson, Andrew. *Latter-day Saints' Biographical Encyclopedia.* 4 vols. Salt Lake City: Andrew Jenson Historical Company, 1901-1936.

Merrill, Milton R. "Reed Smoot: Apostle in Politics." Ph.D. dissertation, Columbia University, 1951.

———. *Reed Smoot: Utah Politician.* Logan, Utah: Utah State Agricultural College Monograph Series, 1953.

Pardoe, T. Earl. *The Sons of Brigham.* Provo, Utah: Brigham Young University, 1969.

Provo, Utah. Brigham Young University. Harold B. Lee Library. Reed Smoot Journals.

Salt Lake City, Utah. LDS Church Archives. Anthon H. Lund Journal.

Shipps, Jan. "The Public Image of Reed Smoot: 1902-1932." *Utah Historical Quarterly* 45 (Fall 1977):380-400.

Eliza R. Snow

Barrett, Ivan J. *Heroines of the Church.* Provo, Utah: Brigham Young University Extension Publications Division of Continuing Education, 1966.

Beecher, Maureen Ursenbach. "The Eliza Enigma: The Life and Legend of Eliza R. Snow." *Sister Saints.* Edited by Vicky Burgess-Olson. Provo, Utah: Brigham Young University Press, 1978.

Clark, James R. *Messages of the First Presidency.* 6 vols. Salt Lake City: Deseret Book Company, 1964-1974.

Life and Labors of Eliza R. Snow Smith. Salt Lake City: *Juvenile Instructor* Office, 1888.

"Miss E. R. Snow's Address to the Female Relief Societies of Weber County." *Millennial Star,* 12 September 1871, p. 578.

Newell, Linda King. "A Gift Given, A Gift Taken: Washing, Anointing, and Blessing the Sick Among Mormon Women." *Sunstone* 6 (September-October 1981):16-25.

Woman's Exponent, August 1886, p. 37.

Erastus Snow

Larson, Andrew Karl. *Erastus Snow: The Life of a Missionary and Pioneer for the Early Mormon Church.* Salt Lake City: University of Utah Press, 1971.

Salt Lake City, Utah. LDS Church Archives. Erastus Snow Journal.

Snow, Bess. "History of Levi and Lucina Streeter Snow Family." Unpublished manuscript of Erastus Snow Family Organization.

Lorenzo Snow

Arrington, Leonard J. *Great Basin Kingdom.* Cambridge, Massachusetts: Harvard University Press, 1953.

Barrett, Ivan J. *Heroines of the Church.* Provo: Brigham Young University Extension Publications Division of Continuing Education, 1966.

Deseret News, 15 December 1899, 20 July 1901.

Improvement Era, June 1919.

Jenson, Andrew. *LDS Biographical Encyclopedia.* 4 vols. Salt Lake City: Andrew Jenson Historical Company, 1901-1936.

Romney, Thomas C. *The Life of Lorenzo Snow.* Salt Lake City: Deseret News Press, 1955.

Salt Lake City, Utah. LDS Church Archives. Lorenzo Snow Diary.

Smith, Eliza R. Snow. *Biography and Family Record of Lorenzo Snow.* Salt Lake City: Deseret News Company, 1884.

Snow, LeRoi C. "An Experience of My Father's." *Improvement Era,* September 1933.

Young Woman's Journal 4:164-165.

Fanny Stenhouse

Bushman, Claudia V., ed. *Mormon Sisters: Women in Early Utah.* Cambridge, Massachusetts: Emmeline Press Limited, 1976.

Deseret News, 8 August 1860.

Salt Lake City, Utah. LDS Church Archives. Journal History, 3 September 1873.

Stenhouse, Fanny. *An Englishwoman in Utah: The Story of A Life's Experience in Mormonism.* London: Sampson Low, Marston, Searle, & Rivington, 1880.

———. *Expose' of Polygamy in Utah: A Lady's Life Among the Mormons.* New York: American News Company, 1872.

———. *Tell It All: The Story of a Life's Experience in Mormonism.* Hartford: A. D. Worthington & Co., 1874.

James E. Talmage

Allen, James B., and Leonard, Glen M. *The Story of the Latter-day Saints.* Salt Lake City: Deseret Book Company, 1976.

Talmage, John R. *The Talmage Story: Life of James E. Talmage.* Salt Lake City: Bookcraft, 1972.

Jenson, Andrew. *LDS Biographical Encyclopedia.* 4 vols. Salt Lake City: Andrew Jenson Historical Company, 1901-1936.

Provo, Utah, Brigham Young University. Harold B. Lee Library. James E. Talmage Journal.

Annie Clark Tanner

Bushman, Claudia V., ed. *Mormon Sisters: Women in Early Utah*. Cambridge, Massachusetts: Emmeline Press Limited, 1976.

Tanner, Obert C., ed. *A Mormon Mother: An Autobiography by Annie Clark Tanner*. Salt Lake City: Tanner Trust Fund/University of Utah, 1976.

John Taylor

Green, Forace. *Testimonies of Our Leaders*. Salt Lake City: Bookcraft, 1958.

History of the Church 7:104-105.

Ivins, Stanley S. "Notes on Mormon Polygamy." *Utah Historical Quarterly* 35 (Fall 1967):309-321.

Minutes of the Trial of John W. Taylor before the Council of Twelve Apostles. Salt Lake City: Mormon Underground Press, n.d.

Quinn, D. Michael. "The Council of Fifty and Its Members: 1844 to 1945." *Brigham Young University Studies* 20 (Winter 1980):163-197.

———. "Organizational Development and Social Origins of the Mormon Hierarchy, 1832-1932: A Prosopographical Study." Master's thesis, University of Utah, 1973.

Roberts, B. H. *Life of John Taylor*. Salt Lake City: Bookcraft, 1963.

Salt Lake City, Utah. LDS Church Archives. Abraham H. Cannon Journal, 6 April 1884.

West, Emerson R. *Profiles of the Presidents*. Salt Lake City: Deseret Book Company, 1973.

John W. Taylor

Jorgensen, Victor W., and Hardy, B. Carmon. "The Taylor-Cowley Affair and the Watershed of Mormon History." *Utah Historical Quarterly* 48 (Winter 1980):4-36.

Minutes of the Trial of John W. Taylor Before the Council of Twelve Apostles. Salt Lake City: Mormon Underground Press n.d.

Roberts, B. H. *Comprehensive History* 4:399-400.

Salt Lake City, Utah. LDS Church Archives. Abraham H. Cannon Journal, 29 March 1892, 2 April 1894.

———. Anthon H. Lund Journal, 27 March 1902.

Salt Lake City, Utah. University of Utah. J. Willard Marriott Library. John Taylor Family Papers.

Taylor, Samuel Woolley. *Family Kingdom*. New York: McGraw Hill, 1951.

———. *The Kingdom or Nothing: The Life of John Taylor, Militant Mormon*. New York: Macmillan Publishing Company, 1976.

Utah Genealogical and Historical Magazine, July 1930, p. 106.

Moses Thatcher

Deseret News, 19 October 1895, 28 November 1896.

Hatch, Nelle Spilsbury. *Colonia Juarez: An Intimate Account of a Mormon Village*. Salt Lake City: Deseret Book Company, 1954.

Ivins, Stanley S. *The Moses Thatcher Case*. Salt Lake City: Modern Microfilm Company, n.d.

Journal of Discourses 26:328

Madsen, Truman G. *B. H. Roberts: Defender of the Faith*. Salt Lake City: Bookcraft, 1981.

Reasoner, Calvin. *Church and State: The Issue of Civil and Religious Liberty in Utah*. Salt Lake City, 1896.

Roberts, B. H. *Comprehensive History* 6:330-336.

Salt Lake City, Utah. LDS Church Archives. Abraham H. Cannon Journal, 14 October 1886, 2 December 1895.
———. Heber J. Grant Journal.
Salt Lake City, Utah. University of Utah. J. Willard Marriott Library. John Henry Smith Journal.
The Thatcher Episode: A Consise Statement of the Facts in the Case. Salt Lake City: Deseret News Publishing Company, 1896.

Chief Walker
Bailey, Paul. *Wakara: Hawk of the Mountains.* Los Angeles: Westernlore Press, 1954.
Brooks, Juanita. "Indian Relations on the Mormon Frontier." *Utah Historical Quarterly* 12 (January 1944):6.
Gottfredson, Peter. *Indian Depredations.* Salt Lake City: Skelton Publishing Company, 1919.
Kelly, Charles. "We Found the Grave of the Utah Chief." *The Desert Magazine*, October 1946.
Neff, Andrew Love. *History of Utah: 1847 to 1869.* Salt Lake City: Deseret News Press, 1940.
Salt Lake City, Utah. LDS Church Archives. Journal History, 26 March 1850, 9 June 1851, 6 April 1854.
———. Sanpitch Stake Historical Record.
———. Brigham Young Office Journal, 29 January 1855.
Van Wagoner, Richard, and Walker, Steven C. "Chief Walker Revisited." *Utah Holiday*, September 1981, pp. 57-63.

Daniel H. Wells
Conference Reports, October 1941.
Deseret News, 3 May 1879.
Hinckley, Bryant S. *Daniel Hanmer Wells.* Salt Lake City: Deseret News Press, 1942.
Quinn, D. Michael. "Organizational Development and Social Origins of the Mormon Hierarchy, 1832-1932: A Prosopographical Study." Master's thesis, University of Utah, 1973.

Emmeline B. Wells
Bushman, Claudia, ed. *Mormon Sisters.* Cambridge: Emmeline Press Limited, 1976.
Eaton-Gadsby, Patricia Rasmussen, and Dushku, Judith Rasmussen. "Emmeline B. Wells." *Sister Saints.* Edited by Vicky Burgess-Olson. Provo: Brigham Young University Press, 1979.
Woman's Exponent, 1 July 1872, p. 29; 1 October 1895, pp. 59-60.

David Whitmer
Anderson, Richard L. *Investigating the Book of Mormon Witnesses.* Salt Lake City: Deseret Book Company, 1981.
Blankmeyer, Helen Van Cleave. *David Whitmer: Witness for God.* Springfield, Illinois, 1955.
Chicago Times, 26 January 1888.
Chicago Tribune, 17 December 1885.
Durham, Reed C., and Heath, Stephen H. *Succession in the Church.* Salt Lake City: Bookcraft, 1970.
Millennial Star 43:421.

Richardson, Ebbie L. V. "David Whitmer: A Witness to the Divine Authenticity of the Book of Mormon." Master's thesis, Brigham Young University, 1952.

Smith, Mary Audentia, ed., condensed by Vertha Audentia Anderson Hulmes. *Joseph Smith III and the Restoration.* Independence: Herald House, 1952.

Whitmer, David. *An Address to All Believers in Christ.* Richmond, Missouri, 1887.

———. "Letter to Joseph Smith III, 9 December 1886." *Saints' Herald* 34 (1887):89

John A. Widtsoe

Cornwall, Rebecca Foster. "Susa Young Gates: The Thirteenth Apostle." In *Sister Saints*, Edited by Vicky Burgess-Olson Provo, Utah: Brigham Young University Press, 1978.

Improvement Era, July 1948.

Pardoe, T. Earl. *The Sons of Brigham.* Provo, Utah: Brigham Young University Alumni Association, 1969.

Parkinson, Raymond Bramwell. "The Life and Educational Contributions of John Andrus Widtsoe." Master's thesis, University of Utah, 1955.

The Gospel in Principle and Practice: An Abstract or Conspectus of Readings. Provo, Utah: Brigham Young University Press, 1965.

Widtsoe, John A. *In a Sunlit Land: The Autobiography of John A. Widtsoe.* Salt Lake City: Deseret Book Company, 1952.

Wilkinson, Ernest L., and Skousen, W. Cleon. *Brigham Young University: A School of Destiny.* Provo, Utah: Brigham Young University Press, 1976.

Wilford Woodruff

Cowley, Matthias F. *Wilford Woodruff.* Salt Lake City: Deseret News, 1909.

Jenson, Andrew. *LDS Biographical Encyclopedia.* 4 vols. Salt Lake City: Andrew Jenson Historical Company, 1901-1936.

Knight, Newell. Journal. Cited in Pearl Wilcox, *The Latter Day Saints on the Missouri Frontier.* Independence, Missouri: By the Author, 1972.

Quinn, D. Michael. "Organizational Development and Social Origins of the Mormon Hierarchy, 1832-1932: A Prosopographical Study." Master's thesis, University of Utah, 1973.

Salt Lake City, Utah. LDS Church Archives. Abraham H. Cannon Journal, 28 March 1894.

———. Wilford Woodruff Journal.

West, Emerson R. *Profiles of the Presidents.* Salt Lake City: Deseret Book Company, 1973.

Brigham Young

Arrington, Leonard J. "Taxable Income in Utah." *Utah Historical Quarterly* 14 (January 1956):27.

Bancroft, Hubert Howe. *History of Utah.* San Francisco: The History Co., 1889.

Burton, Richard. *City of the Saints.* Edited by Fawn M. Brodie. New York: Alfred A. Knopf, 1963.

Carter, Kate B. *Unique Story: President Brigham Young.* Salt Lake City: Daughters of Utah Pioneers, n.d.

Codman, John. *The Mormon Country: A Summer with the "Latter-day Saints."* New York: United States Publishing Company, 1874.

Conference Reports, October 1941.

Deseret News, 14 May 1856, 12 October 1859, 23 October 1861, 18 March 1863, 8 October 1863, 5 August 1879.

England, Eugene. *Brother Brigham.* Salt Lake City: Bookcraft, 1980.
History of the Church 5:2-3.
Jenson, Andrew, *Church Chronology.* Salt Lake City: Deseret News Press, 1899.
Jenson, Andrew. *LDS Biographical Encyclopedia.* 4 vols. Salt Lake City: Andrew Jenson Historical Company, 1901-1936.
Jessee, Dean C. "Brigham Young's Family: The Wilderness Years." *Brigham Young University Studies.* 19 (Summer 1979):474-500.
Journal of Discourses 3:357, 5:99, 9:150, 13:61.
Larson, Andrew Karl. *Erastus Snow: The Life of a Missionary and Pioneer for the Early Mormon Church.* Salt Lake City: University of Utah Press, 1971.
Millennial Star, 3 August 1888, 15 January 1851.
New York Herald , 30 July 1858, 12 August 1868.
New York Semi-Weekly Tribune, 1 April 1870.
Quinn, D. Michael. "The Mormon Succession Crisis of 1844." *Brigham Young University Studies* 16 (Winter 1976):187-233.
Salt Lake City, Utah. LDS Church Archives. Miscellaneous Meeting Minutes, 7 April 1844.
———. Brigham Young Papers.
Salt Lake City, Utah. Utah State Historical Society. Provo School of the Prophets Minutes, 20 July 1868.
Walker, Ronald W., and Esplin, Ronald K. "Brigham Young: An Autobiographical Recollection." *Journal of Mormon History* 4 (1977):19-34.
Wilkinson, Ernest L. *Brigham Young University: The First One Hundred Years.* 4 vols. Provo, Utah: Brigham Young University Press, 1975.

Brigham Young, Jr.
Brooks, Juanita, ed. *On the Mormon Frontier: The Diary of Hosea Stout.* 2 vols. Salt Lake City: University of Utah/Utah State Historical Society, 1964.
Jenson, Andrew. *Latter-day Saint Biographical Encyclopedia.* 4 vols. Salt Lake City: Andrew Jenson Historical Company, 1901-1936.
Jessee, Dean, ed. *Letters of Brigham Young to His Sons.* Salt Lake City: Deseret Book Company, 1974.
Philadelphia Morning Post, 28 October 1869.
Quinn, D. Michael. "The Mormon Church and the Spanish-American War: An End to Selective Pacifism." *Pacific Historical Review* 43 (August 1974): 342-366.
Salt Lake City, Utah. LDS Church Archives. Wilford Woodruff Journal, 17 April 1864.
———. Brigham Young, Jr., Journals.
Utah Genealogical and Historical Magazine 2:94-96.

Zina D. H. Young
Brodie, Fawn M. *No Man Knows My History,* 2nd ed. New York: Alfred A. Knopf, 1971.
Clark, James R. *Messages of the First Presidency.* 6 vols. Salt Lake City: Deseret Book Company, 1970.
Jenson, Andrew. *LDS Biographical Encyclopedia,* 4 vols. Salt Lake City: Andrew Jenson Historical Company, 1901-1936.
New York World, 17 November 1869.
Stenhouse, T. B. H. *Rocky Mountain Saints.* New York: D. Appleton and Co., 1873.
Woman's Exponent 7 (1878): 98.

Photographic Sources

Elijah Abel; 1—Courtesy Harry Phillips. Almon W. Babbitt; 5—Courtesy Utah State Historical Society. John C. Bennett; 10—From *The History of the Saints*. John M. Bernhisel; 15—Courtesy Utah State Hist. Soc. Sam Brannan; 19—Courtesy Utah State Hist. Soc. George H. Brimhall; 24—Courtesy Brigham Young Universtiy. Fawn M. Brodie; 29—Courtesy Utah State Hist. Soc. Hugh B. Brown; 34—Courtesy LDS Church Archives. Abraham H. Cannon; 40—Courtesy LDS Church Archives. Frank J. Cannon; 44—Courtesy Utah State Hist. Soc. George Q. Cannon; 49—Courtesy Utah State Hist. Soc. George Q. Cannon (center, front row) at territorial penitentiary; 55—Courtesy Utah State Hist. Soc. Martha Hughes Cannon; 57—Courtesy Utah State Hist. Soc. Butch Cassidy, age 27. Photo taken as he entered Wyoming Penitentiary, July 15, 1894; 61—Courtesy E. P. Samborn Collection. Wild Bunch at Ft. Worth, Texas. Sitting, L-R: Harry Longbaugh, Ben Kilpatrick, Butch Cassidy, Standing, L-R: Bill Carver, Harvey Logan.; 64—Photo by John Schwartz, winter 1900-01. Courtesy Union Pacific Railroad. J. Reuben Clark; 67—Courtesy LDS Church Archives. Oliver Cowdery; 72—Courtesy LDS Church Archives. Matthew Cowley; 78—Courtesy LDS Church Archives. Richard L. Evans; 82—Courtesy LDS Church Archives. Green Flake; 86—Courtesy Utah State Hist. Soc. Susa Young Gates; 89—Courtesy Utah State Hist. Soc. Susa and Jacob Gates with descendents; 91—Courtesy Utah State Hist. Soc. William S. Godbe; 93—Courtesy Utah State Hist. Soc. Heber J. Grant; 98—Courtesy LDS Church Archives. Jedediah M. Grant; 104—Courtesy LDS Church Archives. Jacob Hamblin; 108—Courtesy Utah State Hist. Soc. Martin Harris; 113—Courtesy LDS Church Archives. Bill Hickman; 118—Courtesy LDS Church Archives. Orson Hyde; 125—Courtesy LDS Church Archives. Anothony W. Ivins; 130, 132—Courtesy Utah State Hist. Soc. Heber C. Kimball; 135—Courtesy Utah State Hist. Soc. Heber and Vilate Kimball with children; 136—Courtesy Daughters of Utah Pioneers. J. Golden Kimball; 141—Courtesy Utah State Hist. Soc. Jesse Knight; 145—Courtesy Utah State Hist. Soc. Harold B. Lee; 150—Courtesy LDS Church Archives. John D. Lee; 155, 160—Courtesy LDS Church Archives. John D. Lee (with neckscarf) sitting on his coffin, firing squad in background; 161—Courtesy LDS Church Archives. Amasa Lyman; 162—Courtesy LDS Church Archives. Amy Brown Lyman; 167—Courtesy LDS Church Archives. Francis M. Lyman; 172—Courtesy LDS Church Archives. Karl G. Maeser; 176—Courtesy Daughters of the Utah Pioneers. Thomas B. Marsh; 182—No known photo exists. David O. McKay; 187—Courtesy LDS Church Archives. Edward Partridge; 192—Courtesy LDS Church Archives. David W. Patten; 196—No known photo exists. Romania Pratt Penrose; 200—Courtesy LDS Church Archives. W. W. Phelps; 204—Courtesy LDS Church Archives. Orson Pratt; 210—Courtesy LDS Church Archives. Orson and Sarah Pratt with children; 213—Courtesy Daughters of Utah Pioneers. Parley P. Pratt; 217—Courtesy LDS Church Archives. Parley P. Pratt and wife Elizabeth; 218—Courtesy LDS Church Archives. Alice Louise Reynolds; 224—Courtesy LDS Church Archives. Willard Richards; 228—Courtesy LDS Church Archives. Sidney Rigdon; 232—Courtesy LDS Church Archives. B. H. Roberts; 239—Courtesy LDS Church Archives. B. H. Roberts in disguise (1884); 241—Courtesy LDS Church Archives. B. H. Roberts—World War I; 245—Courtesy LDS Church Archives. Porter Rockwell; 249—Courtesy LDS Church Archives. Aurelia S. Rogers; 254—Courtesy LDS Church Archives. Ellis Shipp; 257—Courtesy LDS Church Archives. Dr. Shipp (center row on right) and nursing students; 259—Courtesy LDS Church Archives. Emma Smith; 262—Courtesy BYU. Standing, L-R: David Hyrum Smith, Alexander Hale Smith. Sitting, L-R: Major Lewis Bidamon, Frederick Smith, Joseph Smith, III; 267—

442   A Book of Mormons

Courtesy LDS Church Archives. George A. Smith; 269—Courtesy LDS Church Archives. George Albert Smith; 276, 279—Courtesy LDS Church Archives. Hyrum Smith; 282—Courtesy Utah State Hist. Soc. Hyrum, Joseph, and Emma Smith grave from the Smith family homestead window; 287—Courtesy LDS Church Archives. Joseph Smith; 288, 293—Courtesy Utah State Hist. Soc. Joseph F. Smith; 295—Courtesy LDS Church Archives. Joseph Fielding Smith; 303—Courtesy LDS Church Archives. Joseph Fielding Smith and wife Jesse; 306—Courtesy LDS Church Archives. Lucy Mack Smith; 309—Courtesy LDS Church Archives. Reed Smoot; 314—Courtesy LDS Church Archives. Eliza R. Snow; 320—Courtesy LDS Church Archives. Board of Directors of the Deseret Hospital. Standing, L-R; Dr. Ellis R. Shipp, Bathsheba W. Smith, Elizabeth Howard, Dr. Romania Pratt Penrose. Center Row: Phoebe Woodruff, Mary Isabella Horne, Eliza R. Snow, Zina D. H. Young, Marinda Hyde. Front Row: Jane Richards, Emmeline B. Wells; 324—Courtesy LDS Church Archives. Erastus Snow; 326—Courtesy LDS Church Archives. Lorenzo Snow; 332—Courtesy LDS Church Archives. Lorenzo Snow; 337—Courtesy LDS Church Archives. Fanny Stenhouse; 338—Courtesy LDS Church Archives. James E. Talmage; 343, 346—Courtesy LDS Church Archives—Courtesy Utah State Hist. Soc. Annie Clark Tanner; 348—From *Mormon Mother*. John Taylor; 353—Courtesy LDS Church Archives. John W. Taylor; 361—Courtesy LDS Church Archives. Moses Thatcher; 366—Courtesy LDS Church Archives. Daniel H. Wells; 376—Courtesy LDS Church Archives. Emmeline B. Wells; 383—Courtesy LDS Church Archives. David Whitmer; 386—Courtesy LDS Church Archives. John A. Widtsoe; 392—Courtesy LDS Church Archives. Wilford Woodruff; 395—Courtesy Utah State Hist. Soc. Brigham Young; 402, 405—Courtesy LDS Church Archives.—Courtesy Utah State Hist. Soc. Brigham Young, Jr.; 411—Courtesy LDS Church Archives. Zina D. H. Young; 415—Courtesy LDS Church Archives.

Index

A

Aaronic Priesthood, 290
Abel, Elijah, 1-4
Adam, 247, 345
Adam-Ondi-Ahman, Missouri, 271, 321, 334
Adams, George J., 20
Alberta, Canada, 35-38
Alberta Temple, 103, 300
Alger, Fanny, 75
Alpine, Arizona, Cemetery, 112
Amaretti, Eugene, 62
American Red Cross, 27, 170
American River, California, 21, 367
American-British Pecuniary Claims Commission, 69
Angell, Truman, 403
Antelope Island, Utah, 140
Anthony, Susan B., 261
Antipolygamy, 112, 132, 350, 358, 368, 413
Articles of Faith, 344
Arizona Temple, 103
Argentina, 64

B

Babbitt, Almon W., 5-9, 18, 77, 312, 378
Babbitt, Julia Ann, 6, 9
Backenstos, Jacob, 251
Ballard, Melvin J., 28, 152
Baptism for the dead, 4
Baptist Church, 137
Barton, Clara, 261
Battle of Nauvoo, 119, 378
Beadle, J. H., 124
Beaman, Louisa, 289
Beaver, Utah, 62, 159

Beehive House, Salt Lake City, 338, 378
Beehive State Bank, 38
Beneficial Life Insurance Company, 38
Bennett, John C., 10-14, 211-212, 236, 250, 285
Benson, Ezra T., 334
Berkeley (University of California), 226
Bernhisel, John, 15-18, 78
Berry, William S., 242
Betenson, Lula, 65
Bible, 139, 350; Joseph Smith's revision of, 17, 215, 290
Bidamon, Lewis, 266
Bimetallism, 47
Black Hawk War (Utah), 146, 272
Bogard, Samuel, 198
Boggs, Lilburn W., 199, 235, 250, 285
Bolivia, 65
Bonaparte, Napoleon, 333, 398
Bonneville International, 153
Bonneville Mining, 148
Book of Abraham, 290
Book of Commandments, 205, 291, 388
Book of Mormon, 32, 51, 79, 114-117, 137-138, 205, 215, 219, 230, 233, 263, 283, 289, 290, 310, 334, 362, 387-391, 404
Book of Moses, 290
Boynton, John F., 105, 355
Boy Scouts of America, 27, 279
Bowen, Albert E., 35, 69
Brannan, Samuel, 19-23
Bridgeman, Peter, 291
Bridger, Jim, 121
Brigham City, Utah, 335
Brigham City Mercantile and Manufacturing Association, 335
Brigham's Destroying Angel, 119

Brigham Young Academy (Provo), 142, 168, 225, 277, 315, 344, 349, 403. See Brigham Young University
Brigham Young Cemetery, Salt Lake City, 325
Brigham Young College (Logan), 35, 393, 403
Brigham Young Express and Carrying Company, 122
Brigham Young Monument, 401
Brigham Young Trust Company, 55
Brigham Young University, 25-28, 37, 92, 148-149, 179-81, 393. See Brigham Young Academy
Brights Disease, 331, 418
Brimhall, George H., 24-28, 30, 168, 180
Brodie, Fawn M., 31-33, 289
Brooklyn, The, 21
Brown, Hugh B., 34-39, 189
Browns Park (Hole), Utah-Colorado, 62-63
Bryan, William Jennings, 41
Buchanan, James, 14, 139, 398, 407
Bullion-Beck Mining Company, 42, 55
Butterfield, Josiah, 289

C

Cache Valley, Utah, 140
Cahoon, Reynolds, 265, 284
Cain, 128
Caldwell County, Missouri, 198, 311
California, 21-22, 56, 60, 372
Calistoga, 23
Calverly, Bob, 62
Cambridge, Massachusetts, 31
Campbell, Alexander, 11, 126, 193, 219, 233, 321
Campellites. See Alexander Campbell
Camp Douglas, Salt Lake City, 379
Canada, 354, 360, 363, 400, 405
Cane Creek, Tennessee, 242
Cannon, Abraham, 40-43, 50, 148, 197, 362, 368, 399-400
Cannon and Sons Publishing Company, 41, 51, 55

Cannon, Angus, 58
Cannon, Frank J., 44-48, 50, 54, 60
Cannon, George Q., 41-42, 45-56, 95, 102, 175, 215, 297, 301, 307, 337, 345, 354, 358-359, 399, 413
Cannon, Martha H., 57-60
Capital punishment, 305
Carrington, Albert, 52, 127, 413
Carson Valley, Nevada, 129
Carter, Jared, 284
Carthage Greys, 251, 356
Carthage, Illinois, 355
Carthage Jail, Illinois, 230, 251, 266, 286, 294, 300
Cassidy, Butch, 61-66
Catteraugua Indians, 219
Cedar City, Utah, 158, 330
Centerville, Utah, 248
Chapman, Arthur, 65
Chicago Silver Mining Company, 97
Children of Zion, 238
Children's Friend, 300, 307
Church Board of Education, 25
Church Genealogical Society, 304
Church of Christ, 291
Church of Zion, 96
Church Silk Association, 416
Church Welfare Program, 151-152
Cincinnati, Ohio, 3, 237, 286
Circleville, Utah, 62, 65
Civil War, American, 12, 290, 329, 407
Claflin, H. B., 148
Clark, J. Reuben, 35-38, 67-71, 103, 134, 189, 280, 307
Clarkston, Utah, 117
Clay County, Missouri, 195, 220
Cleveland, Grover, 46, 54, 175
Cluff, Benjamin, 26
Coit, Lillie, 23
Colesville, New York, 291
Colonia Juarez, Mexico, 368
Colorado, 47-48, 62, 151
Colorado Stables, 253
Coltrin, Zebedee, 278

Columbia University, 69, 226
Columbus, Christopher, 398
Comprehensive History of the Church, 247
Congress, 8, 17-18, 46-47, 53-54, 243-244, 316, 358
Conner, Patrick, 250
Co-op Furniture Company, 42
Consolidated Wagon and Machine, 175
Contributor, The, 41
Co-op Furniture Company, 42
Co-op Wagon and Machine Company, 55, 99
Coray, Howard and Martha, 312
Cornell University, 226
Corrill, John, 194
Council Bluffs, Iowa, 7-8, 76, 109, 120, 127, 185, 271, 406
Council House, Salt Lake City, 378
Council of Fifty, 7, 17-18, 52, 101, 128, 157, 164, 174, 209, 231, 237, 251, 255, 272, 292, 299, 328, 355, 368, 378, 407
Council of the Twelve, 20, 41. See Quorum of the Twelve
Cowdery, Oliver, 72-77, 115, 198, 206, 219, 233, 263, 283, 285, 289, 291, 387-389
Cowley, Matthew, 78-81
Cowley, Matthias, 79, 188, 363
Cragin Bill, 96
Crooked River, Missouri, 198
Cullom-Strubble Bill, 45, 96
Cummings, Horace Hall, 26-27

D

Danites, 128, 156, 183, 198-199, 252
Daughters of Utah Pioneers, 92
Delaware Indians, 219
Democratic Party, 36, 47, 81, 131, 134, 242-244, 300, 318, 369, 407
Denmark, 328
Depression, The, 317
Deseret, State of, 7-8, 17, 52, 77, 211, 221, 231, 271, 357, 378, 407

Deseret Federal Savings and Loan Association, 38
Deseret Gymnasium, 307
Deseret Hospital, 58, 203, 260, 323
Deseret Iron Company, 328
Deseret National Bank, 99, 134, 367
Deseret News, 41, 51, 58, 92, 95, 174, 179, 209, 230, 260, 370, 373, 407
Deseret Sunday School Union, 52, 181, 300
Diabetes, 216, 248
Diaz, Porfiro, 131
Dingly Tariff, 47
Dixie Mission, Utah, 273, 329
Doctrine and Covenants, 12, 73-74, 79, 117, 183, 193, 215, 233, 235, 263, 286, 301, 389
Douglas, Stephen A., 12, 14
Drummond, W. W., 9
Dusenberry, Warren, 25
Dyer, Alvin R., 189

E

Echo Canyon, Utah, 379
Edmunds Act (1882), 53, 299
Edmunds-Tucker Act (1887), 148
Egan, Howard, 272
Eldredge, Horace, 315
Elijah, 315
Ellison Ranching, 148
Endowment, The, 4, 138, 209, 237, 264, 292, 312, 318
Endowment House, Salt Lake City, 16, 58, 323, 358, 378
England, 138, 229-230, 242, 255, 277, 297, 312, 340, 344-354, 355, 397, 406, 410
Ensign, The, 83, 307
Ensign Peak, 271
Erie Canal, 311
Escalante and Dominguez, 372
Eureka, Utah, 147
Evans, David W., 90
Evans, Richard L., 82-85
Evening and Morning Star, The, 75, 194, 206

Evolution, theory of, 345, 350
Excommunication, 6-7, 13, 22, 31-32, 48, 75, 95, 123, 127, 137, 164-165, 207, 211-212, 237, 301, 342, 364, 369
Extermination Order, 199, 235, 285

F

Farmington, Utah, 255-256, 349-352
Far West, Missouri, 75, 156, 163, 183, 198-199, 207, 220, 284, 291, 296, 355, 388-390
Fast Day, 401
Fayette, New York, 387
Federation of Women's Clubs, 226
Ferguson, Ellen B., 203
Fillmore, Millard, 407
Fillmore, Utah, 164, 166, 174, 374-375
First Council of Seventy, 41, 84, 242, 246, 315. See First Quorum of Seventy
First Presidency, 38, 52, 71, 77, 102-103, 133-134, 137, 139, 152, 160, 164-165, 174, 215, 234, 236, 243, 247, 290, 299, 305, 312, 316, 318, 335-336, 358-360, 363, 369, 400, 404, 414
First Quorum of Seventy, 6, 143, 163. See First Council of Seventy
Flake, Green, 86-88
Flake, James, 87
Florence, Nebraska, 8
Follett, King, 195
Folsom, Amelia, 404
Fort Kearney, Nebraska, 8
Fort Laramie, Wyoming, 122
France, 340, 355, 357
Fraziers Magazine, 291
Friend, The, 307
Friendly Botanic Society, 229
Friendship, New York, 238
Frontier Guardian, 7-8
Fullmer, John S., 7, 312
Fulton, Illinois, 266

G

Gallatin, Missouri, 156
Gates, Susa Young, 89, 180, 393, 404
Gates, Jacob, 90
Gause, Jesse, 234, 291
Genealogical Society of Utah, 92
Gibbs, John H., 242
Gifford, Alpheus, 137
God, 73, 289-290, 345
Godbe, William S., 17, 93-97, 342
Godbeites. See William S. Godbe
Goethe, Johann Wolfgang, 398
Gold, 21-22, 50
Gold plates, 73, 387
Granite Stake, Salt Lake City, 36
Grant Central Mining Company, 55, 316
Grant, Heber J., 36, 71, 98-102, 105, 124, 131-132, 134, 143, 147, 152-153, 170, 175, 188-189, 243-244, 280, 317, 321, 328, 341, 346, 369, 409
Grant Jedediah M., 2, 99-100, 104-107, 166, 341, 379, 404, 412
Grant, Rachael Ivins, 99
Grant, Ulysses S., 96, 214, 398
Great Britain. See England
Green River, Utah-Wyoming, 122, 280
Gunnison, John W., 374

H

Haight, Isaac, 159
Hale, Aroet, 292
Hamblin, Jacob, 108-112
Hampton, Utah, 410
Hannah, Mark, 316
Harrisburg, Pennsylvania, 387
Harris, George Washington, 183
Harris, James H., 383
Harris, Lucy, 114-115
Harris, Martin, 74, 113-117, 198, 205, 263, 291, 388
Harrison, E. L. T., 94-95
Harvard University, 393
Hawaii, 50-53, 296-299, 334, 359
Hawaiian Temple, 103, 300
Hayden, Amos S., 234
Hearst, William R., 83
Hess, John, 256
Heywood, Joseph, 7, 312

Hickman, Bill, 118-124, 156, 379
Higbee, Elias, 236
Hill Cumorah, New York, 114
Hiram, Ohio, 234, 291, 333
History of the Church, 247, 273
History of the Saints: Or An Expose' of Joe Smith and the Mormons, 13
History of Missouri Persecutions, 222
Home Insurance Company, 99, 175
Hong Kong, 81
Hooper, W. H., 52
Hoover, Herbert, 69-70, 318
Hotel Utah, Salt Lake City, 38, 153
House Carpenters of Nauvoo, 3
Hull, Mary Chadwick, 322
Humbug Mine, 147
Huntington, Lott, 122, 124
Huntington, Oliver, 209
Huntsville, Utah, 188
Hyde, Orson, 7-8, 20, 76, 120, 122, 125-129, 137, 183, 199, 208, 215, 221, 271, 284

I

Idaho Falls Temple, Idaho, 280
Illinois State Medical Society, 11
Illinois Wesleyan University, 344
Improvement Era, The, 70, 83, 226, 300, 307, 394
Independence, Missouri, 122, 194, 205-206, 284, 300, 321
Instructor, The, 226
International Council of Women, 91
Ireland, 355
Iron County Mission, Utah, 157
Isaacson, Thorpe B., 189
Isle of Man, 355
Italy, 334
Ivins, Anthony W., 36, 71, 99, 130-134, 327

J

Jackson County, Missouri, 75, 183, 198, 220, 291, 321, 389
Japan, 81, 102

Jensen, Ella, 336
Jerusalem, 128
Jesus Christ, 73, 74, 106, 164, 289-290, 304, 336
Jesus the Christ, 346
Jews, 128, 164
Johns Hopkins University, 344
John the Baptist, 73
Johnson, John, 291
Johnson, Lyman, 76, 163, 327
Jonas, Abraham, 292
Juvenile Instructor, The, 41, 51, 92

K

Kaibab Cattle Company, 134
Kane, Thomas L., 8, 18, 407
Kanesville, Iowa. See Council Bluffs
Kaysville, Utah, 360
Key to Theology, 222
Kelly, Charles, 375
Kimball, Heber C., 3, 20, 135-140, 142, 143, 166, 198, 208, 230, 266, 274, 289, 296, 299, 334, 355, 403, 406, 409
Kimball, Hiram, 121, 265
Kimball, J. Golden, 47, 134, 137, 139, 141-144, 246, 363
Kimball, Sarah, 322
Kimball, Spencer W., 128, 137, 139, 327
Kimball, William H., 379
"King, Priest, and Ruler over Israel on Earth," 52, 358
King, William H., 36
Kirtland High Council, 6, 115
Kirtland, Ohio, 6, 20, 115, 126, 163, 205, 219, 233, 270, 284, 311, 321, 355, 390, 412, 416
Kirtland Safety Society, 20, 115, 137, 220, 291
Kirtland Temple, 3-4, 116, 206, 270, 284, 290-291, 327, 409
Knight Consolidated Power, 148
Knight, Jesse, 145-149
Knight, Lydia, 146
Knight, Newel, 146
Knight Trust and Savings, 148

Knight, Vincent, 289
Knight Woolen Mills, 148
Knopf, Alfred, Publishing Company, 31
KSL Radio, 38, 83

L

Lander, Wyoming, 124
Latter-day Saints Business College, Salt Lake City, 68, 344
Law, William, 13
Law of Consecration. See United Order
Lay, Elzy, 62
Layton, Christopher, 136
Layton Sugar, 148
League of Nations, 70, 244, 317
Lebanon, New Hampshire, 311
Lee, Harold B., 150-154, 307
Lee, John D., 110, 119, 136, 155, 198, 377
LeHigh University, 344
Lewis, David, 375
Liberty Jail, Missouri, 195, 235, 285, 291, 355, 398, 406
Lincoln, Abraham, 300
Lion House, Salt Lake City, 90, 325, 378, 410
Liverpool, England, 315
Logan Cemetery, Utah, 370
Logan, Utah, 367, 393, 410
London Temple, 190
Los Angeles, California, 342
Los Angeles Temple, 81, 190
Los Angeles Times, 33
Luminary, The, 329
Lund, Anthon H., 300, 316
Lyman, Amasa, 22, 51, 88, 162-166, 173, 189, 193, 270, 299, 403
Lyman, Amy Brown, 167-171
Lyman, Francis M., 148, 163, 166, 172-176
Lyman, Richard R., 28, 163, 166, 168-171, 173

M

Maeser, Karl G., 25, 142, 148, 168, 177-181, 225, 258, 277, 344, 349
Mahoning Baptist Association, 233
Mapleton Sugar, 148
Manchester, England, 307
Mann, H. R. Company, 99
Manifesto. See Woodruff Manifesto
Mansion House, Nauvoo, 293, 312
Manti, Utah, 129, 373, 375, 381
Manti, Temple, 381, 409
Marks, William, 236
Marsh, Edward, 184
Marsh, Thomas B., 75, 127, 182-186, 198-199, 271
Masonic Hall, Nauvoo, 12-13
Masonry, 14, 107, 138, 205, 292
Maw, Herbert, 36
McConkie, Bruce R., 304
McKay, David O., 30, 38, 70, 84, 187-191, 290, 305, 307, 317, 365
McKinley, William, 47, 277, 316
McLean, Elenore, 218, 222
McMurrin, Joseph, 246
Meadow Creek, Utah, 375
Meadowville, Utah, 142
Melchizedek Priesthood, 2, 290
Mendon, New York, 404
Mendon, Utah, 410
Mentor, Ohio, 126, 233
Merkley, Christopher, 3
Messenger, The, 20
Messenger and Advocate, 2, 74
Methodist Church, 354
Mexico, 23, 54, 131-133, 280, 330, 360, 367, 372, 400
Mexican Colonization and Agricultural Company, 133
Mexican Revolution (1910), 368
Middleton, George, 168
Miles, John H., 380
Millennial Star, The, 51, 83, 138, 220
Miller, Eleazer, 404
Mississippi River, 265, 270, 286, 378
Missouri, 77, 115, 119, 388
Missouri River, 120

Index   449

Mojave Desert, 173
Mohave Land and Cattle Company, 134
Monroe, James, 272
Montez, Lola, 23
Morley, Isaac, 194, 373
Mormon Battalion, 21
Mormon Portraits, 212
Mormon Tabernacle Choir, 179
Mormon, The, 340
Moroni, The Angel, 388, 409,
Moses, 290
Mountain Meadows Massacre, 110, 157-161
Mount Hope Cemetery, San Diego, 23
Mount Olivet Cemetery, Salt Lake City, 97
Mount of Olives, Jerusalem, 128
Moyle, Henry D., 189
Moyle, James H., 318

N

Napa Valley, California, 23
National Council of Women, 170, 226, 256
National Education Association, 27, 226
National Women's Suffrage Association, 384
Nauvoo, Illinois, 4, 6, 7, 11-14, 16, 50, 87, 109, 138, 146, 195, 201, 208-209, 255, 265, 268, 311, 321, 355, 377, 383, 406
Nauvoo Charter, 7, 13
Nauvoo Expositor, 7, 286, 294
Nauvoo House, 266, 286, 294
Nauvoo Ladies Society, 322
Nauvoo Legion, 13, 105, 157, 355, 378
Nauvoo Neighbor, 355
Nauvoo Temple, 3, 50, 212, 221, 284, 294, 312, 323, 377, 409, 416
Navajo Indians, 375
Nelson, Joseph, 69
New Era, The, 83, 307
Newman-Pratt Debate, 214
New Movement, 165, 342

New York Herald, 214, 340, 342
New Orleans, Louisiana, 237, 383
New Zealand, 79-80
New Zealand Temple, 190
Nibley, Charles, 70
Nibley, Hugh, 31
Nibley, Preston, 245
Nixon, Richard M., 33
No Man Knows My History, 30-32, 289

O

Oberlin College, Ohio, 333
Oakland Temple, 190, 307
Ogden Cemetery, Utah, 48, 186
Ogden, Utah, 186
"Old Tabernacle," Salt Lake City, 378
Omaha, Nebraska, 201
Overland Telegraph, 407
Owen, Caroline, 380

P

Pacific Islands Mission, 22, 80
Page, Hiram, 387
Page, John E., 3, 208
Palestine, 127-128
Palmyra, New York, 114, 219, 289, 300, 311
Panguitch, Utah, 159-160
Parker, Robert LeRoy. See Butch Cassidy
Parley's Canyon, 410
Parowan, Utah, 157, 272
Parrish, Warren, 397
Partridge, Edward, 163, 192-195, 205, 219, 289, 291
Patten, David W., 137, 183, 196-199, 406
Payson, Utah, 146
Pearl of Great Price, 79, 289, 301
Peteetneet, 373
Penrose, Charles, 202-203, 348, 368
People's Party, 242, 300
Perpetual Emigration Fund, 407
Peter, James, and John, ancient apostles, 290

Peterson, Joseph, 350
Peterson, Ziba, 219, 233
Phelps, W. W., 7, 76, 127, 194, 204-209, 231, 291, 355, 389, 407
Phillips, William. See Butch Cassidy
Pierce, Franklin, 8
Piercy, Frederick, 32
Pioneer Jubilee Celebration, 401
Pittsburgh, Pennsylvania, 237
Place, Etta, 64
Pleasant Grove, Utah, 168, 258
Plural marriage, 41, 45, 52, 54, 75, 133, 202, 211-214, 221, 268, 285, 290, 292, 297-299, 301, 317, 322, 340-341, 349-352, 354, 360, 416-417. See Polygamy
Poe, Edgar Allan, 377
Pointer, Larry, 66
Political Manifesto, 59, 243-244, 369
Polk, James K., 7
Polysophical Society, 335
Polygamy, 16, 18, 20, 53, 237, 286, 289, 299, 301, 358, 368, 399. See Plural Marriage.
Post, Stephen, 238
Pratt, Mary Ann Frost, 218, 221, 229
Pratt, Orson, 3, 7, 100, 117, 127, 163-164, 189, 208, 210-216, 221, 289, 297, 312, 327-328, 329, 335, 388, 404
Pratt, Orson, Jr., 329
Pratt, Parley P., 20, 22, 51, 74, 138, 158, 205, 208-209, 212, 217-223, 233, 289, 292, 354
Pratt, Parley P., Jr., 201
Pratt, Sarah, 211-212
Prayer circle, 158, 299, 312
Priesthood, 2, 73-74, 80
Priesthood Committee, General, 152
Primary Association, 256, 323, 349, 358, 385
Prohibition, 317
Provo Cemetery, Utah, 92, 149, 319
Provo Commercial and Savings Bank, 316
Provo Lumber Manufacturing and Building, 315
Provo Temple, 307

Provo, Utah, 345, 351
Provo Woolen Mills, 315
Pulsipher, Zera, 396

Q

Queens College, London, 226
Queen Victoria, 237, 335, 385
Quincy, Illinois, 195
Quincy, Josiah, 312
Quorum of the Twelve Apostles, 38, 50, 59, 74, 80, 84, 100, 102, 106, 115, 127, 137, 143, 152, 160, 164, 174, 183, 188, 198, 208, 211, 215, 220, 230, 237, 267, 277, 299-301, 316, 318, 334, 336, 357, 362, 364, 369, 380, 393, 397, 399, 401, 405-406, 413

R

Ramus, Illinois, 7
Randolph, Vermont, 310
Rawlins, Joseph L., 60
Reaper's Club, 261
Rebaptism, 117
Reformation, 106
Relief Society, 92, 117, 169, 226, 256, 263-264, 292, 307, 322, 385, 417, 418
Relief Society Magazine, The, 92, 169, 226, 300
Reorganized Church of Jesus Christ of Latter Day Saints, 261, 267, 286, 289, 388, 391
Republican Party, 36, 46, 134, 300, 316-317, 369
Reynolds, Alice Louise, 168, 225-227, 349
Reynolds, George, 225
Rich, Charles, 22, 51, 88, 164
Richards, Franklin, 316, 403
Richards, Preston, 35
Richards, Staynard, 69
Richards, Stephen L., 189, 307
Richards, W. A., 63
Richards, Willard, 7, 106, 137, 208, 228-231, 273, 286, 289, 334, 355, 403, 406
Richmond, Missouri, 199, 235, 285, 291, 296, 390

Index 451

Richmond Cemetery, Missouri, 77, 391
Rigdon, Nancy, 236
Rigdon, John, 236
Rigdon, Sidney, 11-13, 126-127, 193, 205, 207, 219, 232-238, 245, 270, 290-291, 321, 389, 406
Roberts, B. H., 31, 36, 134, 142, 239-248, 316, 368-369
Robinson, Louise, 170
Rockwell, Porter, 9, 121, 249-253, 265, 286
Rockwood Albert, 403
Rogers, Aurelia S., 254-256, 349
Rogers, Thomas, 255
Romney, Marion G., 153
Roosevelt, Franklin, 70, 244
Roosevelt, Theodore, 70, 317
Root, Elihu, 69-70
Rotary Club, 85
Roundy, Jacob, 147

S

Sacramento, California, 367
Sacred Grove, New York, 300
Saint George Temple, 90, 398
Saint George, Utah, 90, 131, 134, 144, 159, 274, 330, 331, 408, 410
Saint Louis, Missouri, 205, 207, 255, 270
Saint Petersburg, Florida, 319
Salt Lake City Chamber of Commerce, 42
Salt Lake City Cemetery, 4, 18, 39, 43, 56, 71, 81, 85, 103, 106, 134, 144, 181, 191, 203, 209, 227, 231, 253, 256, 261, 275, 281, 302, 308, 331, 347, 360, 364, 381, 385, 394, 401, 414, 418
Salt Lake City Temple, 3, 41, 305, 336, 378, 399, 409
Salt Lake City, Utah, 122, 203, 222, 231, 342, 351, 379
Salt Lake Herald, 99, 242
Salt Lake Pacific Railway, 42
Salt Lake Tabernacle, 271, 378
Salt Lake Telegraph, 214, 341
Salt Lake Theatre, 99, 280, 378
Salt Lake Tribune, 47, 60, 94, 253, 359, 380

Salt Lake Twentieth Ward, 179
San Bernardino, California, 87, 164
San Diego, California, 23
San Francisco, California, 21, 222, 342, 401, 403
Sanford, Elliott, 54
Sangamon County, Illinois, 367
Sanpete County, Utah, 129, 146
Savage, Charles R., 68, 100
School of the Prophets, 94, 96, 127, 290, 327, 341, 407
Scotland, 188, 211
Scott Amendment, 360
Scott, Walter, 233, 321
"Second Manifesto," 301, 364
Seer stone, 387
Seer, The, 214
Seixus, Joshua, 127, 333
Senate Finance Committee, 317
Seneca River, New York, 193, 387
Shakerism, 116
Shawnee Indians, 219
Sherman, Lyman, 289
Shipp, Ellis, 257-261
Sloan, Edward, 214
Smith, Alvin, 310-311
Smith, Alexander, 263, 268
Smith, Bathsheba, 265
Smith, David H., 263, 268, 289
Smith, Don Carlos, 251, 270, 310, 312
Smith, Emma Hale, 17, 206, 262-268, 289, 294, 313
Smith family homestead, Nauvoo, 268, 286, 294, 313
Smith, George A., 75, 157, 183, 206, 208, 238, 240, 269-275, 277-278, 283, 289, 292, 296, 373-374, 410
Smith, George Albert, 28, 71, 79-80, 188, 270, 276-281, 307, 317
Smith, Hyrum, 208, 219, 230, 265-266, 268, 270, 282-287, 289, 296, 304, 310, 312, 355, 416
Smith, John, 270, 283, 296, 304
Smith, John Henry, 270, 277-278, 330
Smith, Joseph, Sr., 2, 73, 270, 277, 283-285, 289, 310-312, 336

Smith, Joseph, Jr., 6-7, 12-13, 16-17, 31-32, 73-74, 100, 105, 109, 115-116, 119, 136-139, 157-158, 163, 166, 189, 193-195, 199, 205-208, 211-212, 220, 229-230, 233, 236-237, 250-252, 263-268, 270, 283-284, 288-294, 296, 300, 304, 310, 312, 321-322, 325, 327, 333, 354-355, 387-390, 398, 404, 406, 416

Smith, Joseph, III, 263, 267, 289, 391

Smith, Joseph F., 2, 43, 47-48, 53, 100, 102, 133, 137, 148, 166, 170, 188, 216, 225, 243, 253, 270, 274, 277, 283, 294-302, 304, 307, 317, 334, 337, 345, 354, 358-359, 364, 385, 388, 399, 414

Smith, Joseph Fielding, 74, 99, 152-153, 189, 247, 283, 298, 303-308

Smith, Lucy Mack, 267, 289, 309-313

Smith, Mary Fielding, 283, 296

Smith, Mercy Thompson, 354

Smith, Samuel, 283, 297, 310, 312, 404

Smith, William, 208, 219, 266, 283-284, 310-313

Smoot, Abraham, 315

Smoot-Hawley Tariff (1930), 318

Smoot, Reed, 47, 70, 79, 99, 134, 152, 180, 244, 278, 300-301, 314-319, 363

Snow, Edward, 330

Snow, Eliza R., 101, 201, 256, 258, 260, 320-325, 327, 333, 404, 416-417

Snow, Erastus, 131, 159, 174, 214, 273, 289, 321, 326-331, 333, 404, 408

Snow, Lorenzo, 3, 52, 225, 244, 299, 300, 316, 321, 327, 332-338, 340, 363, 368, 396, 403-404

Snow, Warren, 407

Snow, Zerubbabel, 163

Snow Hall, Salt Lake City, 378

Social Hall, Salt Lake City, 378

Society for the Aid of the Sightless, 280

Sowiette, 373

Spanish-American War, 46, 68, 414

Spanish Fork, Utah, 25, 185, 372

Speaking in Tongues (glossolalia), 321

Spencer, Emily, 380

Spencer, Orson, 255

Spiritualism, 165-166

"Spoken Word, The," 83-84

Spring City, Utah, 129

Springville, Utah, 185

Spry, William, 142

Stanton, Elizabeth, 261

State Bank of Utah, 99

Stenhouse, Fanny, 339-342

Stenhouse, T. B. H., 340-342, 416

Stevenson, Edward, 117

Stewart, Levi, 159

Stoddard, Lyman, 109

Stout, Hosea, 106, 208, 379

Stowe, Harriet Beecher, 342

Strang, James J., 13-14, 116, 238

Sugarhouse Park, Utah, 357

"Sundance Kid" (Harry Longbaugh), 64

Swartzell, William, 156

Switzerland, 335, 340

Switzerland Temple, 190

Sword of Laban, 388

T

Taft, William H., 70, 318

Talmage, James E., 68, 180, 247, 343-347

Tanner, Annie Clark, 180, 348-352

Tanner, Joseph Marion, 180, 349-352, 398

Tanner, N. Eldon, 153, 189, 260, 307

Tanner, Obert, 351

Taylor, John, 4, 50-54, 58, 100-103, 128, 185, 208, 215, 221, 230, 296, 299, 330, 353-360, 362, 368, 380, 412

Taylor, John W., 102, 142, 188, 343, 360, 354, 359, 361-365

Teasdale, George, 132

Tell It All, 342

Temple Square, 140

Thatcher, Moses, 59, 79, 243, 316, 327, 366-370

"The Truth, The Way, The Life," 241

Thompson, Samuel, 229

Times and Seasons, 50, 195, 289, 292, 355, 398

Tintic Smelting Company, 198

Tooele, Utah, 100, 109, 174

Truman, Harry, 280

Tullidge, Edward, 214
Twain, Mark, 143-144
Tyler, John, 179

U

Union Cemetery, Salt Lake Valley, 88
Union Pacific Railroad, 413
United Order, 290, 335
University Chronicle, 68
University of Chicago, 30, 226
University of Deseret, 41, 58, 90, 214, 241, 255, 258, 378, 403
University of Michigan, 225, 260
University of Nauvoo, 12-13, 214, 377
University of Utah, 30, 33, 68, 83, 85, 169, 188, 277, 344, 349
Urim and Thummim, 391
Utah, 8, 18, 46, 116, 127
Utah Agricultural College (USU), 92, 393
Utah-California Railway, 42
Utah Central Railroad, 240
Utah Education Association, 27
Utah Expeditionary Force, 122, 129, 139, 158, 164, 173, 272, 297, 379, 407
Utah Historical Society, 33, 133-134, 394
Utah-Idaho Sugar Company, 38, 55, 153, 280, 318
Utah Legislature, 59, 101, 105, 122, 128, 131, 157, 209, 214, 299
Utah Light and Power Company, 55
Utah Loan and Trust Company, 42, 148
Utah Magazine, 94
Utah National Bank, 280
Utah National Guard, 307
Utah Pacific Railroad, 55
Utah Savings and Trust, 280
Utah State Journal, 47
Utah State Penitentiary, Sugarhouse, 42, 54, 159, 335
Utah State University, 354
Utah Territorial Insane Asylum, Provo, 316

Utah Women's Press Club, 261
Utah Woolen Mills, 99

V

Van Buren, Martin, 398
Victoria Institute, 394
Vincent, Dr. George, 169
Voice of Warning, 221

W

Walker, Chief, 371-375
Walker War, 272, 374-375
War of 1812, 114
Warsaw Signal, 266
Wasatch Lawn Memorial Gardens, Salt Lake City, 171
Washington, D. C., 18, 45, 59, 77, 79, 96, 294, 319, 410
Webb, Ann Eliza, 404
Weber Academy, Ogden, 188
Wells, Daniel H., 99, 140, 376-381, 383-385, 409
Wells, Emmeline B., 260, 382-385
Western Bugle, 8
Western Standard, 51
Whitmer, Christian, 387
Whitmer, David, 74-77, 115, 183, 198, 207, 219, 283, 386-391
Whitmer, Jacob, 73, 387
Whitmer, John, 207, 387, 389
Whitmer, Peter, Jr., 73-74, 219, 233, 283, 387
Whitmer, Peter, Sr., 73
Whitney, Newel K., 166, 194, 289, 383
Whitney, Orson F., 96, 99, 243, 273, 377
Widtsoe, John A., 83, 392-394
Wight, Lyman, 208
"Wild Bunch," 63-65
Williams, Frederick G., 136, 207, 284
Williams, Thomas, 94
Williams, Zina Young, 384
Wilson, Woodrow, 69-70
Winder, John R., 300, 304
Winter Quarters, Nebraska, 139, 185, 255, 296, 378

Woman's Exponent, The, 58, 92, 203, 323, 384

Woman's Suffrage, 59, 203, 243, 256, 323

Women's International Council and Congress, 384

Women's Medical College of Pennsylvania, 259

Woodruff, Azmon, 397

Woodruff Manifesto, 42, 45, 100, 351, 399-400

Woodruff, Owen, 396, 401

Woodruff, Wilford, 20, 43, 45-46, 52, 101, 132, 175, 181, 197, 208, 212, 215, 225, 243, 277, 299, 301, 336, 345, 351, 363, 368, 395-401, 412, 417

Woolley, Edwin D., 94, 99, 240, 327

Word of Wisdom, 290

Wordsworth, William, 398

World War I, 35, 69, 245

World War II, 35, 37, 280, 410

Worrell, Franklin A., 251

Wyandot Indians, 219

Wyoming, 8, 62

Y

Yates, Richard, 123, 379

Young, Brigham, 4, 7-9, 17-18, 21-22, 35, 47, 51-52, 73-76, 87, 90, 94, 96, 99, 102, 105-106, 110-111, 116, 119-123, 127, 129, 136-140, 146, 156-158, 164, 174, 180, 183-185, 189, 193, 198, 201, 205, 208-209, 212, 215, 221, 225, 229-231, 237-238, 240, 251, 258, 266-268, 273-274, 286, 289, 299, 312, 315, 322, 325, 329-330, 334, 335, 341, 355, 357-358, 372-374, 377, 378-380, 398, 402-410, 412, 416

Young, Brigham, Jr., 52, 277, 315, 404, 411-414

Young, John W., 122, 404, 412-413

Young, Joseph, 137, 405

Young, Joseph A., 404, 412

Young Ladies' Mutual Improvement Association (YLMIA), 92, 323, 385

Young Men's Mutual Improvement Association (YMMIA), 70, 143, 279

Young, Mahonri, 410

Young, Phineas, 73, 76-77, 137

Young, Seymour B., 246

Young Woman's Journal, The, 92, 203, 226

Young, Zina D. H., 90, 100, 203, 260, 321, 384, 404, 415-418

Z

Zion's Camp, 6, 105, 115, 127, 137, 163, 207, 211, 220, 270, 284, 290, 405

Zion's Cooperative Mercantile Institution (ZCMI), 17, 38, 55, 96, 99, 153, 240, 277, 280, 367

Zion's First National Bank, 153

Zion's Savings Bank and Trust Company, 55, 99, 134, 175